The Cripple Creek Road

The Cripple Creek Road

A Midland Terminal
Guide and Data Book

Edward M. "Mel" McFarland

PRUETT **P** *PUBLISHING COMPANY*

Boulder, Colorado

GUIDE TO PHOTO CREDITS

The following abbreviations have been used for photo credits.

MA or MWA	Morris W. Abbot Photo
AHP	Alco Historic Photo
GCB	Gordon C. Bassett Collection
HB/ESP or EP/HJB	Henry Bender Jr.,/Ernie Peyton Photo
CEB	Charles E. Burroughs Collection
EC	Ed Chonka Photo
CC	Colorado College, Special Collection
CHS	Colorado Historical Society
CCM or CCDM	Cripple Creek District Museum
DPL	Denver Public Library
DPL/OP	Denver Public Library/Otto Perry Collection
WAG	William A. Gibson Sr. Photo
JG or JGC	Jeff Gillapsy Collection
HO or HO/AC	Herb O'Hanlon Photo or HO/Author's Collection
AJ or AJC	Allan Jackson Collection
MM or AC	Mel McFarland or Author's Collection, or Photo
LDM	L.D. Mitchell Photo
WM/BSM	William Monypeny Photo/Brent S. Michaels Collection
PPL	Pikes Peak Regional Library, Colorado Springs
PM	Pioneer's Museum, Colorado Springs
JS	John Sherbak Collection
JAS	John A. Siemon Collection
WSC or WS/EC	Wally Smith Collection or WS/Earl Cochran Photo
USGS	U.S. Geological Survey Photo Library
UPHS	Ute Pass Historical Society
HKV	Collection of Harold K. Vollrath
LLW	Lester L. Williams Collection

Endpapers: Engine 60 leads a mixed train thru upper Ute Pass near Craig Siding in the early 1930's. — Standley Photo, Colorado Railroad Museum Collection.

Facing Title Page: The old and the new; ex-CM 50 and an ex-US Army ex-0-6-0 are posted adjacent to the oil house with three additional US Army engines behind 52's smoke. — DPL

Acknowledgements: The train is almost to Woodland as the conductor and brakeman take in the scenery. The four Rock Island cars will be left at the quarry. — HB/ESP

Jacket Painting: "Bound for Cripple Creek." A west bound passenger train approaches Anaconda Station in 1896. Painting by Mel McFarland.

First Edition
1 2 3 4 5 6 7 8 9

Printed in the United States of America

Library of Congress Cataloging in Publication Data

McFarland, Edward M., 1944-
  The Cripple Creek Road.

Includes index.
  1. Midland Terminal Railway. 2. Colorado Midland Railway. I. Title.
TF25.M47M35 1983   385'.09788'58   82-23038
ISBN 0-87108-647-6

Acknowledgements

THIS BOOK IS A COMPILATION OF THE efforts of many people, most of whom are extremely interested in preserving the memory of the last railroad into Cripple Creek. The ground work was already started when the book on the Colorado Midland, **The Midland Route,** was finished. A review of many of the research centers was quickly complete, including another trip to Washington, D.C. The libraries, historical societies and museums were now quite familiar, and the return visits produced not only Midland Terminal but additional Colorado Midland material. In that light, there are a few conflicting bits of information that have been clarified in this edition.

In Colorado Springs, the Pioneer's Museum, Penrose Public Library, and Tutt Library at Colorado College have received many visits, each adding new material. The Colorado Historical Society and the Western History Department of the Denver Public Library are required stops to any researcher; unfortunately the latter is now almost cost prohibitive to us "non-Denver residents." The Colorado Railroad Museum in Golden is by far one of the West's most valuable resources, and Bob Richardson, along with the directors, staff and volunteers, is continuing to assist the world in preserving our railroad history at a most commendable rate. The Ute Pass Historical Society, and Jan Pettit, is a vigorous concentration of "pure gold." The Cripple Creek District Museum, housed in the old Midland Terminal depot, is an interesting place to visit and work. The U.S. Geological Survey photo library in Denver is a largely unnoticed source for some very unique glimpses at our history.

The number of individuals who have helped me provided not only information, but also photographs and memorabilia, and their support has been overwhelming. In the beginning, Woody Ralston and Jeff Gillaspy opened up their minds and collections, providing a footing for this book. In the area of photographs, Henry J. Bender, Jr., who has preserved a major portion of the valuable photographs of Ernie S. Peyton, provided the basis for a solid illustrative foundation. Harold K. Vollrath, Gordon C. Bassett, Allan Jackson, Brent Michaels, L.D. Mitchell, the DeGolyer Library at Southern Methodist University, Morris Cafky and Dr. Lester Williams opened up their collections to provide glimpses of Midland Terminal scenery.

The number of former employees, and their relatives who contributed, grows even as this is being composed! Tony Vidmar, Ralph Bishop, John Sherbak, John McGrady, Hoot and Jack Sullivan, Lloyd Lunsden, Keith Schooley, Ed Chonka, Jack Buckman, Spencer Marsh, Ted Nulph, Jim Reilly, and a number of others supplied bits of their memories and photographs. The stories of these men are the history of the railroad, and if every one of their recollections could be written it would stretch as far as the railroad ran. I know that there are others around, some of whom were contacted but had no reply, and many others that I was unable to reach. I am sorry that their stories are not included here.

The Golden Cycle Corporation unfortunately culled their files years ago, but Paul Bauer, a longtime official, provided access to company annual reports. In searching the files at the Teller County Courthouse, Fred Campbell, fellow researcher, and I were directed to the files at the Carlton Mill. The Texasgulf Metals plant manager, Charles E. Brechtel, allowed tracing of the system right-of-way maps (about all that exists of MT records at the mill), and he guided us to the two steam boilers in the plant, two ex-MTRy locomotives, and told of a third that was formerly at the Ajax Mine. Holly Sugar Corporation searched their records after it was learned that they had preserved the railroad records, but they found that these records had been destroyed in the late 1960s upon their moving into their new building in Colorado Springs.

A number of rare, unusual, and interesting collections have been included here: however, there is rumored to be yet enough material available for almost another volume on the Colorado Midland-Midland Terminal stashed away here in the Colorado Springs area. I hope you all enjoy reliving the days of steam railroading in the Pikes Peak Region and the Cripple Creek Gold Mining District.

I doubt that my grandmother when she read to Bob Womack when he was near death, or my grandfather when he worked for the Carltons, or Hoot and Judy Sullivan in the early 1950s when they watched my sister and me, had any idea that someday I might put out a volume like this. Thank you all, for the help and inspiration.

Steam hides the locomotive in this view of the movement of Locomotive 60. — WS/EC

Preface

```
┌─────────────────────────────────────────┐
│                                           │
│          THE MIDLAND                      │
│       TERMINAL RAILWAY                     │
│                                           │
│  CRIPPLE CREEK VIA THE SCENIC MIDLAND TERMINAL │
│                  RAILWAY                   │
│                                           │
│        "THE UTE INDIAN TRAIL ROUTE"       │
│                                           │
└─────────────────────────────────────────┘
```

THE MIDLAND TERMINAL RAILWAY WAS not a major railroad, except to those that knew it well. In memories it is known to most as just "The Midland." The stories of it are entertwined with the Colorado Midland, and rightly so, because the two railroads were thoroughly involved with each other. In this text I hope that the relationship between the Colorado Midland, the Atchison, Topeka and Santa Fe, the Midland Terminal and the people of Cripple Creek Gold Mining District and those in Colorado City are more clearly explained.

The structure of this book is patterned after **The Midland Route** because of the relationship with the Colorado Midland. The two companies were the same company on occasion as well as the boldest of rivals at times, but any history of one must deal fairly with the other. When **The Midland Route** was written, the Midland Terminal was almost constantly in mind, but when the suggestion came for the compilation of the material to be presented here, it was almost a surprise. The idea came largely from people who wanted to know why there was not more Midland Terminal in the Midland book. The problem had been solved, partly by those people who provided

me with the additional material I needed. I do believe that I have presented it fairly, however mixed with similar memories from others, in an interesting manner.

The Cripple Creek Road is an ambitious title, but the Midland Terminal was an ambitious railroad. It was first carried on the books as the Cripple Creek Branch in 1891, and fifty years later it was truly **The Cripple Creek Road**, the only railroad in the district.

The two trip sections give you a view of the changes in the nature of the railroad in just over thirty years. It is that latter trip that many will see as familiar. A modern-day trip has not even been attempted, since the Cripple Creek District is again alive and rapidly changing. The differences that can be seen from day to day make today's observations tomorrow's history, and predictions of what it might be like when **The Cripple Creek Road** finally reaches your hands are too unpredictable.

If there can be any dedication of this book, it must be to those Midland Terminal and Golden Cycle Mill people whom I was lucky enough to grow up with.

TABLE OF CONTENTS

BOOK ONE: THE MIDLAND TERMINAL HISTORY
  1.   Early Development   3
  2.   The Growing Years   17
  3.   The Cripple Creek Central   35
  4.   The Golden Cycle Years   49

BOOK TWO: A RIDE ON THE MIDLAND TERMINAL
  5.   On the Colorado Midland   83
  6.   On the Midland Terminal   91

BOOK THREE: ON AN ORE TRAIN
  7.   All Aboard!   113
  8.   On the Way Back   137
  9.   District Switching   149

   BIBLIOGRAPHY   160

   APPENDIX
   Stations and Buildings   161
   Passenger Equipment   167
   Freight Equipment   173
   Maintenance of Way   182
   Locomotives   189
   Listing of Employees   200

   INDEX   212

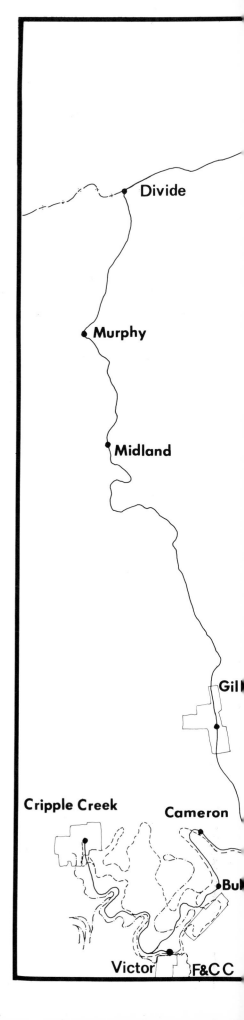

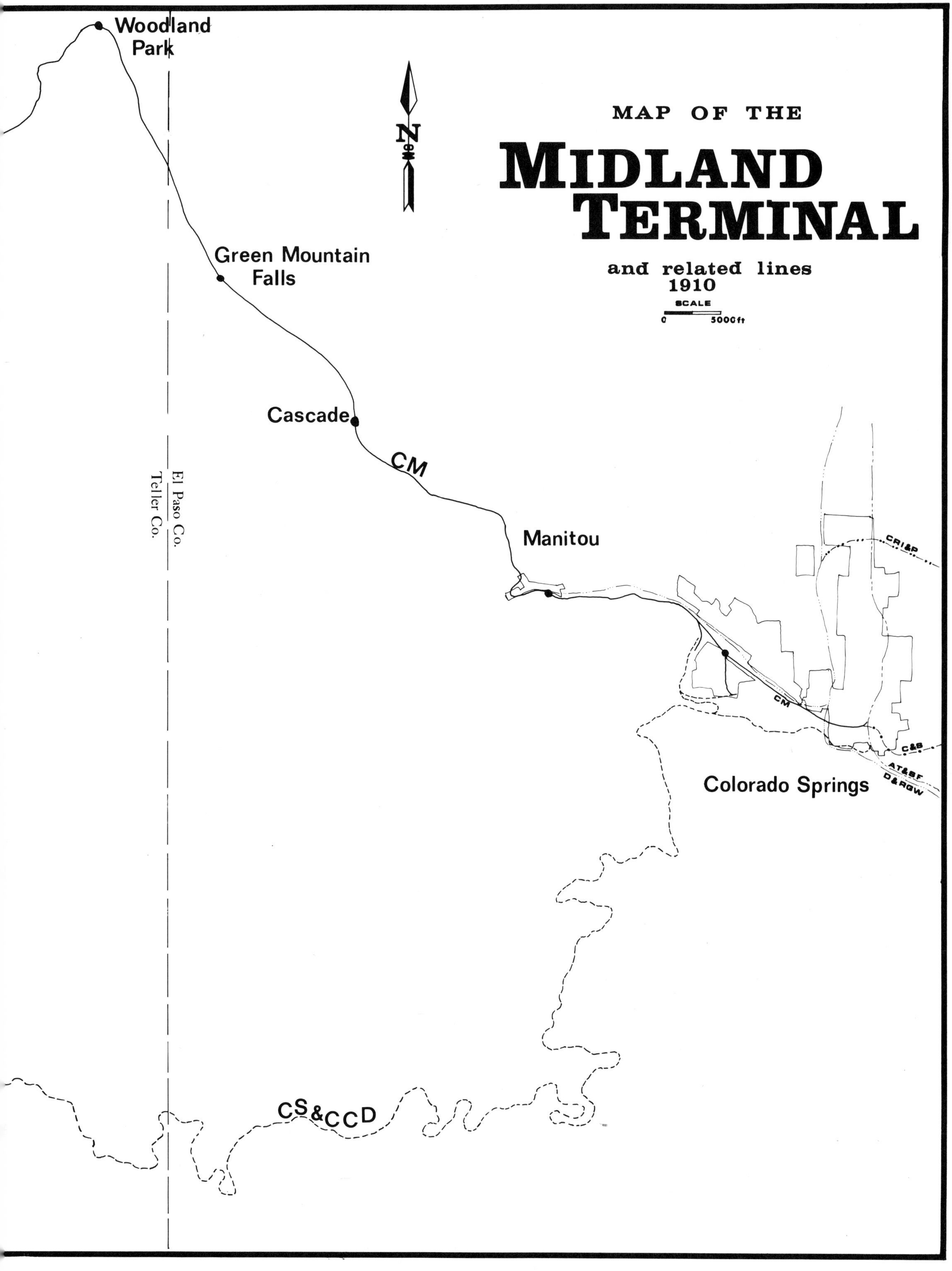

MAP OF THE

MIDLAND
TERMINAL

and related lines
1910

SCALE

0 ——— 5000ft

N

Woodland
Park

Green Mountain
Falls

Cascade

CM

Manitou

El Paso Co.
Teller Co.

CRI&P

CM

Colorado Springs

C&S

AT&SF

D&RGW

CS&CCD

X

Book one:
The Midland Terminal History

Before the MT was built, passengers rode in stagecoaches to Cripple Creek from the Colorado Midland's Divide depot. —
Author's Collection

1. Early Development

Stage coaches met the Colorado Midland trains serving Cripple Creek at Divide and Florissant. A stage meets a train made up of Santa Fe and CM cars, probably at Divide in about 1893. — DPL

T HE 1859 COLORADO "PIKES PEAK OR Bust" gold rush sparked interest in the largely unexplored Rocky Mountains, backbone of the west. The early gold rush activity centered around Cherry Creek, some eighty miles north of Pikes Peak. After the gold fever subsided in the 1870s, the government commissioned several surveys of the western territories. A Hayden Survey team passed through the area behind Pikes Peak, mapping hills and streams and collecting mineral samples in 1873. The high meadows then served mainly as a grazing area.

One of the survey team members, H.T. Wood, found fragments of gold ore on the slopes of Mount Pisgah. A report of the find drew a few prospectors to the area, but little gold was found. In 1878 Henry Cocking and B.F. Requa explored unsuccessfully in the region. Cocking supposedly drove a tunnel in Poverty Gulch but found nothing, and in a short time the area returned to normal. The hills were roamed only by grazing cattle and on occasion by a lone ranch hand.

One of the locale's early ranch hands was a sometimes-prospector named Bob Womack. On several occasions he found surface gold, or float, in the streams. He was adept enough to know that it had to come from somewhere, and he was searching for the source.

In 1884 a few businessmen in the Canon City area, long since passed up by gold seekers, dreamed up a scheme to lure people back. The station agent for the Denver and Rio Grande Railroad was reported to have first spread the word. The stories of Bob Womack, "Crazy Bob" as he was often called in the Colorado City saloons, spread as far south as Canon City. The businessmen heard the tales, as well as the accounts of others from the region, and the plot quickly became popular. The landmark selected was the cone of Mount Pisgah, visible from their community.

The story emerged of a traveler conveniently having come south after visiting the Pisgah region. He reported far and wide that he had found large nuggets in the ground around the peak. The men from Canon City spread the story of the massive find on the nearby slope. The gold rush would bring new money into the area, and Canon City

3

Hundley's Stage Line met the Ute Pass local before the Midland Terminal was built. The old Divide depot is barely visible behind the coach on the right. — AC

businesses, it was hoped, would again thrive. It was a shortsighted scheme that would eventually bring distaste not only for Mount Pisgah, but for Canon City, too.

The people lured by such tales suddenly were faced with the fact that they had been taken in. A few remained in the area, searching for the source of the small amounts of float found in streams. (Unlike the Cherry Creek strike, there was little "free gold" in the Mount Pisgah area. The most common form found in the district is a grayish-yellow ore.) The word quickly spread that the Mount Pisgah strike was not to be a gold camp. The area would not boom—but it would bust anyone who might believe the tales!

In 1885 two land developers, Horace W. Bennett and Julius A. Myers, purchased the area with ranching as their announced goal. The place was renamed the Broken Box Ranch, but the thought of gold development could not have been very far from their minds. Bob Womack remained in the vicinity, occasionally wandering into Colorado City, making the rounds of saloons with his tales of gold in the hills on the other side of Pikes Peak. In October 1886, he filed his first formal gold claim on a hole in Poverty Gulch.

Colorado City was buzzing with activity. The building of the Colorado Midland Railway had brought renewed activity to the old town. New people drifted in every day. The streets and the saloons were full again. The appearance of Crazy Bob and his stories caused no real excitement by comparison to the railroaders' tales of riches. Leadville, over one hundred miles away, was a real boom camp, and Colorado City was again a stop for those on the road to Leadville.

A wagon road had been built through Ute Pass in the 1870s, but it had seen little use since the railroads had been built westward from Denver, and through the Royal Gorge. The building of the Colorado Midland short cut all of those routes. Now Ute Pass and Colorado City were busy again, but it was from the railroad boom, not a gold rush. The number of businesses in Colorado City doubled in less than a year, and the number of saloons doubled twice within a year.

In the meantime, Bennett and Myers were quietly developing a small town called Fremont, which served as a home for a dozen prospectors who roamed the district. The number of test holes in the hills east of the town soon reached into the dozens, most of them unsuccessful.

In December 1890, two prospectors came up from Colorado City to look at the district, E.M. De la Vergne and F.F. Frisbee were guided by George Carr, who worked for Bennett and Myers. The tour included a visit with Bob Womack, and the visiting miners took samples of rock from various parts of the district. In February 1891, the two returned to Fremont planning to explore the areas that showed promise. Womack had worked on a forty-eight-foot shaft and found good ore, but unfortunately it was not on his claim. De la Vergne and Frisbee staked out a claim near the Womack discovery, and Womack quickly filed another claim on his new workings, which he named the El Paso Lode. The winters can be very rough in the high mountains, and the first storm sent Crazy Bob to Colorado City. But De la Vergne and Frisbee stayed in the district to check on several new locations.

The novelty of Womack's discovery was still not

convincing because of Womack's poor reputation. Even though Womack had finally found his lode, the development of the district was hindered because no one believed Womack's story. In the spring, all of the claim holders gathered at the Broken Box to discuss a few common problems. The group finally decided to draw up a good name for their little region that would help to dispel the Mount Pisgah hoax. The name chosen was the Cripple Creek Gold Mining District. De la Vergne was one of the first to use the name "Cripple Creek" in a claim. Cripple Creek, as yet, was the name of the stream running through the ranch, not the name of any town. The town of Fremont began the transition to the town known as Cripple Creek at that meeting, even though the name Fremont was to hang on for several more years.

The spring thaw brought more activity in Colorado City, too. Railroad construction, however, was finished, and those attracted by it were now looking for something to do. A few of these men opened small businesses catering to prospectors, and a larger number made their way into the Cripple Creek District. The little camp at Fremont grew to 250; other camps in the area boasted equal or larger populations.

People moved slowly into the district through the spring and into the summer. The Colorado Midland's agent in Colorado Springs, Samuel N. Nye, was busy telling anyone he could about the news from the gold camp. Harry Collbran, general manager of the Colorado Midland, called Nye into his office after hearing the stories. It was true that the district showed signs of becoming a real gold camp and that the railroad was hauling ore and freight at Florissant in ever larger amounts. However, Collbran did not want the Colorado Midland involved in any new hoax. He asked Nye to tone down his tales of the "pot of gold at the end of the rainbow" over Pikes Peak.

Frisbee was not letting the summer waste away. He shipped nearly a ton of surface ore to Pueblo to be refined. The ore was assayed at $200 per ton. Confidently he contacted Womack and persuaded him to sell the El Paso Lode. The claim was sold for $5,000, but shortly Frisbee sold it to two other Cripple Creek investors, Lennox and Giddings, who added it to their Gold King holdings.

The wagon road up Ute Pass bustled with freight wagons loaded with mining equipment. The wagons, once they reached the district, were often filled with ore and taken to Leadville. The road

Halfway House on the Hundley Stage Line was located at the toll gate on the road through Midland. The MT would eventually come right through this spot in this photo that was probably taken in 1891.
— CHS

from Fremont to Florissant saw use as the main artery into the district. The number of freight wagons on the road increased each week. The small stage line tripled the number of coaches assigned to the route, and still they were not able to keep up with the demand. People were now heading to the district at the rate of fifty per day.

The little camp on the top of Hayden Divide (named by the Hayden Survey team), eight miles east of Florissant, was the next town to boom. The small camp, barely more than a railroad siding in 1890, was called either Hayden or Divide by the local ranchers. The Colorado Midland had tried to give it other names but had settled on Divide. Construction on a shorter road to Fremont was subsequently started. A toll road backed in part by Hundley's stage line, it would cut ten to fifteen miles off the distance from Divide through Florissant to Fremont. The first section was fairly easy to build, but after it reached the mouth of a canyon, the going got rougher.

A toll station was established at the mouth of the canyon and given the name "Midland," since it was about halfway between Divide and the district, and a small community grew up around the station. A few prospectors even scoured the area for any sign of gold. Extra teams, food, water, and even a rugged hotel could be found in Midland only weeks after the town was started. The toll road and the free road from Florissant were still quite busy. In addition, a toll road from Canon City was quite popular. In Colorado City the talk was of a toll road of their own, over the south slope of Pikes Peak, starting at Bear Creek Canyon.

Bear Creek Canyon, a short distance south of the Colorado City business district, was the scene of an early-day route into the front range. General Palmer had commissioned work on the trail, turning it into a high-quality road. The main problem with the road was its destination—an isolated spot in the forest. General Palmer, in the interest of conservation, had the area set aside as a forest preserve. The toll road company proposed to merely extend the road into Fremont.

Meanwhile, on the other side of Pikes Peak, the Clough and Davidson Construction Company was working on a toll road south of Midland along Oil Creek. One and one-half miles south of town it turned eastward up a branch and climbed toward Beaver Park. The toll road required numerous switchbacks to climb from the stream to the top of the ridge three miles south of Midland.

Another construction man from Colorado Springs was busy in the area, but he was not building a toll road. W.S. Stratton, a house builder, was prospecting on the back of Pikes Peak. He met De la Vergne and Frisbee, who interested the builder in a few days' work in the Cripple Creek District. On his visit, Stratton talked with Womack, whom he had met before in Colorado City, and the two made a quick tour of the district. Stratton's interest in the area grew, and after he visited with other local prospectors, he decided to spend the summer.

The same summer, a young man, Charles L. Tutt, was lured into the district. On a hillside near Womack's claim, he staked out the C.O.D. claim, which slowly paid out small quantities of ore. Tutt tempted a close friend, Spencer Penrose, to come west and take a one-third share of the mine. The partnership developed into a most powerful and long-lasting association.

The seriousness of the strikes in the district was finally being felt in Colorado City, as well as in other towns farther away. In fact, the lure of gold occasionally thinned the ranks of the Colorado Midland, as men would take time off to try their hands at prospecting. The majority returned "broke," but a few either found gold or a new job in the district.

A rumor finally began to be spread around the shops that the Colorado Midland would soon be seriously seeking a rail link with the district. In October 1891, the word was out—unofficially—that a survey team, probably from the Santa Fe or Colorado Midland, was working southeastward from Florissant toward the district. A second team was working south from Divide; presumably the railroad company was checking possibilities. But the officials remained quiet on the subject. The Denver and Rio Grande, too, had a team of their own working northward from Florence, east of Canon City. By the end of the year, the Colorado Midland finally acknowledged its two teams working in from the north. The D & RG team reached Fremont on December 19, 1891.

The people in Colorado City watched the economy of their town slide into a continually worsening condition. No longer a staging area for people heading into the goldfields, or for railroad construction, it needed something to get busines going again. A few men developed grand plans for gold mills, since most of the Cripple Creek ore was being shipped over the D & RG or CM to Leadville.

The town of Florence was already the scene of mill construction. The supporters of the proposed toll road through Bear Creek Canyon cheered the mill proposal and stepped up their fund-raising activities. The rally failed, and by February the toll road idea was dead.

The Colorado City businessmen were furious. The Colorado Midland, and their owners the Santa Fe, seemed to be dragging their feet. A newsman from Leadville supported the Denver and Rio Grande route, stating on a visit to Colorado City, that there were other ways of getting into Cripple Creek than by the Colorado Midland. It was not going to be easy for the D & RG either, for their eastern stockholders were blocking attempts to build the branch line. The Colorado City men were not swayed by the Leadville reporter's views, and they kept after the Colorado Midland and the Santa Fe to get going.

In March the Santa Fe asked Colorado Springs resident James J. Hagerman, former owner of the Colorado Midland, to look into the Cripple Creek situation. Hagerman, who was busy with land development in New Mexico, had returned to his Colorado Springs home to rest during the winter, and he did not feel that his health would allow another business venture. Irving Howbert, a business associate of Hagerman and a well-known banker, consented to take his place.

Howbert was knowledgeable regarding railroad problems and could be trusted to make a fair observation. In April, Howbert boarded a Colorado Midland passenger train with a round-trip pass to Florissant. He had been briefed about what he would find between Florissant and Divide, but he was still taken by surprise. Freight wagons were hauling equipment into Cripple Creek from every station from Woodland Park to Florissant. High-quality ore was being shipped out by wagon to the Colorado Midland, as well as over the old wagon road to the mills at Leadville. In his report to Hagerman and to the Santa Fe, the conservative Howbert was barely able to control his enthusiasm.

Harry Collbran personally delivered the report to Santa Fe headquarters in Chicago. He took the time, however, to announce that the Colorado Midland would indeed be building into Cripple Creek before his special car, **The Mountaineer,** left the Colorado City depot. The report was greeted in Colorado City and Colorado Springs with optimism. The officers of the Santa Fe decided to act and ordered a refinement of the Divide to Cripple Creek survey.

The selected survey would start at the Colorado Midland station at Divide, which somehow had

The roundhouse crew of the Colorado Midland, third man from the right, with his thumbs in his lapels is A.P. Schilling who would be a boilermaker and sheetmetal man with the Midland Terminal.
— Mrs. D. Butler Collection

Looking from the hill at Murphy down toward Midland in 1910. — CC

received a new name. The name carried on the contract bids was "Rhyolite." A first section was to be constructed from near the Divide depot to Midland City (as the village of Midland was often called). The grading would roughly follow the toll road, but would not obstruct road traffic. The second section would be toward Beaver Park, and the third section, from Beaver Park to Cripple Creek, was still under study. Three possible routes into the gold camp were being investigated.

The final survey to Midland City was completed in July, and invitations for construction bids were published. The bidding closed in August and again Collbran traveled to the Santa Fe's Chicago offices. On September 1, 1891, Allan Manvel signed the contract with Price and McGavock Construction Company of Pueblo for the grading between Rhyolite (Divide) and Midland City. The bid was well under the surveyor's estimates, and the construction company foresaw completion within four months.

The competition was not waiting either. A new railroad, the Florence and Cripple Creek, heavily supported by the Denver and Rio Grande, announced plans to build into the district using the old D & RG survey. The new company faced a much more challenging route than that confronting the Colorado Midland's branch line.

At the same time a third group of men had started taking matters into their own hands. The men, mostly residents of Colorado City and Colorado Springs, were getting anxious about the Santa Fe's slow action and had formed their own

railroad company. These entrepreneurs explored the possibility of building from various points in the Colorado City area, including the Bear Creek Toll Road route. The group decided that starting from some point along the Colorado Midland further up Ute Pass would be better. But, upon finding that the best route was already taken, they approached the Santa Fe with an idea of building from Midland City. The men, headed by Harlan P. Lillibridge, concluded that they could build from Midland City while the Santa Fe crews worked from Divide.

The new railroad was incorporated on August 9, 1892, as a two-foot gauge line. The Gilpin area, some one hundred miles away, was Colorado's only other railroad of that gauge. The directors of the new line, which was called The Midland Terminal Railway, since the terminus with the Colorado Midland would be at Midland, could not agree on a final name for their railroad. The most common name heard in Colorado Springs was "Cripple Creek Terminal." Lillibridge, his directors, the Colorado Midland, and the Santa Fe would only encounter additional confusion.

Harlan P. "Colonel" Lillibridge, trained as a banker, had worked twelve years with Pacific Ocean shipping companies. In the ten years prior to his arrival in Colorado Springs, he had been active in Great Lakes shipping, Lake Superior iron ore trade in particular. The silver business had attracted him to Colorado, and he was one of the early investors in the Mollie Gibson Mine at Aspen, and served as a director, secretary, and treasurer of that and other prominent Aspen companies. One of his associates, and a neighbor in Colorado Springs, was none other than James J. Hagerman. Soon after the Cripple Creek area began to blossom, another friend, Richard Newell, who had worked with the "Colonel" in Michigan, suggested investment in a new project. Newell, a young man of twenty-five years, had heard of the Colorado City businessmen and their railroad idea. Newell told Lillibridge, who was among the first to appreciate the need for stability in the panic that a "boom" area produces. A railroad, he well knew, would have a real stabilizing effect.

Colonel Lillibridge organized the group of men and helped them to set realistic goals, and he called on Harry Collbran in July. The two men discussed the problems the group faced, and their difficulties were more or less settled by the time they incorporated. Collbran and Lillibridge took the idea of the two-foot gauge railroad to Allan Manvel, president of the Santa Fe railroad. The Santa Fe could not speed up their construction schedule. Due to the growth of the Santa Fe system, money for expansion and improvements was extremely tight. The three men studied the prospects and concluded that a completely new plan might work more rapidly. The unfinished grading from Divide to Midland City became the property of the Midland Terminal group in mid-November. The two-foot gauge road would start at Divide, not Midland City, or Midland, as it was more commonly known. The grading work continued, barely two miles away from Midland.

In December 1892, work on the grade stopped for the winter. The group was stalled by the weather, but that did not stop them from ordering equipment. The Cripple Creek Terminal, as some called it, ordered four Baldwin locomotives, seventy freight cars, and one caboose. An order for ties and rails eventually would be required, but with a Pueblo steel mill producing large quantities of rail only a few miles away, the order was held until more funds were available.

The little railroad seemed finally out of the hands of the Santa Fe-Midland, which suited both groups. Money problems loomed large on the horizon for the entire Sante Fe system. For a few months, the situation remained without much change, but increased activity in the district coupled with the inactivity of the Lillibridge group, eventually brought the Colorado Midland back into the picture.

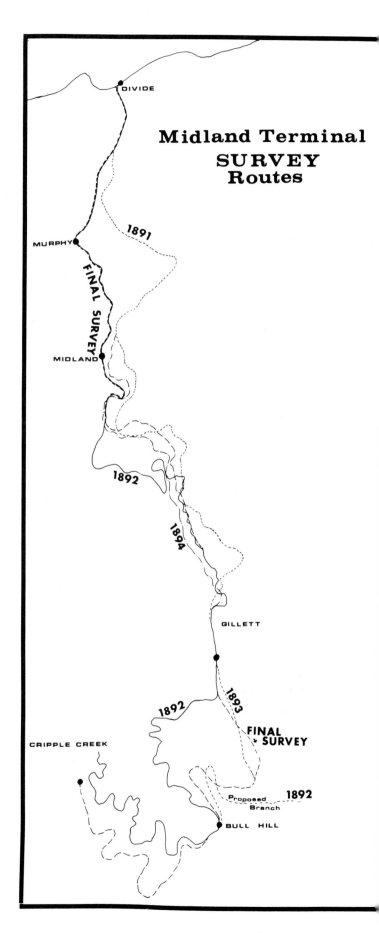

Midland Terminal
SURVEY
Routes

In February 1893, Santa Fe president Manvel died. The new president would have to make some important decisions about the financial problems of the Santa Fe, Colorado Midland, and the Lillibridge group. The Santa Fe directors had been casting a greedy eye on the profits shown by the Colorado Midland. The income was helping the rapidly expanding Santa Fe, and in a few months the usual summer traffic rush would be on, bringing greater revenues from the mining country. If that little group could be persuaded to make a few changes, revenues would be safer.

The Cripple Creek area was growing at a rate of about fifty new people per day. The increased demand was such that the Colorado Midland's Ute Pass local passenger train, **The Suburban,** was expanded and extended to serve Divide, rather than Woodland Park. In April, Collbran took his special car east to meet with the new Santa Fe president. One of the topics for discussion was probably the construction of the little railroad.

Collbran, on his return to Colorado City, called Lillibridge into his office for some interesting news. It was his task to persuade the "terminal" group to reconsider their choice of gauge. The connection at Divide would be much more beneficial to the two companies if they were both the same gauge. Collbran reminded Lillibridge that his would be the

only railroad of that gauge in the area, emphasizing the size value of the larger cars. To help get the stalled construction going again, the Santa Fe and the Colorado Midland would help the "terminal" get through its problems. The alternative that faced the Lillibridge group would be to have the Santa Fe repossess the grading to Midland and resume their standard-gauge construction plans. He would then be faced with competition from the Santa Fe-Colorado Midland into Cripple Creek. The choice was clear, but the directors would have to make the final decision.

The terminal group had constructed nearly a mile of grading above Midland that would have to be abandoned since it was totally unsuited for the larger gauge. A refinement of the earlier Santa Fe survey would take only a few weeks, weather permitting. The group met in May to decide on the Santa Fe proposal.

The directors of the little railroad quickly elected to accept the Santa Fe-Colorado Midland offer. The narrow-gauge grading above Midland was ordered abandoned. Huge quantities of new supplies were diverted by the large companies to the smaller one, and the Midland Terminal, which went by various names (the Terminal, Cripple Creek Terminal, and even the Cripple Creek Railroad), seemed to be back on the tracks again.

The nearly famous view of the Cripple Creek connection, a train that ran between Colorado Springs and Divide before the MT was built, stopped just west of the depot. — MM

In the original Palace Hotel, before the fire, the Pullman Banking and Brokerage had a distinctive office for its Cripple Creek patrons. — DPL

The Santa Fe-Colorado Midland had finally turned the tables on the small company. Only a short time before, the Lillibridge group had been impatient with the large companies, and now the large company had settled the problems caused by the small company's delays.

Ties and rails were quickly scattered along the grade south of Divide. Colorado Midland and Santa Fe workmen could be found assisting the terminal crews all along the grade. A survey team went to work refining the route to Beaver Park. Track laying was expected to start within a month, but the fate of the Santa Fe-Colorado Midland combination was stalled by severe financial problems. In late October rumors were as common as falling leaves. Collbran had been away for a month, which did nothing to squelch rumormongers. The Florence and Cripple Creek and the Denver and Rio Grande were having financial problems, too. One of the rumors stated that David Moffat and Collbran were working on a merger agreement between the F & CC and the Midland Terminal.

If Collbran had merger on his mind, he was not talking. At the Colorado City depot, on his arrival from Chicago, he said, "I don't want to make any newspaper talk, but I want the people to judge by our deeds what we intend to do."

Collbran called for a private meeting with the directors. The group, among other things, settled the name problem. It was officially The Midland Terminal Railway. The company's auditor, William K. Gillett, thought Cripple Creek and Gold Gulch or some other beautifully "euphonious" name would be better than the Midland Terminal, but the other directors won out. One of the other matters discussed was Lillibridge's leadership. A few of the directors felt that it had been proven that their company had been stalled without Santa Fe-Colorado Midland leadership. Colonel Lillibridge was not pleased by their conclusions. His force of character had commanded the confidence required to get the railroad going, but his lack of railroad knowledge may have caused some discontent. Moreover, his mining interests often seemed to undermine his direction of the company. His role as leader of the group faded quickly after the meeting, and he started to look around for someone to buy his share of the Midland Terminal.

The Colorado Midland was soon unloading supplies for the Midland Terminal's construction at Divide. The Sante-Fe-Colorado Midland, or the Santa Fe as many were calling it, had agreed to loan the Midland Terminal engines and equipment, as well as men, until their own labor force could be arranged. On November 10, 1893, six carloads of rail arrived at the Colorado Midland's Colorado City yards. The rail curving machine had not been used in nearly three years, but a twelve man crew worked nearly two weeks to get the rails ready to be laid. Construction at Midland and track laying at Divide started immediately. On December 11, the first passenger train began service into Midland.

A very mild winter brought changes to the Cripple Creek district. One modern convenience arrived in December when the first telephones were installed. The area was now in voice contact with the outside world. To the south, construction of the Florence and Cripple Creek Railroad had started. To the east, in Colorado Springs, a rumor circulated that the Chicago, Rock Island and Pacific would soon be building over Bear Creek Toll Road and the south slope of Pikes Peak, a story which was flatly denied.

Grading on the line south of Midland proceeded at a slow but steady pace. The old surveys had called for from three to seven tunnels. Revisions had brought the estimate down to one 700-foot bore. Contractor Clough suggested another slight change which would reduce the tunnel length to under 500 feet and would speed up the construction schedule by more than a week.

In Colorado City an old, often-heard story was again being dusted off. A new railroad was being announced, the Cripple Creek and Colorado Springs Railroad. The new standard-gauge line would roughly follow the route of the unsuccessful Bear Creek Toll Road. A real novelty of the proposal was the inclusion of a revolutionary idea involving one of the most successful railroads in the Colorado City area, the Manitou and Pikes Peak Railway. The M & PP operated as a tourist railway, but it was no ordinary railroad. It used a cog type drive system common to railroads in the Alps of Switzerland. The cogs help the engine pull (or in the case of the M & PP, push) cars up very steep grades. The Cripple Creek and Colorado Springs proposed to use a cog system on the steepest portions of their railroad.

The news of the Cripple Creek and Colorado Springs had little effect on the Midland Terminal until some of the large mine owners in the Cripple

Creek district started backing it. The mine owners were anxious to get railroad service to their mines. Problems had surfaced in the district that would have an effect on mine production and mining profits, for owners started having serious difficulties with their miners. The trouble involved wages, working conditions, and hours, and was directly related to labor organization.

The influx of men into the area included a large number of workers from eastern industrial areas. In the East, labor groups were showing their strength, but in the West the idea was new. A few radical labor organizers traveled into the district to promote unionism.

Violence was not new to Cripple Creek and the district, but in the form it took now, it was a threat even to the railroads, which became a target. The strikes against the mines were often the scene of beatings and shootings. Strikes closed many mines, and on more than one occasion shut down grading on the Midland Terminal. The violence prompted a call for the state militia, and Cripple Creek now had a public relations problem, because people with families no longer wanted to move into the district. In time the situation cooled, but problems were not settled.

On the Midland Terminal, construction of the twin timber trestles above Midland had finally been finished and grading was complete to Beaver Park. The railroad had plans for this relatively flat, high mountain meadow. The spot was ideal for construction of the railroad's shop and main yards, in railroad terms a division point. Yards, coal, water, shops, and even a small roundhouse were in the plans for this new town named Gillett.

The construction crews were busy erecting the new depot, coal trestle, and water tank when the track laying crew popped out of the valley north of town. The rails would be reaching the new town for the July 4, 1894 celebration. The scene in Cripple Creek that day was much more exciting, because the first train on the Florence and Cripple Creek pulled into town.

The section between Midland and Gillett had kept the Midland Terminal from reaching Cripple Creek as early as had been planned. If the original schedule could have been followed, it would have been a Midland Terminal train into Cripple Creek in spring, beating the F & CC. The country between Midland and Gillett was the roughest terrain the Midland Terminal would cross, and the steepest. The grading from Gillett to Bull Hill was completed

The Cripple Creek Express into Cripple Creek passes over the Twin Bridges above Midland with Colorado Midland equipment in the 1890's. Timber is visible on the hillside behind the coach, a major industry in the area. — AC

Gillett yards were fairly busy in 1906, and there was even a Short Line yellow box car near the coal trestle, as well as another, and an MT box car on it. The Montecarlo can be seen on the hill above town. In 1965 this area was extensively damaged by a flash flood and little can be found of it today. — CC

very quickly. A final climb from Cameron to Bull Hill required a lengthy loop. Construction crews were already half way to Victor, and the depot at Independence was finished when the track crews reached Bull Hill in early November. The Florence and Cripple Creek trackage was now in sight, but the area on the northeast slope of he district was already being served by the Midland.

The F & CC's territory was about to be invaded. The Midland Terminal was not rushing toward Cripple Creek, but was advancing carefully. Passengers were arriving at the Cameron and Independence depots from all parts of the district and from points east. Four trains daily served Gillett and the district, two passenger trains and two freights. Working south from Independence the grading was high on the hillside in the area of F & CC tracks. The line then dropped very slowly as it made a big swinging "C" around the valley. It curved into an "S" above Victor where the right-of-way skirted the north edge of the hillside town.

Trouble had flared in Independence as the track laying crew passed through town. The Midland Terminal had been given permission to cross the Black Wonder claim on a fifty-foot right-of-way, but one of the three claim owners was irate when the news of the agreement reached him. He did not approve of his partners' actions, and Sylvester Yeoman was awarded $125 damages to his portion of the claim. A cabin remained on the property, forcing the railroad to make a sharp turn.

Richard Newell, Jr., chief engineer for the Midland Terminal, traveled to the cabin in his private car on December 19, 1894, with an order to move it or tear it down.

Newell's train stopped on the dangerous curve, only a few feet from the cabin. In the coach, leased from the Colorado Midland, was Newell's brother, John, and several railroad employees. Newell stepped down from his car and walked to the cabin. As a man opened the door, Newell reached into his pocket for the court order. There were three men in the cabin, but none was Yeoman. A man at the cabin door reached over, picked up a 40-60 Winchester and fired it at Newell from about three feet. Newell was knocked back, mortally wounded; he turned and made a couple of steps before he fell. The conductor started quickly for Newell, but the man in the cabin stopped him. Then the man closed the cabin door, and the conductor and two other men ran to Newell, but he was already dead.

The train rushed to Victor, where the deputy sheriff was called aboard for a return trip to the cabin. Inside, A.W. Van Houten was found packing to leave. The three men were arrested and placed on the train, which headed for Colorado Springs.

In Colorado Springs Yeoman was found and arrested. Van Houten, who had only been using the cabin, had been leasing two nearby claims. He was charged with murder, and the two other men and Yeoman were charged as accessories. In

One of the earliest known photographs of the right-of-way in the district. The cabin near the tracks is likely to be the site of the murder of John Newell Jr. at Independence. — PPL

The earliest Independence depot was on the north side of the tracks. It was later moved to the south side, and even later another depot was built to replace it. — PM

addition to his Cripple Creek problem, it was found that Van Houten was a fugitive from Aspen.

Construction stopped until the issue died down, but crews were working again in a few days. The cabin was torn down, and the trouble with the curve was solved. Lillibridge and John Newell accompanied Newell's body to Cleveland, Ohio, for the funeral.

The murder of Newell marked the end of a long chain of events involving Newell, Lillibridge, and the Midland Terminal. Lillibridge was brought into the Midland Terminal by Newell, but only a short time before the shooting, Lillibridge had sold his Midland Terminal stock to W.K. Gillett. Now for the first time since the group was formed, neither man was part of the railroad. On the other hand, Collbran, who had been with the Colorado Midland, was now general manager of the Midland Terminal. Gillett, who had been with the

Santa Fe in Colorado Springs, was now superintendent, major stockholder, and had a town named after him. W.E. Bailey replaced Newell, starting a few days after the shooting.

The Midland Terminal had finally reached the Cripple Creek District, even if it would not reach the town for another year. The Cripple Creek District was still growing, and the railroad was growing with it.

Construction Progress

Divide to Midland	Completed on	December 11, 1893
Midland to Gillett	Completed on	July 4, 1894
Gillett to Victor	Completed on	December 16, 1894
Victor to Anaconda	Completed on	August 25, 1895
Victor to Victor Jct.	Completed on	August 25, 1895
Anaconda to Cripple Creek	Completed on	December 19, 1895

15

Midland Terminal ad copy. — AC

Colorado Midland 42 was used in the Cripple Creek District until the Midland Terminal received their own engines, shown here at Victor. — DPL →

A short passenger train winds through the mines between Cripple Creek and Victor not long after the Midland Terminal was completed. The first car behind the locomotive is CM 113, which was rebuilt into a combination car in 1903 — Allan Jackson Collection

2. The Growing Years

THE SANTA FE MIDLAND WAS ABOUT to receive a return on the loans to the Midland Terminal by the end of 1894. Freight cars, passenger "varnish," and locomotives from the Santa Fe and Colorado Midland could be found all along the Midland Terminal, from Divide to Independence.

The Midland Terminal started in 1895 with eight buildings and about twenty miles of track. Plans were already being drawn up for additional buildings at Divide and for four additional depots. Equipment orders were placed for locomotives, boxcars, and a few way cars. The Midland Terminal would look like a branch line of the Santa Fe–Midland until that equipment was on hand. The year looked very good, even the unpredictable weather was cooperating.

In January construction started on a small reduction mill on a slope southwest of Gillett. A track was run up to the Summit mill from the end of the wye. The plant was nearly ready for operation by early summer.

In March the Colorado Midland and the Santa Fe faced a new challenge. The Colorado Midland

bondholders were not happy with the new Santa Fe leadership, for the Santa Fe had gone through some tremendous changes since the Silver Panic and Manvel's death. The bondholders felt that the Colorado Midland was not being treated fairly, and they decided to choose a new leader for their railroad. They selected George W. Ristine to replace the Santa Fe-appointed official in May 1895. One of Ristine's first actions was to inspect the Cripple Creek operations of the Midland Terminal. On June 1, changes were initiated that included the little railroad. Ristine supported the Midland Terminal, but he decided that too much valuable energy was being exerted for the amount of revenue gained. He announced that the Midland Terminal would be required to furnish their own freight cars and locomotives after January 1, 1895.

Nonetheless, the Colorado Midland would continue to support the small railroad for some time. Likewise, the Denver and Rio Grande was supporting the Florence and Cripple Creek. In the Cripple Creek District the casual observer would not know that there were four railroads involved, because he would think the area was served by the Colorado Midland (or the Santa Fe) and the Denver and Rio Grande. The D & RG, which had been converting to standard gauge, and had an abundance of narrow-gauge equipment for the F & CC to use. An equipment lease to the F & CC would last for nearly another decade. Competition between the MT and F & CC increased as the Midland Terminal built into areas previously served by only the F & CC. The only factor influencing moderation was the extremely rapid growth of the district. The two railroads were operating at almost full capacity, and competition between them was offset by the fantastic growth rate.

A grand event was scheduled for August 24, 25, and 26, 1895, at Gillett. An arena was constructed inside the racetrack, northwest of town. The 5,000-seat arena would be the site for a gala bullfight. The promoter, Joe Wolfe, billed it as a "Great Mexican Bull Fight." Humane society members and church and civic leaders from Denver to Cripple Creek lodged letters of protest. Wolfe, a small-scale con-artist and former hotel owner and manager in Cripple Creek, advertised the event throughout the state. A special train was chartered over the Santa Fe and Colorado Midland to bring in spectators. Three thousand people were ushered into the arena for the Saturday show, but the event was stopped when the first bull, a rather range-weary one at that, was killed. The sheriff arrested the entire company. The Cripple Creek constable, an investor in the company, arranged to have the crew released with minimal fines.

On Sunday only 300 showed up for the affair. The big event turned into a comedy when the bulls failed to meet the bullfighters in battle. The event was far from any standard for a real Mexican bullfight, and the sheriff repeated the arresting procedure. Monday's fight was cancelled, and Wolfe departed the district very quickly, leaving everyone holding debts.

The Colorado Midland's ticket office in Denver and Colorado Springs refunded bullfight tickets for several weeks following the event. The railroads involved, however, hardly expected to benefit greatly from the spectacle, since passenger trains were already filled to capacity. The Colorado Midland and the Santa Fe occasionally watched such promotions along the Midland Terminal with sheer frustration.

The Colorado Midland's main problem with the Midland Terminal was damage to equipment. Inexperienced crews were continually putting cars and locomotives to the ground. Track work and maintenance were typical for branch-line railroads that were laid quickly. Boxcars were battered in normal service. In the district most boxcars were filled with rough stone for shipment to mills in Denver, Leadville, Pueblo, and even Florence. The trip from mine to mill could be as far away as Aspen in rare cases. In addition to this damage, the number of ore-laden cars passing over the rails often caused moments of panic for railroad security and local law enforcement officers. High-grade ore cars were often guarded enroute, for boxcars were frequently broken open, often causing heavy damage to the car, and the ore removed. The art of "high grading," as it was called, was a way of life in the district, and railroads were not the only target. The number of damaged freight cars in the Colorado City yards reached into the dozens by early summer 1895. The car and paint shops went on twelve-hour shifts to catch up.

The Cripple Creek's popularity continued to grow. Headlines in eastern newspapers began to carry the story of the district into financial centers much separated from the West. The Colorado Midland's passenger and freight revenues rose briskly as the number of cars on the suburban train and connecting trains increased. The Ute Pass **Suburban** was eliminated, becoming the **Cripple Creek Express,** even though it did not even reach that town. A new suburban service operated only in the district, and residents could now travel on a train, either MT or F & CC, to almost any part of the district on a regular schedule. The Colorado Midland regularly borrowed coaches from the Santa Fe to augment their limited number of cars, and the Midland Terminal announced the construction of a large brick depot for Cripple Creek. The $2,000 cost was covered by the Colorado Midland.

Colorado Midland crews operating on the Midland Terminal were starting to wonder about the operations on the little line. The Midland Terminal gained several new names among the roundhouse and train crews in Colorado City. "The Pea Vine," "Midland Terrible," and the "Great Shake" were some of the recorded nicknames. Numerous minor accidents caused by poor track, and mistakes caused by unadequately trained Midland Terminal men, increased each week. The novelty of having an engine or car on the ground

Locomotives often left the tracks in the district; however, it was vandalism this time when CM #15 left the rails, as well as at least one box car. — AC

did nothing for Colorado Midland men's confidence in the road.

The operational problems finally began to smooth out as track crews neared Cripple Creek in the fall. In October another story made front page news in the district. A new railroad was proposing to purchase the Midland Terminal, Florence and Cripple Creek, and a large section of the Denver, South Park and Pacific. The plan of the Denver and Colorado Southern was very grand, and the new company proposed to rebuild the D, SP&P from Denver, to a dual-gauge railroad as far as Slaghts, north of Divide. They would build a fifteen to twenty mile connection from the station to Divide, and the F & CC, like the other narrow-gauge road, would be rebuilt with three rails. Other tales speculated that the road would then be extended southwest to the San Luis Valley, and possibly even into the San Juans. The stories of the great development were quickly allowed to fade into memory as other schemes proved more feasible.

On February 7, 1896, the Midland Terminal's first two engines arrived at Colorado Springs. One week later the two were ready for their official dedication. In an elaborate ceremony the **W.K. Gillett** (#1) and the **H. Collbran** were presented to

the public. The **Collbran** (#2) was posed for the press between a highly polished Santa Fe passenger 4-4-0 type locomotive and the Colorado Midland #1. The brightly polished **Collbran** and the **Gillett** as well as CM #1 were all products of the Schnectady Locomotive Works, but the new engines were visibly larger.

E.E. Rittenhouse, Midland Terminal Trainmaster, presented a short oration, followed by Colorado Midland Master Mechanic Al Humphrey. The Colorado Midland mechanical department had drawn up the specifications for the Midland Terminal engines. Once the introductions were completed, the two locomotives were steamed up and taken to the Santa Fe depot in Colorado Springs. The two were on display there for several hours before they returned to Colorado City; the railroad had commissioned a local photographer to record the event. The two were dispatched to Divide for duty the next day. The next three engines, **B.P. Cheney** (#3), **J.A. Blair** (#4), and **J.B. Dennis** (#5) arrived within a few days and were placed into service without as much glory.

The Colorado Midland repairmen were even happier when 200 boxcars, four flatcars, and three cabooses arrived. The old equipment was severely

strained, for a traffic boom was underway on the eastern end of the railroad. The Midland Terminal was finally able to present their proud marquee "The Cripple Creek Short Line" to residents in the Pikes Peak Region and the Cripple Creek District.

The Midland Terminal was quite a bit shorter than the route over Florence and Cripple Creek, but another line was about to steal their advantage. The Colorado Springs and Cripple Creek District Railway was incorporated on February 29, 1896. W.S. Stratton, W.S. Jackson, Irving Howbert, Jimmy Burns, and I.L. Lindsey were the gentlemen responsible for the district's newest railroad. The Beaver Creek Air Line, as it was commonly known, still had a few major problems that needed working out, including the development of a more realistic route.

Colorado City finally received the news that they had been waiting for in March. The first major gold reduction mill was to be built across Fountain Creek from the town. The Colorado–Philadelphia Mill would bring more of the ore from Cripple Creek into town. The mill was heavily supported by two of the most interesting men from the district, Spencer Penrose and Charles L. Tutt, who named the mill for their past and present homes. The Colorado City businessmen, along with the Colorado Midland and Midland Terminal railroads, were elated. Colorado Springs, a short distance to the east, would not permit **any** industrial development of this type. The mills in Pueblo, Florence, Denver, and Leadville were not very happy with the prospects of a new milling community either. In addition, the owners of the Colorado Springs and Cripple Creek District Railway informed the public that another new mill,

Engine 1, the W.K. Gillett, named for the same man who would have a station named after him was finally engine 54, one of the first of the original engines to be scrapped. — AHP

(Right—top) Engine 2, the H. Collbran, named for one of the most important members of the leadership of the railroad was eventually numbered 55, which would eventually donate its boiler to the Carlton Mill. — AHP

Engine 3, the B.P. Cheney, named for an early investor in the company and eventually a Vice President would finally be engine 56. — Alco Historic Photos

Engine 5, named the J.B. Dennis in honor of some long forgotten individual, was one of the first order of locomotives. It was given number 58, after two other renumberings. The engine was one of the last engines to see use, after an entire career on the MT. — All, Alco Historic Photos.

20

the Portland Mill, was to be constructed south of Colorado City, and would be served by their railroad, exclusively.

The owners of the Florence and Cripple Creek gathered to organize another railroad. The Golden Circle Railroad Company was incorporated on April 15, 1896, to operate a wholly owned narrow-gauge extension into the upper reaches of the district.

A disaster struck the center of Cripple Creek ten days later. On April 25, 1896, a fire destroyed a multiblock area of the gold camp business section. The wooden structures, which dated back in most cases to early settlement, were rapidly reduced to piles of embers. Mine owners and businessmen quickly announced that the area would be rebuilt and set about to do so. Plans were soon presented for new, brick buildings.

Four days later another conflagration destroyed an area much more extensive than the earlier fire, including most of the recently started construction. In response, special relief trains were organized in the towns along the front range. Carloads of clothing, bedding, and nonperishable food were dispatched from Denver, Colorado Springs, Pueblo, and smaller communities. Several teams of doctors were rushed into the area. Donations were shipped into the stricken community without charge.

Cripple Creek started to rebuild before the ashes were cold. The Florence and Cripple Creek and the

Midland Terminal were realizing tremendous bonuses from the tragedy. The mines and mills were busy, and now there was the influx of materials to rebuild the town. The lumber mills around, already working from dawn to dark, rushed to fill orders for building materials. Carloads of brick arrived from as far away as Ohio. One of the benefits of the railroad's prosperity was the announcement of construction of a fine grand hotel. The new National Hotel was financially backed by none other than W.K. Gillett. The   — P

(Right—below) Two unidentified Midland Terminal locomotives with, among other cars, a Short Line box car on their way to Cripple Creek at the turn of the century. — A

The Colorado-Philadelphia Mill was processing center for the first loads of ore in Colorado City, brought down on the Midland Terminal. It was directly west of the Colorado Midland yards. — PPL

Midland Terminal even raised wages and cut back working hours for most of the train crews.

The Midland Terminal was gaining ground. The little branch line was on fairly stable financial footing by late summer. The Colorado Midland and the Santa Fe were finally able to recover some of their earlier losses on loans to the Midland Terminal. Construction of servicing facilities at Gillett strengthened the company's position over the Colorado Midland. The Colorado City yards would still be visited by equipment from the Midland Terminal until larger changes would occur than those represented by the yards at Gillett. The Colorado Midland's grip on the Midland Terminal was starting to slip again.

The independence of the Midland Terminal may have had something to do with the loss of another of its early backers and officers. Collbran started to look for someone to buy his Midland Terminal shares in late summer. In October, David Brown of Aspen bought out Collbran. The tidy sum allowed Collbran to expand his investments into other lucrative areas. In a few weeks Brown was elected president of the Midland Terminal in a special election, and he immediately had to face several new problems.

Competition between the Midland Terminal and the Florence and Cripple Creek was taking on rougher terms. The two were now in a position to serve many of the mines and mills jointly, and the Midland Terminal was putting in tracks to mines

that had been the exclusive customer of the F & CC. Mines were not about to deny service, since they benefited from the competitive freight rates offered by the two. The F & CC developed a new weapon against the MT in 1896. A subsidiary of the F & CC, the Golden Circle Railroad Company, was incorporated as a railroad of either standard or narrow gauge. The decision to build in standard gauge was waved under the nose of the Midland Terminal. The line, however, was built narrow gauge and was connected with the parent F & CC at Victor. The railroad was constructed to serve the numerous mines and towns on the hills above Victor, Goldfield, and Cripple Creek. In Cripple Creek another less obvious form of competition was being built.

The latest attraction in southeast Cripple Creek was the construction of an electric railway. The Cripple Creek District Railway was built as an electric interurban, but with the additional feature of trackage connecting Cripple Creek with the other small towns in the district. The standard-gauge line had plans to compete with the steam railroads, and it ordered a variety of freight cars in addition to the usual electric coaches. In Colorado Springs there was talk of an electric railroad between Cripple Creek and Colorado Springs. The rumor mill was now proposing that the Beaver Creek Air Line dig a tunnel rather than their proposed cog, or tram line. A suggestion was offered that the company ought to drill a twenty-

The Hundley Stage at the depot at Cameron, or Grassy, depending upon the date carried the Cripple Creek passengers over Hoosier Pass in the days before the arrival at the "gold capital". — PM

mile-long tunnel through Pikes Peak to connect with the Cripple Creek District Railway. Steam locomotives would be useless in such a long tunnel, and electricity would be the only "logical" choice—not that a twenty-mile-long tunnel was all that "logical." One other suggestion was to use cable cars, loaded cars pulling empties back to Cripple Creek.

The hostility between the Midland Terminal and the Florence and Cripple Creek prevented expansion of the Golden Circle near Goldfield. The narrow-gauge line had surveyed a route to lower Goldfield with quite a loop, but it required crossing the Midland Terminal. The Golden Circle construction crew reached the Midland Terminal's right-of-way in late August 1897. The attitude of both parties prevented any negotiation, and a second event a few weeks later only made the problems between the two railroads more hostile.

The Strong Mine had been one of the first mines in the Victor area served by the Florence and Cripple Creek. Midland Terminal tracks crossed the Strong property, but they had no access to the ore bins. The Midland Terminal had made overtures to the Strong owners; however, when they contacted the F & CC, the narrow-gauge company ruled against any access. MT Superin-

tendent Jesse Waters was not ready to give up.

Waters prepared a team of track layers and drew up a fantastic scheme to foul the F & CC's connection at the Strong Mine. The crew started in the dim light of early morning, and by the time the sun was barely over the hills to the east, the crew had laid a very crude trackwork **over** the F & CC tracks at the Strong ore bins. Once the tracks were in place, the crew lowered by cable several Colorado Midland boxcars down the trackage. The trackwork was not secure enough to support an engine, but it would hold empty boxcars.

The Florence and Cripple Creek was not about to be outflanked, or unequaled in outlandish activity. A train that was doing switching in the area was dispatched at speed. It entered the Victor yard at a high clip, scattering Midland Terminal track workers and a number of spectators. The Florence and Cripple Creek locomotive, pushing several Denver and Rio Grande boxcars, knocked the standard-gauge cars off the crude trackwork. The incident managed to turn several D & RG and CM cars into kindling. Once the rails were blocked, another string of narrow-gauge cars were backed over another track that the MT had crossed, preventing the standard-gauge line from either adding to the pile, or retrieving the cars.

Near Strong Junction looking up to Independence #2 and Portland mines, between Victor and Goldfield. — AC

The incident ended with an agreement between the two lines, as well as an opening for the F & CC to settle one of their problems. The Golden Circle was still separated from the F & CC north of Victor, by MT right-of-way. The F & CC took a page from the MT book by preparing a special crew. A combination track and bridge gang was made ready just after Christmas 1898. On New Years Day the crew started working on a bridge over the Midland Terminal right-of-way near Goldfield. They waited until a regular passenger train passed before starting. The courts were closed due to the holiday season and nothing legal could be done until they reopened. The bridge was finished and in use by the time legal recourse could be taken. The reaction to this incident was much less hostile than that taken by the F & CC at the Strong Mine a few months before.

The rivalry between the two railroads continued tumultuously while the new competitor made progress in its move into the district. The Colorado Springs and Cripple Creek District Railway had completed their final survey from Colorado Springs to Cripple Creek. The route started at the mouth of Bear Creek Canyon, and fortunately the survey team had ruled out almost all of the earlier proposed routes. The new survey was quite

unique in that it contradicted standard railroad construction practice. Nearly all railroads follow a natural water course. The Colorado Midland follows the path of Fountain Creek up Ute Pass, as an example. On the other hand, the CS & CCD traveled across water courses, which caused the railway numerous construction problems. The number of tunnels, high and long trestles, and a grade carved out of hillsides slowed the progress toward Cripple Creek. On the positive side, the rails of the streetcar line passed through areas as yet untouched by either the narrow gauge or the Midland Terminal.

In the spring the construction of spurs to different mines exploded with a burst of activity. The standard-gauge line was starting to have an impact on the narrow gauge, but with the increased activity in the district, both railroads were still doing rather well. One result of the fantastic growth of the district was the division of El Paso County, which stretched from the prairie nearly into South Park. Cripple Creek was selected as the new county seat of Teller County. The dividing line between the two counties crossed over Pikes Peak.

A most unusual problem began to show itself in the deeper gold mines in the district. The average

25

Engine 6, named the D.R.C. Brown in honor of the president of the railroad, has its formal builders photo taken before it leaves the Schenectady, NY plant. — Alco Historic Photos

mines were anywhere from fifty to one thousand feet deep. The Standard, a relatively new mine, struck water while following a rich vein. This difficulty had not been encountered by most of the shallow mines, but as each mine reached a lower level the problem of water became serious. A few of the mine owners decided that a drainage tunnel, bored into the core of the mountain, might drain off the excess liquid.

On the Midland Terminal a few of the crews had been diverted to work far from their home road. The center of Colorado, principally the area around Leadville, was suffering from another type of moisture problem. A winter storm had set in during late January and closed most of the railroads, including the Colorado Midland. A few of the men who normally worked on the Midland Terminal found themselves working on the Colorado Midland relieving crews who were stranded. The schedules returned to a more normal one with the onset of spring.

The equipment list on the Midland Terminal reflected the good fortune of the times. Locomotives number 6 and 7 arrived in 1898 and 1899, but Colorado Midland locomotives were still a common sight in the district. The Florence and Cripple Creek was operating quite prosperously, and when a rumor started to circulate that the F & CC **and** the Midland Terminal were being sold, it encountered hearty disbelief. Officials from both of the companies flatly denied any truth to the story.

On August 21, 1899, a fire struck Victor. The flames turned the center of the town into a furnace. Unlike Cripple Creek, there were mines among the businesses, and even those were victims. The

huge Gold Coin complex, near the Midland Terminal's depot, was destroyed, all surface buildings leveled. A few miners sought out the mine tunnels for safety, for several tunnels were interconnected with other mines, and no lives were lost in the mines, at least during the fire.

The F & CC depot was destroyed, and the Midland Terminal's building suffered heavy damage. The red brick structure was gutted, but the heavy walls survived. A dozen or more cars were burned in the yards, but no locomotives were lost.

The relief effort was not as spectacular as that for the Cripple Creek fire, but help arrived from Denver, Colorado Springs, and Pueblo on special trains. Victor immediately started to rebuild. The majority of the new buildings, as had been the case in Cripple Creek, were rebuilt using red brick, looking more like an eastern city than a mining community. The Gold Coin mine was even rebuilt with the red brick, looking like just another office building.

In October the stories of the sale of the railroads surfaced again. It appeared that an old scheme was about to be repeated, but with a more realistic twist. The formation of the Denver and Southwestern Railroad Company was announced in mid-October, but it was not incorporated until November 18, 1899. The company united all of the steam railroads in the district (MT, F & CC and their Golden Circle, and the Canon City and Cripple Creek), the La Bella Mill, Water and Power Company, as well as the Colorado Trading and Transfer Company, and partial ownership of several mining companies. Of particular interest

Midland Terminal 7 had already lost its cab name when this group posed with it in Independence, but unusual is Colorado Midland excursion car 3, which had received windows. The car was built as an open car, but was used in the district occasionally on the suburban runs. — Author's Collection.

On August 21, 1899, Victor burned, and the MT's depot was damaged, but not destroyed. — CHS

Barely visible is the red and cream brick Victor depot, without its roof, above the word Victor, ten days after the fire. The businesses had moved into tents, while some started to rebuild. — CCDM

After the August 21, 1899 fire which destroyed downtown Victor many people picked through the remains. — CCDM

On the hill above Victor, on a short spur off the main line, not long after the arrival of the MT, a man unloads ore into a Santa Fe box car. The Sante Fe had a large interest in the MT. — DPL

was the inclusion of Albert E. Carlton, Spencer Penrose, and Charles L. Tutt in this company. Carlton's Colorado Trading and Transfer had placed him in a position of power in the district. Penrose and Tutt's mining and milling interests also put them high on the list of the district's leaders. The new corporation, actually a holding company, also included a large number of eastern investors. Each of the companies retained an identity under the D & SW ownership, but several managerial functions were consolidated.

The Denver and Southwestern control of the railroads in the district brought a quick solution to many of the problems of competition, at least for a short time. The still small electric railway, and the new railroad being built toward the district, would temper that. The D & SW proposed changes in the Florence and Cripple Creek. One of the plans included having the F & CC's shops relaid with a third rail to handle Midland Terminal equipment. The Midland Terminal's agreement with the Colorado Midland was continued, but under an emergency basis only. In a few cases the CM would do emergency repairs. In normal circumstances any equipment that needed repair work would be shipped over the Rio Grande or Santa Fe to Pueblo, and on to the shops at Florence.

The Denver and Southwestern worked to get the highest return from each of the member companies. The operations of the narrow gauge and standard gauge were adjusted so as not to conflict with each other. A rivalry bantered on between the two groups even though the leadership had been unified. The narrow-gauge lines had the best service connections in the district, while the standard-gauge carried most of the inbound freight.

The company holdings were all showing some form of profit. The peak of the gold production in the district was recorded in 1900 at close to $18,000,000. Stratton's Independence, one of the most famous mines in the district, was sold to Venture Corporation, Limited, of London, England, for $10,000,000. At one time A.E. Carlton, of the Denver and Southwestern, was reported to have turned down an offer to buy the Independence, at a cost of only hundreds of dollars.

The construction of the new railroad concerned Carlton, as well as the other owners of the D & SW, but for the present the building of the electric line presented a major problem. Running the line up Bennett Avenue blocked access to the main office of Carlton's Trading and Transfer. A court order failed to stop progress; in fact it only seemed to exaccerbate the distress. Carlton fumed for nearly a week while the street in front of his building was reduced to a construction site. Alternative access proved limited, but the company survived, and activity returned to normal.

Business on the Midland Terminal in the district had slowed, while traffic to Divide was up. A number of spur tracks and yards were expanded. Divide, Bull Hill, Independence, and Victor received additional yard space. The Bull Hill yard more than tripled in size, and additional tracks to nearby samplers were expanded. Sections of main line trackage were scheduled to be dual gauged for access by all of the D & SW railroads. Colorado Midland coaches were no longer used on interurban, or suburban passenger trains. The trains ran hourly, or every half hour, with fifteen to twenty trains per day. The depot at Independence had to be moved across the tracks, away from encroaching mine tailings. The Midland Terminal was making many major, and minor changes, adjusting to the new ownership as well as changing conditions in the district.

The electric line between Cripple Creek and Victor pulled many customers away from the suburban trains of the D & SW's F & CC. The line connected with the new railroad from Colorado Springs at Cameron, near Hoosier Pass, in 1901. A second connection was planned toward Victor, by way of Goldfield. The "Short Line," as the new Colorado Springs and Cripple Creek District Railway was called, would soon have complete access to the district. A number of the mines quickly transferred their business to the new railroad. The D & SW suffered somewhat with the arrival of the heavy competition, as well as a slight decline in mining activity.

A fire destroyed the El Paso Mill in July. The operation of mills and samplers in the district was becoming a financial gamble. The construction of the new mill in Colorado City was completed, and the Short Line was hauling large quantities of ore to the site. The Midland Terminal and Colorado Midland quickly noticed a drop in their shipments. The Metalic, National, and Union mills in Florence passed into the hands of the United States Reduction and Refining Company, owners of the Colorado-Philadelphia and the new Standard mills in Colorado City. They planned to phase out

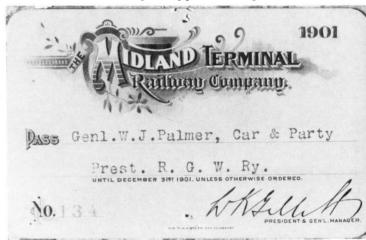

General Palmer's 1901 pass on the Midland Terminal. — PM

Colorado Trading and Transfer was a busy place when Cripple Creek was growing, and it continued to be busy for decades as is evident in this photograph taken in about 1910. — PPL

A switching traffic jam has #204 surrounded by narrow gauge F&CC equipment at the Eagle Sampler, but everyone seems to be more interested in having their picture taken than getting moving. — PPL

the Florence mills in favor of the newer mills in Colorado City. Smaller district mills and samplers were quickly losing out to the larger companies. The reduced production of the mines and increased competition was just too much for the small mines. Colorado City, with four large, modern mills was about to replace Florence as the district's primary milling site.

Short Line construction of new trackage was unmatched by even the rapid growth that had occurred when the first tracks were laid to the mines. The railroad construction included a short branch above Colorado City to the Standard and Colorado–Philadelphia mills, offering mine owners complete non-CM or MT service to all of the Colorado City mills. The new railroad was quickly gaining strength. To quote A.E. Carlton, "These are strong men."

In November the D & SW decided to challenge the strength of the competition. Fares between

Cripple Creek and Colorado Springs were cut. The Short Line reduced their rates by a similar amount. The two railroads continued to undercut each other's fares for nearly nine months.

The construction of a drainage tunnel for the district was well underway. Many of the mines had reached the level that the Standard mine had established as the depth limit. If deeper mines were to be developed, a drainage tunnel was required. A drainage company had been formed, subscriptions were collected from the mines who would most benefit, and construction started.

The impact of the rate war between the D & SW's Midland Terminal and the Short Line was putting a strain on the owners. The D & SW found that the CS & CCD owners had much more strength than had been suspected. The rate war collapsed in September, a major victory for the Short Line.

Albert E. Carlton had moved into leadership of the D & SW, as well as the company digging the drainage tunnel. His financial and political influence had expanded his business holdings into banking as well as mining. While moving into a prominent position in the state Republican party, he worked to keep a criminal in jail. Van Houten, convicted of the murder of Newell, was attempting to have his case retried. Carlton's influence kept the case out of the Colorado Supreme Court.

A serious problem erupted on March 17, 1903. The first of a new series of walkouts by miners in the district shut down most of the mines. Mining disruption brought immediate distress to the area's railroads. One month later, the F & CC, MT, and the CS & CCD were all forced to lay off large numbers of employees. The strikers returned to work in mid-April, and most of the railroaders who had been furloughed returned to their jobs.

Labor unrest was nothing new to the district, since it had presented itself nearly ten years earlier. The problem, however, was about to turn violent again. Shootings and "accidents" were common, but suddenly the targets were often as not union organizers as well as opponents to the unions.

The operating headquarters of the D & SW was moved to Cripple Creek, which seemed more appropriate than having it at one end of the railroad. Company shops, however, were relocated to Canon City. The firm was in real trouble and about to collapse. The rate war, as well as the mining labor troubles, had a severe impact upon its financial stability. Eastern investors were screaming over their losses.

The Cripple Creek Central Railroad Company, also a holding company, was formed by a few of the owners of the D & SW in September 1904. Several original owners of the D & SW elected to sell out, and in October a proposal for sale was drawn up. Since those making the offer were largely those about to decide to accept it or not, the new company's offer was received favorably. It can be assumed that only the eastern investors had any complaints. In December the D & SW defaulted on its debts, and the Cripple Creek Central took over.

The Colorado Militia was summoned several times to Cripple Creek when labor difficulties arose. Here they are assembled at the Terminal Hotel at Midland in the late 1890's. — Glenn Kinnaman Coll.

Camp Goldfield, Colo. Oct. 1903.

Camp Goldfield of the Colorado Militia, just below the
Portland mine, was the result of labor difficulties in the
district. The mine owners and the miners had continual
problems until about 1905 when the miners who were giving
the owners trouble were shipped out of the district. — CHS

F.L. Ransome's view of the LaBella electric plant and the
Golden Cycle Mine extends up to two strings of ore cars at
Bull Hill. The engine visible at the bottom of the picture is in
the F&CC yards. — USGS

3. The Cripple Creek Central

The Golden Circle depot at Independence, scene of an explosion in 1904. — AC

THE CRIPPLE CREEK CENTRAL WAS IN firm control of the remains of the Denver and Southwestern in early 1905. Labor unrest in the district had finally reached its peak in 1904 with an explosion at the F & CC depot at Independence at about 2:27 A.M. on June 6, 1904. Thirteen miners from the Findley Mine were killed. The Western Federation of Miners was suspected, the state militia was dispatched, and the union leaders along with many of the members were rounded up and shipped out of the state. The labor problems were not over, but the situation cooled considerably.

The Colorado Springs and Cripple Creek District's rate war with the Midland Terminal had attracted the attention of several other large railroads. Rumors started the rumble in Colorado Springs of a potential sale of the Short Line to the Chicago, Rock Island and Pacific. On December 15, 1904 the CS & CCD was sold to the Colorado and Southern. The C & S, itself a rather young

railroad, had been formed from several small standard and narrow-gauge lines most of which were having financial problems. The road was not absorbed into the C & S system, but was operated as a separate company. The Colorado and Southern already owned half interest in the Colorado Midland, but was looking for a way out of that situation. The Cripple Creek Central approached the C & S with an offer to establish joint operation of all of the Cripple Creek District's railroads. Many of the mines were on a decline and competition would only hurt the railroads.

One of the first developments of the joint agreement with the C & S was consolidation of MT and Short Line use of the Cripple Creek depot. To avoid confusion Midland Terminal locomotives were renumbered from 1 through 7 to 201 through 207. Passenger trains on the Short Line began running over Bull Hill to Victor and on the Cripple Creek over the Midland Terminal, rather than by their own tracks over Hoosier Pass. On the

Colorado Springs end, CS & CCD trains shifted to the Santa Fe depot. The two roads cooperated as if they were under the same owner.

In November 1905 a fire destroyed the Florence and Cripple Creek–Midland Terminal shops in Canon City. A Midland Terminal locomotive and one from the Florence and Cripple Creek were saved from the inferno. The loss to the Cripple Creek Central was not as severe a blow as the decline in mining in the district. Many of the small mines had either been closed or swallowed up by larger operations. The number of mills in the district dwindled to six, to four in 1906, and by 1908 to two, the Independence and Portland. The larger mills in Colorado City had almost completely taken over the processing of Cripple Creek ores. The bigger mills in Florence declined almost as rapidly as those in the whole district. One mill, the Telluride in Colorado City, was opened and soon closed, because its treating process was not adequate to remove all of the gold from the ore. The mill shut down, but was soon purchased and reopened as the Golden Cycle Mill. It was owned by the same men who operated the Golden Cycle complex near Goldfield. A fire destroyed the roasting section and ball mill, but it was immediately rebuilt with the latest equipment and an enlarged capacity. Nearby, three mills the Colorado–Philadelphia, Standard, and the Portland, were barely operating.

Older mills in the district were challenged by the expansion in Colorado City. In 1909 a new mill was built at the Independence, just above Victor, and 1910 saw an experimental mill erected at the Portland mine. The small mill used a new process for concentrating the low-grade ores into a high-grade mixture before refining by traditional means. The "flotation" process enabled many of the low-profit mines to remain open, rather than close due to a lack of high-grade ores. The process would revolutionize milling of district ores and increase the area's lifespan.

The Colorado–Philadelphia and the Standard mills closed in 1911, and the last of the mills in Florence was ready to close. The F & CC was handling most all of the mine switching in the district, but most of the ore was being shipped to Colorado City. Ore was transferred to standard-gauge cars at Walker Transfer near the Eagle Sampler and shipped over the MT to the Golden Cycle Mill.

In 1911 the Cripple Creek Central approached the C & S with an offer to lease the Short Line, in the name of the F & CC's Golden Circle. All traffic that had been routed over the MT would be diverted to the Short Line. The MT would become only a connection with the Colorado Midland, and an emergency route to Colorado City. Alarmed at the change since they relied tremendously on the Cripple Creek traffic, the CM could do nothing to prevent the switch in services.

The Florence and Cripple Creek was only a

While the horses feed box cars were loaded by hand with ore for the mills in Colorado City, here a CM, MT and CS&CCD car are being loaded. — PPL

The Cripple Creek Union Depot, after the consolidation of all of the railroads in the district. Prominent is the walkway over the tracks south of the building. — CHS

M 55.　　　　　　　　NO.　　　　　　S. K. NO.

VOUCHER.

E COLORADO SPRINGS AND CRIPPLE CREEK DIST. RY. CO.

To　　　　THE MIDLAND TERMINAL RAILWAY　6º　DR.

Colo. Spg. Colo.

AUDIT No. 777H

Sept 1906　　190

To adjust September remittance made to CS&CCD in error by M T conductor, W. L. Harrison.　　　　$20.35

APPROVED:

TRAFFIC MANAGER.

APPROVED:

GENERAL MANAGER.

ROVED:

GENERAL SUPERINTENDENT.

APPROVED

ASST. TO GEN'L MANAGER.

APPROVED FOR PAYMENT.

AUDITOR.

ACCOUNT	AMOUNT
onductors	20	35

RECEIVED,　　NOV - 7 1906　　190　, FROM

THE COLORADO SPRINGS AND CRIPPLE CREEK DISTRICT RAILWAY COMPANY

Twenty and 35/100------------------------------------ DOLLARS,

IN FULL PAYMENT OF THE ABOVE ACCOUNT.

THE MIDLAND TERMINAL RWY, CO.

$ 20.35

CASHIER

NOTE.—The receipt to this Voucher must be dated and signed by the individual or company in whose favor the Voucher is made, or when signed by another person, the authority for so doing must in all cases accompany

ghost of its former self when flooding closed the line between Canon City and Victor. An earlier flood had erased a substantial stretch of the original alignment, but a higher route was built to replace that section. The 1912 flood wiped out more of the original roadbed and small sections of the newer route. The flood caused serious concern in the Cripple Creek Central offices. All equipment on the south end of the railroad was moved to the Canon City shops until a decision could be made on further disposal. Canon City and Florence were extremely disturbed about the situation, and business leaders in the towns demanded that the railroad be reopened.

Jesse Waters, president and general manager of the Cripple Creek Central, was killed in a railroad accident on the Midland Terminal near Victor, while the F & CC matter was being studied. Henry Blackmer, who had been the general attorney of the Midland Terminal since the 1890s, moved into Waters' office. It was under his leadership that the F & CC filed for, and was granted permission to abandon the section south of Victor.

The Golden Circle and the remaining sections of the F & CC north of Victor were combined and reorganized as the Cripple Creek and Colorado Springs Railroad (Colorado Springs reflected the old CS & CCD, under lease to the F & CC). Large portions of the F & CC roadbed inside and out of the district were scrapped. The portion between Victor and Florence was turned into an automobile road, following lengthy and heated discussions with business leaders in Victor, Florence, and Canon City. A small amount of the equipment was retained in the district, but the Short Line and Midland Terminal absorbed most of the traffic. The usable portion of the roadbed was quickly converted to standard gauge, the small sections that had already been converted, to dual gauge. Narrow gauge was about to completely vanish from the Cripple Creek District. A few surviving narrow-gauge passenger cars, which had been used in suburban service, were remounted on standard-gauge trucks. The diminutive cars looked even smaller when mixed with the larger gauge equipment.

A.E. Carlton's interests had moved him to take over the faltering First National Bank of Cripple Creek, the First National Bank of Canon City, as well as the City Bank of Victor. Carlton and his wife lived in a large, but modest penthouse suite in the First National Bank of Cripple Creek. At one time

The Bull Hill depot bright and fresh after its move from Anaconda in 1912. — PM

he had held a sizable portion of the Colorado–Philadelphia and Standard mill stock, but recently he had invested in the Golden Cycle mill in Colorado City. Early success with the El Paso Tunnel had been short-lived, for the mines were soon reaching into the depth drained by that tunnel. The Roosevelt Tunnel was started in 1907 and would drain an area much deeper. Carlton was not one of the initial subscribers in the project, but when it ran into difficulty he was called upon for help. He salvaged the bore, completing it as far as the El Paso mine in 1910. The ultimate goal, Portland #2, was not reached for another nine years, but the tunnel, which was drained at an average rate of 6,000 gallons per minute, was successfully draining mines as soon as it reached the El Paso.

In 1914 the Cripple Creek Central leadership, a group of prominent businessmen and friends, moved to form a very powerful syndicate. The group included the Carlton brothers, Albert E. and Leslie G., Charles M. MacNeill, Charles L. Tutt, E.P. Shove, Spencer Penrose, and other, but less colorful district leaders. Their prime acquisition was the Cresson Consolidated Gold Mining and Milling Company, a rather lackluster, but consistently producing mine. The group soon added the Golden Cycle Mining and Reduction Company, United Gold Mines (a Carlton group), and the Cripple Creek Central.

The Cresson produced Cripple Creek's single most sensational find in April 1914, the Cresson Vug. A "vug" or geode, is loosely described as a rock that has had its center dissolved, resulting in a hollow core often lined with pure crystals of the predominant mineral. The Cresson Vug was as big as a house of that era and produced nearly $1,000,000 in pure gold. Several other vugs were discovered in the district, but nothing as amazing

A group of men pose on the Cripple Creek wye after one of the many winter storms. The rotary was used to clear the lines in the district on numerous occasions as late as 1948. — AJ

Rotary B has arrived in Cripple Creek and has partially cleared the wye in a cleanup after the 1913 storm. — AJ

The office of the Tutt-Penrose empire in its very early days was merely this frame structure. Left to right the men are Bela Kadish, Spencer Penrose, Ed Newhouse, and Charles Tutt. The empire would eventually include the Midland Terminal, Golden Cycle Mill, as well as the Manitou and Pikes Peak Railroad. — PPL

as the Cresson find. A special train, guarded by a team of sharpshooters, hauled the ore out over the Midland Terminal. A heavy door was installed at the entrance to the vug, and it was guarded until the vug was completely stripped of gems.

The Cresson find was discussed continually for the next year, but in truth the district's decline was accelerating. The next few years showed that the pattern was leading to an end of the glory days. People were starting to leave the area almost as fast as they had arrived twenty years before. A result of the slump in activity was the impending death of one of the state's largest railroads.

On April 21, 1917, Carlton attended an auction at the Colorado City office building of the Colorado Midland Railway. The railroad was to be sold for scrap. In an interesting maneuver he purchased the remains of the Colorado Midland for the syndicate from under the hands of a close friend, B.P. Morse of Denver, one of the largest railroad

scrap dealers in the West.

The new president of the Colorado Midland, A.E. Carlton, directed his general manager, J.J. Cogan, to examine the railroad and draw up a list of needed improvements. Cogan had been with the various Cripple Creek railroads and was the general manager of the Cripple Creek Central. The CM was in a frightful condition. Freight equipment was only in adequate-to-poor condition, and track maintenance had been grossly insufficient. Engines that could safely run over the track were too light for economical operation.

The Colorado Midland was interchanging cars with the C & S, Santa Fe, Denver and Rio Grande, and the Cripple Creek lines. A program was started to purchase a few good used, preferably almost new cars while scrapping started to clear the yards of worthless equipment. A plan was considered for the purchase of new American Locomotive Works engines for Carlton held several hundred shares of

On the Short Line at an unidentified tunnel, #203 (ex MT #3) derailed while cutting through a small snowdrift in about 1916. — Author's Collection

that locomotive company's stock. A deal was negotiated during a vacation trip to Florida.

The Colorado Springs newspapers praised Carlton and his syndicate for their efforts to rebuild the Colorado Midland. Locomotives of the other Cripple Creek lines were soon found in service on the Colorado Midland, replacing older and smaller engines. The largest of the CM locomotives were concentrated on the eastern end of the line. The lightest of the engines were set aside to be scrapped or sold, but a few returned to running on the Midland Terminal. Crews from the Short Line were furious about trading their engines for the older locomotives.

The Cripple Creek and Colorado Springs, the old Golden Circle, had assumed the lease on the Short Line when the F & CC was finally dissolved. The Cripple Creek and Colorado Springs acted as a unit of the Cripple Creek Central just as the Midland Terminal was doing. The Colorado Midland, even though not officially part of the Cripple Creek Central, acted as an equal partner to the CC & CS and MT. In a few circumstances it was treated as a subordinate.

In June 1917, the Midland Terminal received operating rights over the Colorado Midland from Divide into Colorado Springs. The MT had not regularly operated any freight trains over the CM. In an interesting consolidation, on July 21, 1917, the CC & CS leased the MT, putting all of the railroads with the exception of the Colorado Midland, under one controlling body. The CC & CS was acting as the railroad function of the Cripple Creek Central. MT locomotives were renumbered 41 through 47, to avoid any confusion with the Colorado Midland locomotives 201 through 205. Colorado Midland engines 1 through 10 were renumbered 61 through 70 to avoid confusion with the Short Line locomotives. The new numbering of the MT engines lasted only a short

An unidentified Midland Terminal locomotive with a short work train on the Short Line. The train includes the Cripple Creek ditcher, an Ingoldsby dump car, and one of the Short Line cabooses. — Author's Collection

Engine 54 is very grimy as it sits in the Colorado Midland yards in Colorado City in 1919 with its CM style headlight. The MT was using the yards while the owners waited out the CM's problems. — DPL

In the late teens the district had started to slow down, a short suburban train is visible on the F&CC's trestle, and a long string of cars waits on the MT siding between Elkton and Cripple Creek. — PPL

time, and for the fourth time they were renumbered, this time 54 to 60. The newest numbers placed them inside the Colorado Midland's scheme without any confusion. The CM operated locomotives numbered 41 through 47, and their locomotives 49 through 53 were newer, but similar to the MT locomotives.

In August the Midland Terminal main line, just above the F & CC's old main line between Cripple Creek and Victor, was studied. The narrow-gauge tracks were still in place and had not been used in almost four years. The two grades were compared, and the MT grade was selected as the better alignment. The old F & CC rails were taken up and the grade turned into an automobile road. The few remaining narrow-gauge locomotives and cars were sold, and all remaining three-foot gauge trackage was removed. The Cripple Creek Central (otherwise known as the CC & CS) was all the same gauge for the first time.

A fire on the Short Line destroyed Bear Creek trestle. The CC & CS, routing all traffic over the CM, decided to discontinue their use of the costly Short Line between Colorado Springs and Cameron. Carlton, at this time, was arguing with the United States Railroad Administration over their treatment of the Colorado Midland. The Midland Terminal traffic was minimal, shipments in and out of Cripple Creek were declining and had been for a year. Shifting of Short Line traffic to the MT was only cost effective, and the Colorado and Southern, irritated over the CC & CS's actions, wanted to meet with Carlton. The C & S demanded that the Cripple Creek Central immediately repair the trestle, and if it was not done, they would end the lease. The C & S's demands went unheeded. The line was not reopened, nor any work done on the trestle, and the C & S terminated the lease. The C & S then ordered the CS & CCD bridge crew to rebuild the Bear Creek trestle, and the road was ready to be reopened, under C & S control again, on July 15, 1918.

The Midland Terminal was relatively unaffected by the loss of the Short Line equipment. The Colorado Midland, however, took several days to direct the equipment that they were using back to Colorado Springs. The two railroads indicated a noticeable loss of freight to and from the district. The Colorado Midland only suffered from the loss for a short time, but larger problems loomed on the horizon.

In August 1918, the Colorado Midland ran its last regular train. The closure was a result of the takeover of the railroads by the USRA. Cripple Creek lines were not affected by the takeover. In a few days the Midland Terminal started to rent the Colorado Midland from Divide to Colorado Springs and all of the facilities along the line for $5,000 a month. The MT even began using a few of the better CM locomotives, including the largest engines on runs into Cripple Creek. Short trips were also made into South Park, and the MT continued operating the popular wildflower excursions, routing them to Gillett. The Midland Terminal took over in Colorado City, absorbing a few of the Colorado Midland employees. Colorado Midland equipment was still being interchanged, and several locomotives were rented out to various railroads and industries on a per-diem basis. Some of the locomotives had been sold or scrapped in late 1917 and 1918. A few of the cars that Carlton had purchased in 1917 had never arrived at Colorado City for repainting by the time they were again resold. The Colorado Midland yards in Colorado City became a giant, used equipment yard.

The Cripple Creek Central (or CS & CC) was now comprised of only the Midland Terminal and the ghost of the Golden Circle. The Golden Circle was only a railroad because it owned rights-of-way, but eventually found the Midland Terminal received ownership of that, too. A series of corporate shifts liquidated the CS & CC as well as the Cripple Creek Central.

The Midland Terminal moved some of their equipment into the Colorado Midland's yards, trading several of their old cars for better CM cars. Management decided to sell every piece of equipment that was not absolutely necessary. The yards were clogged with extra equipment, almost all of it suitable only for scrap. Surplus was moved to the unused tracks in every available space inside buildings as well as on some of the tracks in the Short Line yards, already loaded with unused CS & CCD equipment. Interestingly, Short Line locomotives were being stored at the Colorado Midland yards.

The war had slowed business in the district, but not as severely as had been expected. Many of the young men that had worked in the mines found themselves fighting in Europe. The one single factor that was hurting the railroads in the district most, more than the war, was progress. Passenger traffic from Colorado Springs into the district, and

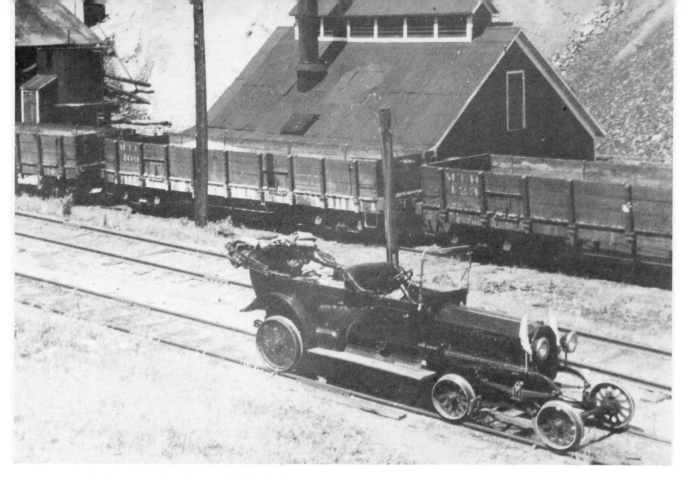

The open touring car was the Midland Terminal's VIP and inspection car, seen here at the Mary McKinney mine near Elkton. It was in an earlier version that Jesse Waters met his end when he met a steam engine running at high speed. — Author's Collection

suburban service in the district, was falling weekly to new lows. The old narrow-gauge cars, which were now running on their standard-gauge trucks, saw reduced service. The automobile and truck were cutting into railroad business.

The Carlton people were busy with the problems of the Colorado Midland and Carlton's other investments suffered from his attempts to return the Colorado Midland to a working railroad. The many problems of the Midland Terminal were minimal when compared to other difficulties facing Carlton's men.

Traffic over the Midland Terminal's suburban trains picked up after November 21, 1919. A fire quickly spread through the old car barn in Cripple Creek, and six of the Short Line's electric cars were lost. The 4:00 A.M. fire was so rapid that the building was fully enveloped in flames before the Cripple Creek fire department could start pumping water. Two employees lost their lives, trapped inside the building. Surviving equipment was not able to maintain even a small portion of the schedule. Steam equipment was tried, using passenger cars, but the attempt was futile. The suburban service could not be operated profitably, and replacement equipment was out of the question, since costs

could no longer be recovered.

The president of the United States announced in December 1919 that government control would end in March 1920. The Cripple Creek Central owners, and Carlton, studied the resumption of operations over the Colorado Midland. Consolidation of the Cripple Creek lines, the Short Lines included, with the Colorado Midland was a certain consideration. A large number of the Colorado Midland cars, as well as Midland Terminal cars, had been scrapped or sold. Only the best equipment and locomotives had been retained. The Short Line equipment, now relatively idle, might be available. A sale, similar to the Colorado Midland auction in 1917, was scheduled for the Short Line.

One plan was to sell the Colorado Midland to the Santa Fe. In a series of inspection trips, a group of Santa Fe officials toured their former property. A purchase might save the railroad from scrapping, which at that time was a growing certainty. The financial condition of the syndicate was under a severe strain as a result of World War One. Cripple Creek slowly returned to normal, but gold production was far below what it had been ten years earlier. The members of the syndicate had used their assets to expand into other fields: oil, sugar, copper, and diverse investments. Sales of the Colorado Midland would alleviate them of a problem; however, it was not to come about.

The Santa Fe was a powerful, modern railroad, quite unlike the earlier corporation that had owned the Colorado Midland. It would cost many Santa Fe stockholders' dollars to make the antique CM as modern as the rest of the system. The money could be used to a better advantage to expand the Santa Fe into a more profitable line. The Chicago, Rock Island and Pacific, a Colorado Midland customer since 1888, sent an inspection team to Colorado Springs in April, 1920. Two maintenance crews were dispatched from Colorado City in late April; the first cleared the tracks, while the second made small bridge repairs and occasionally added new ballast. The second crew reached Leadville at about the same time as the Rock Island inspection crew arrived from Denver in Colorado Springs.

The trip over the railroad was made in the private car of Charles MacNeill, **Mather,** and a Rock Island business car. The team consisted of J.E. Gorman, president of the Rock Island, Charles Hayden, chairman of the board of directors, I.E. Fritch, superintendent of maintenance-of-way, and three other officials. While MacNeill did not accompany the team, A.E. Carlton and Spencer Penrose traveled along.

Rumors circulated that the Colorado Midland would be purchased, along with the San Pedro and Los Angeles, helping the Rock Island link Chicago with Los Angeles. The Rock Island team quickly killed any speculation of a purchase. Hayden stated flatly, "There is nothing to this report in any way, shape or form. The Rock Island has no intention in the world of buying the Midland."

The group traveled over the Colorado Midland to Leadville, where they transferred to the Rio Grande and headed for Grand Junction. **Mather** was taken off the train at Grand Junction, and the Rock Island men continued on to Salt Lake City. Carlton and Penrose planned to travel to New York for the Republican National Convention, for his brother figured prominently in the political party. Natural influences interrupted the trip, however, since the Grand and Gunnison rivers were flooding. The car was returning to Pueblo by way of the Rio Grande's southerly route. Glenwood Springs was unreachable, and the train was stalled on the railroad near Whitewater, Colorado. Carlton and Penrose attempted to leave by way of a handcar, but it barely cleared the water. Carlton made his way through the water, but slipping, he twisted his ankle. The men eventually found their way to the convention.

In May, the Short Line was in full operation again. The C & S announced the event with quite a bit of fanfare. The news was more of a shock within a few days, for the Colorado and Southern let the town know that the Colorado Springs and Cripple Creek District Railway was being closed. The words were followed by several months of intermittent operations. All of the equipment was brought into the Colorado Springs yards by the end of the summer.

In the summer, following serious study of the results of the Santa Fe and Rock Island, the situation was brought under investigation by the Carlton syndicate. The mines were now operating at a rate of less than one-half of the prewar production. The cost of labor, and increased costs in general, were cutting deeply into mining profits. Automobiles and trucks were daily taking revenue away from the rail lines. The Colorado Midland could not reopen, because the syndicate could not afford to rebuild and re-equip it into a competitive railroad under the circumstances. It was decided that the Colorado Midland would be scrapped without further delay. Several considerations were studied. Just how might sections of the Colorado Midland be useful to the Midland Terminal?

The Colorado Midland from Colorado Springs to Divide was the only portion deemed serviceable and necessary to the operations of the Midland Terminal. The remaining equipment would be either absorbed into the Midland Terminal or scrapped. A large number of cars were left in the Colorado City yards until a use for them could be found.

Carlton studied an attempt to purchase the Short Line, with the possibility of abandoning the longer Midland Terminal route. The decision to continue using the MT was largely the result of a lesson in economics. The MT had a serviceable route, with a few small towns providing revenue. The Short Line needed repairs and upgrading, plus only a few small camps, not providing much in the way of revenue. The MT, however, needed somehow to do something to improve its financial posture. All potential markets were studied. The construction of facilities along the line to serve non-mining activities emerged as a definite possibility. The conversion of present facilities was an even better prospect, plus elimination of older, unused facilities. Ice-houses, new stock pens, as well as new sidings, were planned. New orders of gravel by the Rock Island railroad prompted a study of opening a new quarry, as well as reopening some of the old gravel pits.

In the winter of 1920-21, J.J. Cogan located men to operate the scrapping train. Many of the men were former "wreck train" crew members or came from the bridge and building department. The newer rails and switch ties were salvaged for use on the Midland Terminal, as were almost all of the hardware items. Most of the ties and bridges were just left in place, but a few of the bridges were scrapped for timbers. The right-of-way was donated to the state for use as a highway, and simple grading would allow the old road bed to serve as an automobile roadway. A portion of the Colorado Midland served as part of the Pikes Peak ocean to ocean highway. On April 28, 1922, the Colorado Midland was finally dissolved. The old grade was soon feeling the passing of east and westbound wheels, this time rubber tires unguided by steel rails. Colorado's new highway system was built on the graves of many old railroads, not just that of the Colorado Midland.

MIDLAND TERMINAL RY.

F. C. MATTHEWS
GENERAL FREIGHT & PASSENGER AGENT

COLORADO SPRINGS, COLO.

June
Twenty-third
1 9 2 1

The City Council of Colorado Springs,
City Hall,
Colorado Springs, Colorado.

Gentlemen:

      I am instructed on behalf of the scenic attractions of the Pikes Peak region to ask if you cannot change your order prohibiting solicitation by representatives of such attractions at the city auto camps, such as Prospect Lake. Our various representatives have been going to these camps, giving out literature and information to the people stopping at those places; all of which has been received by them very gratefully as their purpose in coming to this region is to see what we have to offer.

      If the people who come to the Pikes Peak region are prohibited from getting the information they desire without burdensome effort on their part, it will undoubtedly restrict the good that our publicity work endeavors to accomplish.

      I would like to ask if there is not some way of handling this matter so that the business of the scenic attractions, which is covered by a very large investment, cannot be taken care of in this respect.

Respectfully yours,

F. C. Matthews

FCM:RP

The Colorado Midland was officially gone, but much of the equipment stayed on with the Midland Terminal. It was rather unique, but the MT even operated a dining car between Colorado Springs and Cripple Creek for a short time. The financial condition of the Cripple Creek Central (or CC & CS) was such that the equipment remained lettered for the Colorado Midland for many years. The passenger equipment was quickly repainted, receiving highest priority. A few cars only received a quick coat of black paint over the old letterboards. In a few years the cars that made the transition to MT passenger service were completely repainted in green. The old CM cars that were destined for M-o-W service remained maroon until that was covered by mineral brown or tuscan.

The offices used a variety of old Colorado Midland forms and reports, on occasion lining out the old name, often not. The forms used by the Midland Terminal became a strange collection of old F & CC, Short line, CC & CS, and Colorado Midland relics. A few of the CM men stayed on with the MT, but most of them either retired or moved on. The majority of those who departed found jobs on the Santa Fe, Union Pacific, or Southern Pacific; very few joined the ranks of the Denver and Rio Grande Western.

A sale was announced for October 16, 1922. The Short Line was finally being sold for scrap. Equipment of questionable condition littered the old Colorado Springs yard. A few items were still stored in the MT's Colorado City yard. A Carlton representative was on hand with a check for what was thought would be the sale price, but in the crowd stood a man with fire in his eyes. The little man from the South had come to Colorado Springs and had firmly established himself as a power in the area's coal industry.

One of the most intense competitors of the Carlton-owned Pike View Coal Company was W.D. Corley. He had a definite dislike for the "King of Cripple Creek" and his empire. The bidding passed the Carlton estimate, and in dismay when it stopped, Corley was the only person to exceed the Carlton bid. Corley had bought the remains of the Short Line out from under the man who thought the deal was only a formality.

Carlton was still looking at the prospects of operating the Midland Terminal on the difficult grades in Ute Pass. The four percent grades were quite steep, and the Short Line was less steep. Corley quickly rejected any chance for Carlton to buy his railroad. He had plans for turning it into a toll road. The automobile was becoming a much more popular mode of travel than the train. Corley planned to cash in on the shortest route to the gold district. The dreams of the old Bear Creek Toll Road were about to be rekindled, some thirty years later. Carlton made an offer to purchase the locomotives, and some of the equipment, now useless due to the conversion of the grade. Corley set a stiff price knowing that Carlton could pay it, if forced. However, Carlton was far from willing to concede to Corley's demands. The engines would never again be seen pulling a train in Ute Pass. In a few years the remaining Short Line engines, which were still stored in Colorado City, were declared worthless and sold for scrap iron.

Corley made one other challenge. The old plan for a railroad to the summit of Pikes Peak from Rosemont was revived, but as a toll road. Corley requested permission to build a road through U.S. forest land. The road would avoid the Penrose-owned Pikes Peak Auto Highway. The Corley toll road to the summit of Pikes Peak was not acceptable to the U.S. Forest Service. The Corley Mountain Highway was eventually sold to the government, becoming the Gold Camp Road from Colorado Springs to Cripple Creek.

All passes. — Dan Abbott Collection

1924   NO. A 2112

MIDLAND TERMINAL RAILWAY

PASS Mr. J. J. Livingston,
ACCOUNT GA, C&NW Ry.

UNTIL DECEMBER 31st 1924. UNLESS OTHERWISE ORDERED
AND SUBJECT TO CONDITIONS ON BACK

VALID WHEN COUNTERSIGNED BY MYSELF M. E. O'BRIEN OR R. S. GILL

COUNTERSIGNED BY

GENERAL MANAGER

1927   NO. A 503

MIDLAND TERMINAL RAILWAY

PASS
ACCOUNT
Mr. F. G. Morss,
Engr. & Pur. Agent,
Uintah Ry. Co.

UNTIL DECEMBER 31st 1927. UNLESS OTHERWISE ORDERED
AND SUBJECT TO CONDITIONS ON BACK

VALID WHEN COUNTERSIGNED BY MYSELF A. J. BUTLER OR R. S. GILL

COUNTERSIGNED BY

GENERAL MANAGER

The new Motor Car 101 waits on the Divide platform in about 1938, the car had yet to be "streamlined". — L.W. Moody Photo, John McCall Collection

4. The Golden Cycle Years

Passenger engine 59 with ex-CM tender waits eastbound at Victor. In the background are three ex-CM Hanrahan cars, converted to single door cars. — DPL

THE MIDLAND TERMINAL RODE INTO the early 1920s as the last surviving railroad in the Cripple Creek District, as well as the last of the Colorado Springs home railroads. The district itself was in serious trouble.

Early leaders in the district were now either old and dying or had moved on to other financial dealings. The city of Colorado Springs had changed from health resort to major financial center to tourist mecca. Major stockholders in district mines lived on the wide, tree-lined streets in north Colorado Springs, or in the new community called Broadmoor. Count James Pourtales had attempted to run a dairy on the expanse of land at the base of Cheyenne Mountain. A casino was built on the land in 1892, changing the area into a suburban area. Spencer Penrose bought the area and built a fine, luxurious hotel in 1917 on the site of the old casino. Penrose and his associates used their income from the district to bring drastic changes in the Pikes Peak Region.

The population of the Cripple Creek District had

had been declining since the start of World War One. In 1920 the population was at about 5,000, or less than five percent of what it had been at the peak some twenty years earlier. Colorado Springs at the same time was growing.

The Midland Terminal, actually in superior condition, saw upgrading of some of the old trackage inherited from the F & CC and the Short Line. Rails, and money for other improvements, had been made available through the abandonment of the Colorado Midland. Twenty miles of worn tracks were to be relaid with heavier rails. The railroad, however, was moving in a direction that spelled its own end, for the Midland Terminal was becoming dependent upon the output of Golden Cycle-owned mines in the district. The Carlton syndicate was gaining control of many of the district mines.

The reduction in the number of working mines and the modern automobile were making the Midland Terminal's passenger service almost unnecessary. The MT outrageously owned seventeen passenger cars at a time when the average passenger train was only three cars. Meals were even available for a while in the old ex-CM dining cars. A study was started to cut back the expense of operating even these small passenger trains.

Ownership of major mines in the district was being consolidated. Forty mines were producing ninety percent of the gold, and four groups owned these mines. In 1922 the Carlton–Penrose syndicate lost a valuable member, Charles M. MacNeill. His death, however, had more of an impact on the group's copper mining investments than on the gold mining. The railroad and gold mining investments of the syndicate had taken on a minor roll as each of the leaders of the group started to develop his own interests. In a parallel pattern, each member's activity slowly increased the financial arena covered by the syndicate. The old Cripple Creek syndicate now had nationwide interests. The scope of the group eventually caused it to disperse. Each of the members remained in close contact, but their varied interests caused them to place many of their old Cripple Creek affairs in the hands of subordinates. Two of the men almost completely lost concern in the district. However, the core of the syndicate, Penrose, Carlton, and Tutt, retained an active interest in their Cripple Creek investments. Each of the men held interests apart from the old syndicate.

Penrose's activities were the most interesting. The flamboyant Penrose, and his associate Tutt, were among the first in the old gold camp. The two young men turned their mine, the C.O.D., into an empire. They had wisely invested their tremendous revenues from each of their ventures. Penrose, the more visible of the two, was turning the Broadmoor area into an entertaining resort. The Broadmoor Hotel was the center of a vast development that included a golf course, park land, grand homes, and a zoo. His interest in the Midland Terminal was only part of his railroad empire. A few years earlier Penrose and some friends, including Carlton, had invested in a land development south of Colorado Springs near Florence.

A small town was built northeast of Florence named Penrose. The area was touted as prime fruit growing land, to rival the fruit industry on the western slope near Grand Junction. One of the unusual aspects of the plan was a short railroad, the Beaver, Penrose and Northern. It is obscure if the railroad ever planned to extend north toward Colorado Springs, but the line did haul a small amount of freight and a few passengers. The southern terminal was on the D & RGW's line to Canon City, at a point called Beaver. The northern end was at Penrose. On occasion Penrose, Carlton, or one of the other syndicate members could be found riding on, and even working on the little railroad.

The officers of the Midland Terminal were working to keep the red ink off their ledger books by developing various industries along the road. The old resort areas had died, many of the fine old hotels became seedy firetraps, while others became mountain tuberculosis centers. The farmers and ranchers along the line were never actively recruited by the Midland Terminal until district activity declined. The problems were of a more common nature than one may suspect. The decline of the district had forced the residents in the area back into an agricultural role. The tremendous decline in population also caused a depression in the market for farm products in the district. The Midland Terminal could help farmers deliver their products to new markets. New cattle pens were built at Gillett and even at Cameron, once a resort and recreation center on the edge of the mining district. Old stock pens were refurbished, and the reconditioning of a few old stock cars once used by the Colorado Midland also occurred. Ice ponds were established at Divide. Refrigeration cars were built from old boxcars, as well as from old Colorado Midland vegetable cars.

The earnings of the Midland Terminal dropped as fast as the earnings of the district mines. In 1923 the railroad saw its last profitable dollar until 1929.

In the summers after the close of the Colorado Midland, an attempt was made to keep the traditional wildflower excursions alive, but by comparison to earlier endeavors they were almost disasters. In June 1923 a tour was arranged from Colorado Springs into Cripple Creek. Seven passenger cars and two locomotives hauled eager tourists up Ute Pass to the mining camp. It was a sight, the likes of which had been memories the old Ute Pass residents had nearly forgotten. The trip, however, was not as popular when it was repeated.

The Golden Cycle Mill was also noticing slim times. Daily newspaper accounts alternately reported the boom or decline of activity in the district. Ores from Leadville and other Colorado mining camps were starting to find their way to the Golden Cycle as the mills in those camps declined. The company actively searched for new business. An experimental flotation process with a 200-ton-per-day capacity was shelved until a power problem could be resolved. The Golden Cycle Mill had been obtaining power from a private power company, as had the Midland Terminal. The city of Colorado Springs was consolidating all of the privately owned power plants into a city-owned system. A new rate structure was introduced, a substantial increase over that of the previous company. A plan was recommended for the construction of a coal-fired power plant for the mill and the railroad shops owned by the Golden Cycle. The new plant would be in operation by late 1925, at the Pike View mine north of Colorado Springs.

A coal miners strike in the East was severely hurting the whole country, but the Pike View and Corley mines were being spared, since they were both nonunion operations. Rivalry erupted again when Carlton raised wages and added bonuses for his miners. Corley was forced to follow suit, and he even considered raising the ante, but did not.

The new Golden Cycle flotation process plan was pushed back until 1929. However, some of the preliminary work was started in 1926. Ore from all over Colorado would be required to keep the mill up to minimum operating capacity. A capacity of 200 tons per day was far above the level produced by the district.

In early summer 1925 a new development stirred activity in the MT yards. A railroad had been removed from the syndicate's empire, the Beaver, Penrose and Northern, and another was about to be added. The B, P & N had barely managed to survive as a toy, and reality forced the scrapping of the project, even though the little town of Penrose would live on. Spencer Penrose approached Zalmon Simmons, owner of the Manitou and Pikes Peak Railway, about the potential purchase of his quaint little line. The M & PP had been in operation longer than the MT, but both of the railroads were suffering from declining markets. The M & PP relied entirely on the tourist trade, which had seen better days. On July 25, Penrose and his associates again found themselves the owners of different gauge railroads, and a streetcar line. The M & PP shops were consolidated with the MT shops, and all major work on the equipment

would be accomplished in Colorado City. The problems of operating the tourist line were added to the other problems facing the leaders of the Midland Terminal.

The population of the district continued to decline in the late 1920s. But, the population of Colorado Springs, which had dropped in the period following World War One, started to climb in the mid 1920s. Construction of new and impressive buildings in Colorado Springs was matched by the destruction of many of the fine, but derelict buildings in the district. The number of operating mines in the district dropped to near two dozen. The Golden Cycle Mill was operating at one-half capacity, even though construction of the flotation tanks continued. The Portland Mill in Colorado Springs had been closed, and their district mill was about to close. Ore production dropped below the $4 million level in 1926, and below the $3 million level in 1929.

Cripple Creek Gold Production

1891	$60,000	1908	$16,230,525
1892	$687,310	1909	$15,350,143
1893	$2,020,400	1910	$15,987,819
1894	$3,256,000	1911	$15,988,684
1895	$6,970,000	1912	$14,006,741
1896	$9,100,000	1913	$14,335,520
1897	$12,000,000	1914	$13,551,931
1898	$16,000,000	1915	$16,189,727
1899	$21,000,000	1916	$14,399,941
1900	$22,500,000	1917	$12,533,177
1901	$24,986,990	1918	$10,508,705
1902	$24,508,311	1919	$7,668,729
1903	$17,630,107	1920	$5,839,803
1904	$21,307,953	1921	$5,288,423
1905	$22,357,432	1922	$4,402,218
1906	$16,288,291	1923	$4,161,306
1907	$13,148,152		

Locomotives were upgraded by the Colorado City shops starting in 1926. Included in the rebuilding were Worthington feed-water heaters and other experiments to the road engines to increase their efficiency. The effort looked to be futile, since traffic was declining at an alarming rate. The railroad had lost $21,720 in 1926 and $45,518 in 1927. An austerity program started in 1928, and the elimination of the passenger runs in the district was planned. To increase shipping, the MT cut rates on ore loads, and the Golden Cycle reduced milling charges in 1927. The loss in 1928 was only $6,401.

The Midland Terminal stopped operation of one of the district's longest running trains in 1929. The automobile had finally forced the end of the MT's suburban train. Revenues from the passenger business between Cripple Creek and Colorado Springs continued to drop. The cars on the suburban special in the district were the former F & CC narrow-gauge cars on their standard-gauge trucks. The cars were moved to Midland and Colorado Springs for company use. The cars at Midland were put on the ground for use by the section gang. The cars in Colorado Springs were employed for storage, except one, the former F & CC 60 which was sold to a company man for his own use. He had it placed in his yard where he used one end as a shop, while children played where hundreds of district residents had once ridden through the gold country.

In the fall of 1929 the system failed; the stock market crashed. The country moved rapidly into an economic depression. The impact, however, was not so severe in the district, which was actually on the verge of a minor boom. A few of the marginal mines had reopened in 1928, but in 1929 and 1930 more reopened. A trust in gold, and the need for any kind of work helped bring a little prosperity to an area that had been in a depression long before the rest of the country. The railroad actually saw a profit of $2,798 in 1929.

The Midland Terminal and the Golden Cycle Mill continued to operate, almost on a day-to-day basis. The mines were producing small quantitites of medium-grade ore, and quite a bit of low-grade ore. The mill was receiving quantities of waste rock from the mines, shipped on the chance it might contain enough gold to pay for its own processing. The gold mining companies were calling for a set, government supported, gold price that would help keep them in business. Ore from all over Colorado was now normally seen at the Golden Cycle Mill. The earlier decline in mining had forced the reduction of coal shipments into the district, but as

The passenger train is about ready to leave for Cripple Creek, on one of the last runs in 1931. Visible on the side of the boiler is the superheater that was installed in the late 1920's. — LDM

Motor 101, in its original configuration, rolls eastbound past the coal trestle in Colorado City. The streetcar heritage of the car is clearly visible, which was "streamlined" later. — UPHS

activity increased so did coal shipments. One commodity that was ominously increasing was the amount of gasoline being shipped into the district.

In 1931 the leadership of the Midland Terminal shifted from one Carlton brother to the other. On September 7, A.E. Carlton died from an illness which had weakened him in the late summer. Leslie G. Carlton moved over to control the Cripple Creek Central, which was still the official owner of the Midland Terminal. One of his first changes was the elimination of the costly steam passenger service between Cripple Creek and Colorado Springs. A passenger car was added to the daily freight runs during the summer and fall, when a few passengers, usually tourists, only half-filled the car. Master Mechanic McKay, always looking for new ways to save money, had been working on an idea for several years. The answer to the problem was suggested by numerous other railroads, but the solution for the Midland Terminal was difficult due to financial conditions. McKay had an idea when the the train crews, and many of the tourists, complained about the situation. It would take several years before the idea could germinate into a new form of transportation on the Midland Terminal.

In the district the mine owners called for a new drainage tunnel, lower than the Roosevelt. The average depth of the mines was 1,000 feet, with the water at the 2,000-foot level. Eight of the largest producers, however, were at or below that level. The Portland #1 was at 3,100 feet and was

spending quite a bit of money on pumping.

A rehabilitation program started on the Midland Terminal in 1933. In a stroke of good fortune the federal government finally set the price of gold at the rate of $35 an ounce, almost $15 over the earlier unsupported rate. The number of operating mines immediately started to increase. Old companies were revived and again put into operation, including Carlton's Pharmacist. Carlton also had a few plans for the Midland Terminal, including the dissolution of the last of the remains of the Cripple Creek Central and its consolidation with the Golden Cycle Corporation.

In 1934 the MT's upgrading program was accelerated. New 90-pound rails and over 30,000 new creosote ties were laid in Ute Pass, as well as sections beyond Divide and in the district. In the shops a streetcar from the Colorado Springs and Interurban emerged as a motor powered coach, #101. The odd car, obviously of streetcar heritage, but with a strange truck-like nose, would start making daily runs between Colorado Springs and Cripple Creek with up to eight passengers, light freight, and mail. A second car was on hand and would be modified as soon as the first car proved its worth. The decline of the Colorado Springs streetcar system had made the two cars available at very low cost. The scheme of Master Mechanic McKay reduced the cost of operating the mail service to Cripple Creek to a fraction of the earlier rate. The main function of the Midland Terminal steam locomotives was pulling ore cars; in 1934 the MT hauled 85,000 tons more ore than in 1933.

The Golden Cycle, still operating their old cyanide process, expanded the flotation portion of the mill from 200 tons per day to nearly 600 tons per day. Two new storage tanks, and an additional section of old trackage, doubled the yard capacity above the mill. Two new roasters and a new crusher made the Golden Cycle Mill one of the largest and most modern mills in the West.

Improvements on the Midland Terminal continued into 1935. Two high bridges above Manitou, as well as three others near the district, were filled with waste rock from the area and rock from the Pikes Peak Fuel mines at Pike View. Trucks hauled the waste rock from the little town north of Colorado Springs to the trestle site by way of a road to the company-owned lime kilns above Manitou. The freight cars on the railroad were in miserable condition. A number of steel dump cars, purchased used, augmented the older wooden cars. The MT had 257 pieces of freight equipment in 1936.

A flood on Memorial Day in 1935 destroyed a large section of Colorado Springs. Spring rains had saturated the ground until an afternoon cloudburst turned the placid Monument Valley Creek, and to a lesser extent Fountain Creek, into walls of water. The flood swept down Monument Creek from north of Pike View, cutting off the Chicago, Rock Island and Pacific's Roswell yards, stripping the Monument Valley Park that Palmer had started nearly sixty years before, washing away bridges and all access to Denver just above the Rio Grande depot. Fountain Creek flooding was not as severe. However, high water created problems in

The old Short Line yards in Colorado Springs were devastated in the Memorial Day 1935 flood. Visible is the old CS&CCD engine house and the MT's bridge over the D&RGW. A number of old freight cars had been in the yards during the flood. — AC

The flood destroyed the D&RGW and CRI&P bridges north of the depot at Colorado Springs, and devastated the Monument Valley Park. — AC

Spencer Penrose has a front row seat in the tiny Zoo Special, built by M&PP and MT shop men. The engine and car were designed by Master Mechanic William McKay of both railroads. — JGC

M&PP, a dimutive locomotive and car of the cog railroad towers over the tiny cog railroad engine built for the Cheyenne Mountain Zoo. — JGC

Motor 102 churns out onto the turntable, ready for a mail and freight run to downtown Colorado Springs or Cripple Creek. — UPHS

the Midland Terminal yards and along the tracks toward Colorado Springs. Monument Creek washed away the bridges of the Denver and Rio Grande and the Midland Terminal, just north of the junction with Fountain Creek. The flooding continued southward as far as Fountain. Colorado Springs had never seen destruction like this, although Pueblo had been flooded by a similar storm thirteen years before. Crews started to repair the roads and railroads immediately. Old Colorado City was connected with Colorado Springs by only one bridge. The railroads were operating almost normally within two weeks, but damage would be visible for several years.

Operations at the Golden Cycle Mill were immediately cut back. The water that had done so much damage to the highway and road system had also washed away some of the tailings ponds and created a huge lake above the mill. Access to the mill eventually returned to normal, but ore shipments from other parts of the state were cut off for several weeks. The Midland Terminal maintenance-of-way and bridge crews worked rapidly to repair the damage from Woodland Park to the Santa Fe yards.

The shop men, as well as the train crews found themselves working on Manitou and Pikes Peak equipment and trains. A number of the MT employees switched over to working full time on the M & PP. In the early thirties M & PP popularity with tourists had declined, but the purchase by Penrose had brought a new vitality to the line. The

colorful Penrose promoted the entire Pikes Peak region as a tourist mecca. The Colorado City shops assisted the Manitou shops of the M & PP in designing and building a small gasoline powered coach for the same general purpose that the MT had built theirs, cutting costs. Master Mechanic McKay, who held that position on both railroads, also came up with an interesting little cog engine for Penrose's latest railroad. Soon after the purchase of the M & PP someone, probably McKay or Penrose, dreamed up an idea for a connection between the Broadmoor Hotel and the Cheyenne Mountain Zoo using a cog engine. The small engine and car would be based on the M & PP, and would allow hotel guests to visit Penrose's zoo.

On the Midland Terminal the second of the streetcars went into operation in 1937. The car handled mainly freight and mail, but a passenger or two could be carried. The car augmented and on very rare occasions ran as a second section to car 101. The two cars, 101 and 102, provided what was left of passenger service. Freight service was minimal and declining. A mill opened near Cripple Creek in 1936, hoping to provide an option to non-Golden Cycle owned mines, but it only lasted until 1937. The Elkton mine suffered from an underground fire in July 1937, but the timbering was rebuilt. United Gold Mines shipped several carloads of very high-grade ore during the year, but most of the ore shipped was of below average concentration. Ore shipments were down, but due to a few high-grade shipments, and the increased price of gold, the ore was more valuable.

Cripple Creek Gold Production

1924	$5,500,000	1932	$2,177,707
1925	$5,050,000	1933	$2,001,883
1926	$5,885,892	1934	$5,690,934
1927	$4,081,208	1935	$5,054,400
1928	$3,100,000	1936	$5,322,260
1929	$2,843,495	1937	$5,575,338
1930	$2,837,384	1938	$5,654,244
1931	$2,729,201	1939	$5,369,567
1932	$2,177,707		

A repair program had been started rebuilding the old wooden ore cars, and the program continued into 1938 converting seventeen old boxcars and a stock car into open ore cars. The older cars, like the locomotives, would eventually need replacement. In 1938 one more locomotive was added to the roster, locomotive 61. The American Locomotive Company engine was purchased from the Chicago and Illinois Midland for $11,325.56. The engine was built in 1910 for the Chicago and Alton, but it was in very good condition. The locomotive was needed to supplement the older engines, which required frequent repairs due to their age. McKay's first impression was to use it in Colorado City switching ore cars to the Golden Cycle. An interesting observation about this particular locomotive is that it is nearly identical to a class of locomotive that A.E. Carlton wanted to buy for the Colorado Midland in 1917. A search was started for other additional engines for the MT. One limiting factor was size, for the curvature of the track restricted engine size. The 61 immediately developed derailment problems, and a trailing truck was added. The additional wheels improved its ability to stay on the rails when backing.

In September company president Leslie G. Carlton died. Seven years after his brother's passing, the leadership of the company moved to Merrill E. Shoup, son of a former Colorado governor. Shoup would be the last president of the Midland Terminal, serving as the Golden Cycle president well beyond the last days of the railroad.

Shipments of ore had declined 6.8 percent from 1936 to 1937, and 8.4 percent in 1938. The value of the ore was the deciding factor. The output of many mines was handled by truck, and the railroad cut back trackage to the mines. In a few of the years trackage was added, but largely it was declining. Shoup speculated that without the tunnel the Golden Cycle and the Midland Terminal would not be needed. The mines controlled by the corporation were at a point of maximum development.

Help for the Midland Terminal came from the East. An extensive project for the rebuilding of the

Locomotive 510 has had the C&IM removed from the tender, and will soon become Midland Terminal 61. The locomotive was originally built for the Buffalo and Susquehana, but the railroad folded before the locomotive was delivered. — CHS

SUBJECT : Ballast Reports-

FAIRBURY - March 26, 1937.

L H McAlpin - Roswell

    Effective April 1 we will again receive granite ballast from the Midland Terminal Railway Co. for points east of Goodland. Arrange to handle ballast as it was done last year. In this connection we will require wire report addressed to W H Dicks, E D Sheehan, and this office giving information as follows:

        A - Date
        B - No. Cars loaded
        C - Where billed to
        D - Total cars loaded since first of month
        E - No. empty cars on hand

    This report to be made at the close of each day so we will receive in this office the next morning. File 305

cc- W H Dicks
    E D Sheehan

                       C G Adams

Chicago, Rock Island and Pacific in eastern Colorado and western Kansas required large amounts of new ballast. One of the Rock Island's major sources of ballast had been the Colorado Midland, and they had occasionally purchased the red, decomposed granite from the Midland Terminal since 1917. The new program would require massive amounts of rock. Large quantities of rock were available from the three sites, including the pits at mile posts 25 and 38. A larger quarry was planned between Murphy and Midland. The Rock Island furnished from ten to one hundred cars a week for ballast shipping, and on a few occasions the Midland shops made repairs to the cars before they could be moved up the line to the quarries. The project provided the funds to purchase another ten miles of used 90-pound rails between Colorado City and Midland.

    The Midland Terminal was busy again. In the region the Cresson, which had started as a fairly lackluster hole, had become one of the district's notable mines. The mine had no railroad access, other than the coal which was delivered to the base of a tramway above the mine. A substantial increase in the lower levels was producing large quantities of medium-grade ore. One other mine had become a high producer, the Ajax. The developments, and further mining of the lower levels required completion of the drainage tunnel, now named Carlton Tunnel.

    In April 1919, the Golden Cycle Corporation set

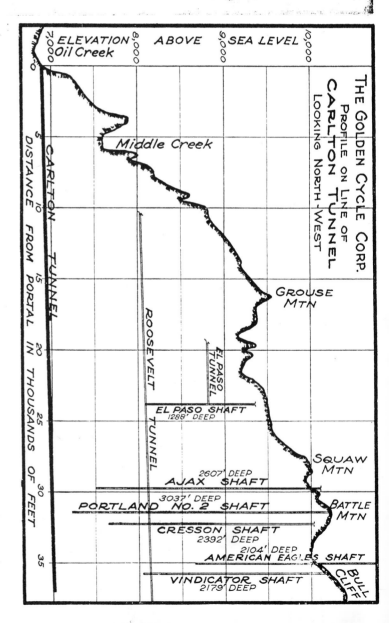

Carlton Drainage Tunnel Dedication

Cripple Creek - Victor Kiwanis Club
HOST

SEPTEMBER 4, 1939   ONE TO FOUR P. M.

aside one million dollars for the construction of the tunnel. Alfred Bebee, vice-president of the corporation, acted as project director. He had been the superintendent of the Cresson for nine years previous to the tunnel start. John Austin, a well-known tunnel builder, came to Cripple Creek to act as superintendent of the construction. Work

finally started on July 13, 1939, nine miles south of Cripple Creek. One hundred men worked to complete the tunnel. As with many of the developments in the district, some of the old-timers were heard to say, "This will add twenty years to the life of the district."

The tunnel was dedicated on September 4,

1939, and Cripple Creek came to life again. Newspapers recorded the event with grand and glorious style. Dignitaries paraded through the streets of the town. The officials of the Golden Cycle and Midland Terminal traveled to Cripple Creek by rail. The trip might have been the last run of the Midland Terminal's business car **Cascade**, which was originally one of the Colorado Midland's business cars.

The event preceeded the death of another Cripple Creek leader by a few months. In early December 1939, the best-known man in Colorado Springs died, Spencer Penrose. The colorful man made a mark in Colorado that will probably never be erased. He came to the district in 1891, and along with Charles L. Tutt, developed the C.O.D. mine. The investments he made produced the Broadmoor Hotel, Cheyenne Mountain Zoo, Will Rogers Shrine, Cheyenne Mountain Highway, and made many other things possible. He had put money into virtually all of the local railroads: Colorado Midland, Short Line, Beaver, Penrose and Northern, Manitou and Pikes Peak, Mount Manitou Incline, and even the Denver, and Rio

Grande Western. Penrose had been a powerful influence in the Colorado Midland and the Midland Terminal. In addition to all of these roads he held stock in several other national railroad companies. The El Pomar Foundation, created by Spencer Penrose, is still a powerful influence in the state of Colorado.

The Midland Terminal hauled 29,875,149 tons of freight in 1939, the greatest part of it being ore from Cripple Creek. The same year saw a number of small changes started around the Colorado City shops. Business car #100, the **Cascade**, had been sold and became a cabin near Chipita Park. Locomotive 53, which had been Colorado Midland 53, was retired and made ready for scrapping. It was moved to a spot near the old oil house as a stationary boiler. A pair of ex-Copper River and Northwestern 2-8-2 locomotives, numbered 62 and 63, were purchased. The two had been used on the railway on the south coast of Alaska, and the trip to Colorado was lengthy; one went in service in 1941 and the other in 1942. The engines required extensive rebuilding including new trailing trucks and tenders, which were

Car 100, the Cascade, served the Midland Terminal owners through the two Carltons, and then was retired. — CHS

Alco builders photo of Copper River and Northwestern shows the locomotive that would become Midland Terminal 63, and shows the numerous differences between the two owners' preferences. — Alco Historic Photos.

(Left) In 1921 Cascade looked quite sedate, the depot, the Cascade House and the distinctive Ramona Hotel would all be gone within a few more years. — JAS

Fresh from shopping, locomotive 62 rolled out onto the turntable bright and sparkling, loaded with coal, and ready to go to Bull Hill for the first time. — UPHS

Daily Report of Ballast Loaded on Midland Terminal Railway

Colorado Springs, Colo., April 15, 1943

P. E. STRATE,
FAIRBURY, NEBR.

L. L. LUMPKIN,
TOPEKA, KANSAS.

Following cars of granite ballast were loaded this date for the Rock Island:

CAR NO. AND INITIAL	NET WEIGHT	STATION BILLED TO	REMARKS
R.I. 100477	129860	LIMON COLO	
R.I. 100362	134040	DO	
R.I. 100518	136200	DO	
sufficient number of these cars wil be qeighed at Colorado Spring			
ITY until we are satisfied that the average agreement weight of			
10,000 will be assured.			
		E. F. Schumm Agent	

CORRECT:................................

Contractor

ROSWELL - Jan 19, 1940

Mr F. Nugent, Supt

Your memo 17th file 305 with regard to the ballast we received from the Midland Terminal Railway.

The ballast would be loaded in Midland one day and delivered to us the next day. It being 25 miles from point the ballast was loaded in MT to where it was weighed on MT and 3 miles from point where weighed to point where delivered to us in D&RG yards at Springs.

The Midland loading reports are made up in their Dispatchers Office showing car number and net weight, then mailed to us and Clerk checks Wts and show destination to their loading reports mailing one copy your Office and six copies to Mr Underwood who signs them and later mails them to you. Their Dispatcher weighs the ballast and makes their loading reports.

L. H. McAlpin

Fairbury - March 10, 1947

File 278

Messrs. L. B. Close
M. J. Contant
A. Erickson
T. J. Keane
Wm. Roberts
A. L. Loy
L. H. McAlpin
C. I. Hansen.

I wrote you on January 16th, advising regard movement of one Midland Terminal Railway wood gondola car with arch bar trucks from Colorado Springs to Chicago for delivery to Iron & Steel Products Company via the Nickel Plate.

The number of cars involved has been increased to 100 and these cars will be moving at the rate of about five cars per week and same instructions apply to all these cars.

It should be understood under no circumstances must these cars be trained elsewhere except next to caboose.

Please instruct all concerned accordingly.

J. H. Mullinix

3-14-47

Locomotive 53 pulling dump cars at Midland on one of the locomotive's last assignments before retirement. — DPL/Otto Perry Collection

Ex-US Army 4064 at the storage track next to the coal trestle in 1948. — HB/ESP

USA locomotice 4028 in Topeka before shipment to Colorado on the Santa Fe. — W.A.G.

brought along when they were converted from oil to coal.

World War Two brought an interesting, but tragic set of events to the district. The government ordered the closing of the gold mines, but due to the importance of other minerals, the operation of the Golden Cycle mill was needed. A small amount of gold ore was moved through the mill as part of the reduction of other ores. The railroad industry in general was short of experienced men. A number of Midland Terminal men moved on to other railroads as they were laid off due to a lack of business, or left on their own due to the low salaries. A few remained with Colorado roads, but many moved to California. A new army post was being built south of Colorado Springs, Camp Carson. A few of the boiler men and maintenance-of-way men went to work on the construction job, many never to return to railroad work.

The machine shop was kept busy turning out small parts for military contracts, under subcontract to Aircraft Mechanics, a local aviation supplier. The two new locomotives were brought up to prime condition by men who were producing parts for single-seat fighter planes and giant four-engined bombers.

A few of the mines were allowed to return to operation in late 1942, but the shift to work was very slow. The mines were short of young men. The Midland Terminal operated with a limited crew. In 1940 there were over 1,000 miners working in the district, but only 200 miners worked in the mines by the start of 1943.

Business was way down on the railroad as a result of the cut in mining. In 1941, 30,669,525 tons of freight were hauled, but in 1942 that was down to 22,782,052 tons. The war-years tonnage barely added up to the 1942 tonnage. The end of the war, however, brought some new enthusiasm. A burst of activity resembled the 1930s' boom, but was on a much shakier basis. A used steam shovel was added to the roster. Purchase of 120 used self-clearing gondola cars solved problems with the old wooden cars. Many of the old wooden cars were rebuilt, from rebuilt cars that had been rebuilt from cars that dated back to 1887. A shortage of cars had been a problem in the late 1930s, mainly due to difficulties created by the decrepit cars.

The Midland Terminal was quick to take notice of the availability of a large number of small, but powerful, new locomotives. The 0-6-0 type locomotives had been produced in large numbers for the United States Army from a United States Railroad Administration design. Two of the engines were purchased in 1945 for $22,000, plus four more were ordered. The locomotives, added to the three that were on hand when the war started, allowed the older locomotives to be rested, or used for light work. The two new locomotives were in service by mid-1947. Old locomotive 54 was retired in November 1946; partly scrapped it would provide parts for other locomotives. Locomotive 55, after it was dumped on the ground at the Midland gravel pit, alternately saw repair work, and stripping, as if the railroad could not decide just what to do with it. In October 1947 the locomotive was finally listed as scrap.

In a very unique chain of events, Merrill Shoup was elected to the board of directors of the Denver and Rio Grande Western. It was probably the first time that anyone had served as an officer or board member of both the MT and the D & RGW at the same time. It must have caused the ghosts of the Colorado Midland to stir, because a series of

The roundhouse crew lined up on the turntable a few days before the abandonment for a remembrance photograph; the men from left to right are: Buck Wilkins, unidentified, unidentified, John Manick, Ed Weller, Sam Bayless, Billy Henderick, unidentified, Harvey Cline, Charlie O'Brien, Jimmy McGrady, Sammy Crain, and in the front is Keith Schooley, Carl Otto, Andy Schooley, and Jack Buckman. — UPHS

Seen from the road, 55 looks pretty sad, with its coal and sand on the ground, unfortunately when it was replaced on the rails, it was dumped again in a matter of minutes. — PM

events in the year following the election led to the demise of the Midland Terminal.

On May 11, 1947, floods in Ute Pass washed out the grade in fourteen places, severed U.S. Highway 24 in several places, and took lives in Manitou. At one point high water invaded the Colorado City yards and nearly destroyed the road bridge at 21st Street near the roundhouse. The railroad bridges over Fountain Creek (just east of the yards) and at Monument Creek were slightly weakened. The railroad reopened two weeks later, but the highway in Ute Pass took longer to repair. In August more heavy rains brought another closure due to flooding, which was almost as severe.

A strange turn of events in 1948 spelled the end of the Midland Terminal. The employees of the Colorado Midland and Midland Terminal were not strong on unions, referring largely to the number of problems with the miners unions in the district at the turn of the century; but also they were neither non- nor anti-union. Many of the employees belonged to the various unions, but since the number was small, they were carried as a local, part of a larger shop, the D & RGW's in Denver.

The average value of the ore being taken from the district dropped from $10 a ton in 1939 to near $6 in 1948. In 1941, 1,300 men worked in the mines, but in 1948 there were only 300. The non-ore freight shipments declined to nearly zero after the war. To add to the problem the shop men asked McKay for a raise and hourly readjustments. The men asked for 25 cents more an hour, plus a forty hour, five day week, rather than their forty hour, six day week. As a comparison, Midland Terminal mechanics received $1.04 an hour while D & RGW mechanics received $1.39 an hour. The other shop men were paid as follows: Carmen 91.25 cents an hour, helpers 82.25 cents an hour, and maintenance men received 68 cents an hour. Most Denver and Rio Grande Western men doing the same jobs were paid from thirty to fifty cents an hour more. McKay flatly refused to discuss any increase. The request then went to Shoup, who also turned the men down. He stated that up to the action taken by the outside union men, he had received no complaints from his employees. It was his opinion that all of the men could use a raise, but that the company was not in a position to raise anyone's wages, and that he would definitely not raise the wages of just a few.

ROSWELL — Febr 12,1948

File 3479 219

Mr. J. H. Mullinix:

Attached bill for the Midland Terminal
Ry Co for the amount of $ 4.55# for repairs to Eng
truck brass Eng 4026 Jan 16,1948.

Eng 4026 arrived here on train 33 Jan 16th
with R.F.Eng truck brass babbit all gone. Had no mandrel
here or nothing to make one to rebabbit the brass. Had
to take it to the Midland Terminal to have them do the
work and furnish material. Pls handle for payment.

L. H. McAlpin

In the late 1920's and early 1930's when this picture was taken, Independence had almost vanished. The Vindicator mine, likewise was only a shell of its former glory, and only the Midland Terminal remained to serve the mines. — PPL

The Golden Cycle Mill, as seen in 1939, shows the immense amounts of tailings generated by the smelter. The roasting building is the most prominent with its nearly flat roof covering nearly an acre of ground. — PPL

Golden Cycle Sno White Lime was a product of the lime kiln in Manitou. The lime was needed in the mill and the excess was a valuable sideline. — PPL

William McKay and Merrill Shoup with the Inspection Car, date and location unknown, but the car looks freshly painted, as do the ore cars behind them which were purchased in 1935. — PM

The shop men felt that they had an honest complaint, and called for a strike. McKay warned the men of the hazards of their choice, but the men decided to go out on strike anyway. On April 16 the men started their strike. The other employees were forced to take furloughs, since the railroad could not run without the shop men.

The leaders of the strike met with McKay and Shoup before and after the strike started, but within a few days the meetings were called off. In mid-May talks resumed. On May 19, Mike Butler acted as mediator for the two sides in a long meeting. On May 20, at the same time that a Golden Cycle Corporation Board of Directors meeting was being held, the strike was settled. The strikers and the other employees would receive a ten-cent an hour raise. Unfortunately, at the board of directors meeting, the officers had voted to petition for abandonment of the railroad.

A site had been selected previously in the Elkton area for construction of a completely new mill. The old Golden Cycle Mill in Colorado City would be closed and scrapped, a portion of the equipment would be used in the new mill, to be named the Carlton Mill, in honor of the Carlton brothers. All mining operations by the Golden Cycle Corporation in the district would stop until the new mill could be opened. The Golden Cycle announced repeatedly that the closing of the mill and the Midland Terminal was **not** a direct result of the railroad strike. In the words of Shoup, "because of economic conditions which have come into existence since the construction of the railroad and the mill."

The plan for closing the Midland Terminal attracted much attention among area residents. The end would bring the closing of the last of the Cripple Creek railroads, plus the end of a Colorado City railroad and mill tradition. Permission to scrap the railroad was granted on August 25, 1948. In December the railroad was sold to Commercial Metals Company as scrap, but that scrapping would not take place until after several additional weeks of operation. Two more old locomotives

In 1947 the Denver and Rio Grande Western was building a new overpass in south Colorado Springs. One afternoon the erecting crew brought their "big hook" back to the yards with the boom up, with this result to the Midland Terminal's tracks over the yard. Fortunately the MT had access via another route to the D&RGW's yards. Looking east in the upper view, the overpass, which had survived the 1935 flood, looks like a broken toy. — Both, PPL

Crossing the Last Trestle

— Denver Post

had been scrapped, 57 was retired in June 1948, and 56 in September 1948. Old 52, which had been Colorado Midland 50, last of the CM engines on the MT, had been retired also. Four more U.S. Army locomotives were on the property, one of which was about the enter service when the abandonment came. Of the four, two were in their military colors, one was about to be placed in service, and one other had just started service. Exactly half of the new locomotives were seeing service on the railroad.

The first of the "last trips" featured world-famous journalist Lowell Thomas, who had grown up in Victor. The trip included engine 59 and two cars, a combination car and observation car 29, which had been Colorado Midland #111. A winter storm chilled the event. The January 27, 1949, trip

was marked by the ground breaking at Elkton for the new Carlton Mill.

A second "last trip" was planned by the Rocky Mountain Railroad Club, headquartered in Denver. The first challenge was convincing the Midland Terminal of their interest, second was to secure two additional cars for the run. The enthusiasm and dedication of the trip organizers, including a former MT employee, brought success. The victory was celebrated on February 6, 1949, behind locomotive 59. The old passenger locomotive, originally MT number 6, pulled two ex-D & RGW combination cars, and two ex-CM cars. The trip was grand and glorious, the train loaded to capacity with railroad enthusiasts. Photographers and area residents lined the route, braving the cold weather. The excursion was

Engine 59, returned to its former function as a passenger engine for this excursion for Lowell Thomas, and his groundbreaking of the Carlton Mill. The cold January day brought additional chills thru to those who realized that this was one of the last times that they would see this railroad run, after over fifty years. — PM

The last special trip on the Midland Terminal in 1949 was the Rocky Mountain Railroad Club's excursion, shown here on the wye at Bull Hill. — GCB

successfully completed, even though only the engine crew knew that old 59 was on its last legs. The veteran locomotive was one of only three of the early MT engines to last until 1949. It had stalled once on the way up Ute Pass, and the men kept their fingers crossed until they reached Divide, on the return trip. The engine not only finished this trip, but made a couple of additional freight trips.

The railroad ran a few more freight runs before the mines shut down on February 15. Trucks were already hauling material that should have been moved by train. The two ex-CR & NM locomotives, 62 and 63, were loaded with spare parts and on their way to Mexico. The former U.S. Army locomotives would be leaving for Virginia soon. On February 19 the last freight pulled into the Colorado City yards. The train had pulled out of the yards at 11:30 A.M. and returned at a few minutes after 5:00 P.M. with only thirty-one cars, four of which were loaded, a caboose full of the supplies from the depots, and a small team of men from one of the Colorado Springs radio stations. Four locomotives sat in the yards after the run, 58 through 61, all the others were gone. On February 20 Commercial Metals started scrapping. A few spur tracks in the district were taken up starting in June, but the majority of the work was now starting.

On February 21 excitement tested the Ute Pass area as the scrapping trains started four fires. Twenty-five men fought the most stubborn blaze near Cascade.

The last of the Cripple Creek railroads was erased by spring. Lowell Thomas returned to Cripple Creek in 1951, but the railroad was gone. A passenger car caravan escorted Thomas, a Golden Cycle stockholder, to the district, and a parade down Bennett Avenue marked the start of the festivities leading up to the dedication of the Carlton Mill. A special visitor came along with Lowell Thomas, his father Dr. H.G. Thomas, long-time doctor in Victor. The elder Thomas had served the community some forty years earlier. At about 3:30 P.M. on March 12, 1951, the switch was thrown that applied power to the machinery at the new mill. A live radio broadcast was carried nationwide after the ceremony.

In the district and all the way to Colorado Springs the old railroad grade returned to its natural state. Teller County quickly converted the grade from Midland to Gillett to a rough road. The Golden Cycle Mill was razed, except for its rather tall smokestack, remaining as an informal monument to Colorado City's fifty years as a mining center. The men who worked for the Golden Cycle were offered similar jobs in the new mill, but most of them rejected the offer and

Once it was here, now it's gone; the wrecking crew pulls up the rails into the Divide depot. Diesel power can be seen behind the cut. — HO/AC

(Left) Engine 59 and the caboose head for the roundhouse after the last freight run in 1949. All remaining equipment was brought to the yards, and the road was then turned over to the scrapper. — PPL

The wrecking crew has cleared Tunnel One and in a short time there will be no rails at the depot. — HB/ESP

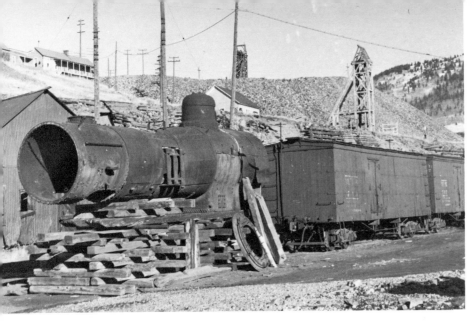

Waiting in the yards in Victor, one of the three former locomotive boilers waits to be moved to either the Ajax Mine or the Carlton Mill. In the background are two former Hanrahan refrigerator cars. — LLW

The scrapping train has just reached the west end of Engleman Trestle. Manitou residents daily gathered to watch the progress of the destruction. — HB/ESP

In 1961 the old Colorado Midland–Midland Terminal Engleman Trestle came down. Interestingly it was taken down in about the same sequence as it was built. Story has it that the spans were sold to a Utah mining railroad, or mysteriously vanished. — PPL

looked for other jobs. The employees of the Midland Terminal as a whole retired or shifted to other employment. The mill operated at Elkton for roughly ten years before it, too, was closed.

Today sections of the railroad can be seen, but as Woodland Park and the other Ute Pass communities grow, more of it is lost. The old line from Midland to Gillett is now a wide, paved road. Tourists yearly curse the highway department for building only a one-lane tunnel on the road, last Midland tunnel to be used for vehicular traffic. The road from Gillett, past Blizzard Point to Bull Hill, is a graded road, here and there the old parallel grade has grown over with grass.

The Cripple Creek District is again bustling with activity. The Carlton Mill, once an operating mill, then closed for nearly twenty years, is again in operation. The new machinery concentrates the ore, rather than completely refining it as in the old days. Two ex-Midland Terminal locomotive boilers served as stationary boilers in the building while it was in operation in the old days, but there is no plan to refire them. One other boiler was used in the Ajax mine, and another was reported to be used in a building in Colorado Springs. The four boilers were probably from the locomotives numbered 52-56. However, no record has been found of exact numbers, the only clues being certain scars and patches.

One cannot end this tale without wondering what might have happened **if**. The most popular scheme relates to a comparison with the D & RGW's Durango and Silverton operation. The Midland Terminal's locomotives were either dispersed or cut up, but a Colorado Springs group wanted to save MT 60 as a memorial, but to no success.

The Colorado Midland and the Midland Terminal are gone, as is each of the Cripple Creek roads. The only reminder of the Carlton syndicate's railroad empire is the still popular Manitou and Pikes Peak, which on special occasions rolls out its last steam locomotive. In Cripple Creek a narrow-gauge line operates along the old MT grade from the original Anaconda (then Bull Hill) depot near the Cripple Creek Museum, strange little reminder of just what this area has lost. Someday that, too, will be gone.

The Commercial Metals scrapping crew has reduced the Colorado City yards to rubble. — LLW

Locomotives number 62 and 63 with their new NOM numbers and lettering at the Colorado City yard ready for shipment to Mexico in 1948. — Herb O'Hanlon Photo/Author's Collection

Ah, there is no glory in it. Engines 59 and 61 are being cut up for scrap in the Colorado City yards in March 1949. — PM

Indistinguishable from its days on the Midland Terminal, 55 was old US Army 4064, which was never used by the MT. The lead truck on the three locomotives that were used was taken off in Virginia. The engine was photographed in October, 1954. — MKV

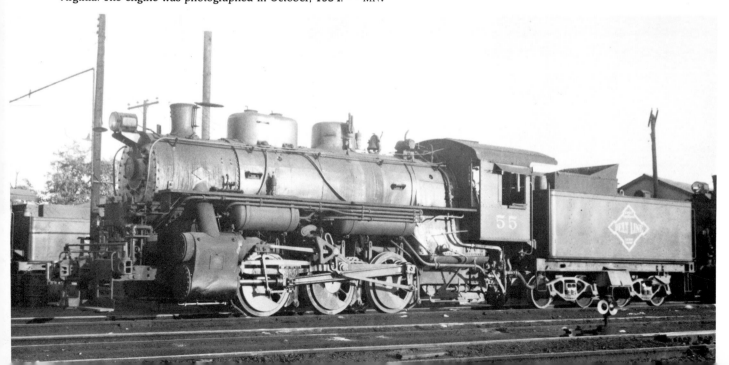

The new Carlton Mill near Victor was dedicated after the Midland Terminal was long gone, but the lower black smokestack is directly above the two ex-MT boilers. — PPL

Lowell Thomas turns the switch to start operations at Carlton Mill near Victor on March 12, 1951. Seated behind him are Ethyl Carlton, Albert E. Carlton's widow and Merrill Shoup — PPL

The last Midland Terminal boilers to see steam are in the Carlton Mill, near Victor, the far boiler is suspected to be from locomotive 55, while the closer one might be from any one of three locomotives. — Mel McFarland Photo

The old office building, machine shop and oil house at Colorado City only two years before the fire that destroyed the central feature of the old years. — PPL

The Colorado City office building the day after the fire in January 1953 is a silent reminder of the two railroads it served. — PPL

The railroad tracks remained for another ten years, but the office building was pushed into its former basement the day after the fire. Unintentionally, the old machine shop received major damage when a part of a wall from the office building fell through the end of the shop. — PPL

The tracks led to the old railroad yards for several years. The Golden Cycle had hopes of selling the facility to an industry that would use the buildings. This photo was taken days after the office building burned. — PPL

Not much was left in Gillett in the spring of 1949. The old right-of-way had already been converted to a one lane road. — HB/ESP

A three car passenger train, eastbound for the Santa Fe
depot in Colorado Springs. — DPL/Otto Perry Collection

Book two:

A Ride on the Midland Terminal

Introduction

THE MIDLAND TERMINAL, THE FIRST standard gauge railroad in the Cripple Creek District, did not operate passenger trains there until the Colorado Midland closed, but the Colorado Midland passenger department was responsible for the equipment and the crews.

Our trip on the Midland Terminal takes place in late summer or early fall of 1908. The fine train, made up of Colorado Midland coaches, leaves from the small Denver and Rio Grande station in Colorado Springs. Along the way, you will learn what is going on in the area served by the Colorado Midland and the Midland Terminal, items of importance for these railroads.

The D&RGW depot in Colorado Springs was a busy place, with trains of the Midland Terminal and Rock Island added to the Rio Grande's daily runs. It is hard to tell if any of these cars are Midland bound. — AC

5. On the Colorado Midland

THE AFTERNOON SUN WARMS THE STONE Denver and Rio Grande depot in Colorado Springs. The stained glass windows cast a strange pattern on the well-worn oak floor. At least a score of people wait for the **Cripple Creek Express**. A few rest under the covered waiting platforms on either end of the building.

The small depot, built nearly twenty-five years ago, has been enlarged to accommodate the twenty trains that use the building daily. Denver and Rio Grande trains that leave Denver bound for Pueblo, Durango, Salida, Leadville, and Salt Lake City pass through Colorado Springs. In addition to the Colorado Midland trains up Ute Pass and Cripple Creek, the Chicago, Rock Island and Pacific trains stop here.

The C, RI & P has a ticket office in the old Rio Grande eating house and hotel, just north of the depot. The track closest to the depot is that of the Rock Island. Colorado Springs is the farthest west that a Rock Island train travels into Colorado; however, trains do run from Limon to Denver and from here to Pueblo. An eight-car passenger train departed the station for Chicago an hour ago.

A Denver and Rio Grande passenger train bound for Salt Lake City left the depot a few minutes ago. A large number of the passengers now boarding the **Express** were on that train. The sound of a whistle and the sight of a small train backing northward stir activity in the crowd. The two cars and the locomotive almost glow in the sun after a brief shower has dampened the train.

The storm, typical for this time of year, has moved to the east almost as quickly as the Rock Island train to Chicago.

The short train, coach #253, combination car #11, and the locomotive, a 4-6-0, #14, is backing up to a car spotted on a track on the far side of the yard. Colorado Midland car #111 was converted from a coach to an observation car and is the only observation car owned by the railroad. The cars that the Colorado Midland uses on the through trains to Grand Junction are the fine Pullman observation cars. The #111 is often used for the Colorado Midland's special wild flower trains. The Denver and Rio Grande regularly brings a Pullman car or two, sometimes including an observation car, to Colorado Springs for the **Express**. Today the number of through passengers to Cripple Creek is very small, and there are no Pullman fares.

The train has been spotted on track three. The passengers gingerly walk over the wet platform to the train. The tracks at one time were three-rail, but seven years ago the narrow-gauge rail was taken up.

The Colorado Midland is offering a special fare for all points in Ute Pass, but it is high compared to the fares charges only a few years ago. The Midland Terminal and the Short Line had a very vicious rate war several years ago. Trains were full, but the two railroads were losing money on every fare, and a truce was finally called. The fare today is fifty cents for all points in Ute Pass.

The Colorado Midland equipment on the train is

generally over twenty years old. The coach shops regularly remodel and upgrade the cars as they need it. The #111 was rebuilt only three years ago. The older coaches have been modernized with vestibules. However, the cars on this train still have open platforms.

The seats in the observation car fill quickly. The interior is cherry wood and hard white oak. The seats are large and comfortable. The upholstery is plush maroon, accenting the highly varnished maroon and gold color on the outside of the car. The windows provide an excellent view of Pikes Peak as we wait for the train to start moving. The glass in the clerestory is French embossed. The sashes are mahogany, finely polished. The ceiling paneling is mahogany with gold trim. Car trimmings are bronze. Four double center lamps of polished brass provide lighting, which is not needed in the bright afternoon sun. The carpet is rich Wilton with a pattern of reds and browns that shows almost no use at all. The windows on one end of the car light up the first two rows of seats. A white linen covering protects the upholstery from the bright sun. Two heavy wicker chairs are in place in the platform, firmly anchored to the car.

The interiors of the coach and the combination car are similar but show much more wear than the observation car. The conductor's announcement of the final boarding can be heard as we step into the observation car after our quick tour of the train. The cars are lightly loaded for this time of year, but we have observed that this car is nearly full. The windows on the end of the car frame the arrival of another train, but the passengers barely hear the sound of the engine's whistle.

The train jerks to a start, and the cars roll to the right and left as the train navigates through the Denver and Rio Grande's yards to their Manitou branch. A short freight train can be seen eastbound on the Colorado Midland track that climbs over the Denver and Rio Grande main line to the south.

The train groans to a stop a short time after crossing Monument Creek, but the pause is only momentary. We soon resume speed but now on the Colorado Midland, entering Colorado City—a town that dates back to the 1850s. Today several gold reduction mills operate here. Florence was formerly the center of Cripple Creek ore refining, but since the Colorado City mills were built, the situation has changed. The two oldest mills are the Portland and the Colorado-Philadelphia. The

Colorado-Philadelphia is on the west end of the Colorado Midland's yards with the newer Standard Mill, while the Portland Mill is over the hill to the south of the train.

On the hillside not far from the railroad appear the large buildings of the Golden Cycle Mining and Milling's Colorado City mill. Chemical reduction works are a class of industry common to mining regions. In the Golden Cycle Mill, the ore is crushed to a sand. The sand is roasted to drive off volatile impurities, after which the sand is dumped into large rotating barrels. In the barrels, the "pulp" is mixed with a solution of cyanide of potassium. The gold is gradually dissolved into the solution, which is drained off. The precious metal is precipitated off using zinc or some other agent. The precipitate is gently roasted and finally is melted into gold bars. The waste products are known as tailings. On the hillside below the mill a field is covered with tailings in the form of a rusty looking sand.

The Golden Cycle was built in 1902 as the Telluride Mill. The old mill originally used a bromine process. In a mill of this type, the bromine compound was used rather than cyanide of potassium to release the gold, but more was left than removed. The mill was closed after a short time, and the buildings were sold to the Golden Cycle, which operated a successful mill near Goldfield. A fire last year destroyed the old roasting and separating buildings, which have now been replaced with more modern, larger buildings and equipment. A long line of Short Line, Midland Terminal, and Colorado Midland cars can be seen behind the mill.

The fine tailings dust covers everything, and a gust of wind blows a steady stream of sand into Fountain Creek.

The operating headquarters and shops of the Colorado Midland are located along the edge of Fountain Creek. The Midland's shops and craftsmen have the capability of building their own equipment and are now busy keeping the hundreds of boxcars used to ship the ore off the scrap line. The Midland Terminal originally used these facilities, but since the Cripple Creek Central moved the Florence and Cripple Creek shops to Canon City, that has changed. The major repairs and servicing on MT equipment is done in the F & CC shops.

The afternoon freight train from Florissant arrived a few minutes ago. The two engines are still

In 1906 the Telluride-Golden Cycle Mill had a fire in the roaster building and it also destroyed the processing area. In this view, taken before the fire spread, the roaster building is completely engulfed in flames. The mill buildings were rebuilt to more modern specifications. — CC

connected with the long line of assorted cars. The train is sixteen cars long, mostly CM cars, but there are a couple Santa Fe cars and a lone C & S car. A dozen men and a family of four are waiting to board our train at the small Colorado City depot.

Southwest of the depot are the two mills owned by the United States Reduction and Refining Company—the Colorado–Philadelphia and the Standard. The company owns at least one of the mills at Florence, but none of their mills are doing very well. The larger mines are almost completely converted over to using the Golden Cycle. The Standard Mill uses the chlorine process. The four mills in Colorado City can process nearly 1,200 tons a day in ore which is one of the highest capacities in the country. The output of the mines is currently closer to 800 tons a day, leaving the mills rather short, and the companies are considering shutting down one or more of them.

The train slowly pulls away from the depot after the short stop. The engine carries the train smartly out of the yards, picking up speed as it climbs away from Fountain Creek. The Denver and Rio Grande and the interurban line follow the creek, so the climb for them is not necessary. The Colorado Midland's survey into Ute Pass requires that the train start climbing immediately after leaving the Colorado City yards. The red and brown spires of the Garden of the Gods stand proudly in the hills to the north, clearly visible from our window.

The Garden of the Gods is one of the most popular natural attractions in the Colorado City area. Indians considered the spot sacred. The springs in Manitou are another sacred location in Indian legend. A number of the springs have been commercialized, but most are still free. The Colorado Midland serves bottled Manitou water in its dining cars.

The community hidden back in the valley was largely the dream of Dr. William Bell. Bell came to Colorado with General Palmer, when the general was building his railroad. Dr. Bell's fine home can be seen to our right just before we pass through that big cut ahead. The Colorado Midland's depot, like the doctor's home, and the D & RG's depot, is constructed of stone. The depot has a superlative view of the little community. The center of town and several of the fine springs are a few short blocks away.

The train whistle signals our arrival, and after a short pause we are rolling again. A few of the interesting buildings in the center of town can be seen more clearly, like the big bottling works. A few passengers have boarded and all of the seats in the observation car are now filled except for those on the platform. The smoke from our engine is blown out over the town. A smaller stream of smoke is visible in the canyon ahead as we enter the first of the tunnels above Manitou.

The Manitou Iron Springs is one of the region's popular resorts. One of the attractions in the district is the source of the smoke. The Manitou and Pikes Peak cog railroad is located just to the west of the curving trestle near tunnel two. The tiny locomotive is backing down from the engine house as we pass. The trains make daily trips to the summit of Pikes Peak pushing a small coach half the size of ours. The engines back all the way down the mountain. The area is lined with shops, fine summer homes, hotels, and even a castle.

The cog railroad's depot is located near the point where the Indians' Ute Pass trail reached Manitou. The trail climbs over the hills to near Cascade. The train swings away from the canyon past a small boarded-up depot. The old station formerly served Manitou Iron Springs and provided access to the cog railroad.

The town of Manitou is well below us now. The band shell is clearly visible in the park on the west end of town. The view is suddenly blocked by another tunnel, and the scenery has changed as we exit. Now we are looking down a deep canyon toward a quarry. The train enters yet another tunnel, and quickly another. Finally another change in scenery, after what seemed like five minutes of darkness. We can now look down a steep canyon toward the old Leadville wagon road that winds along the creek up Ute Pass. The road was carved out of the granite in the 1860s and 1870s replacing the old Indian trail over which it was very difficult to get wagons.

The train is climbing at a rate of four feet per hundred. At each lookout between the tunnels, Fountain Creek can be seen far below in the bottom of Ute Pass. Beyond the stream, high on the opposite side of the valley, are cliffs of lime and sandstone resting on the granite. The wagon road climbs to nearly the same level as the railroad near Hanging Rock Cut.

A long train is held up for us at Crags siding. The eastbound **Eastern Express**, running a little behind schedule, is waiting for us to pass. The westbound trains had priority over the eastbound ones. We could not safely get rolling if we had to

Engine 57 occasionally pulled a passenger train when 59 was out for repairs, and this must have been the case on August 3, 1930. — DPL

The resplendent Ramona Hotel was starting to look rather ragged in 1924. The MT was still hauling in a few summer tourists, but more were driving up in their touring cars. — John Siemon Collection

In late 1931 the last passenger train under steam charges up Ute Pass, near Crystola, largely unnoticed by the public. — UPHS

stop for them. The train is pulled by a polished locomotive, #205, one of the Colorado Midland's crack passenger engines. A baggage, baggage-mail, diner, two Pullman tourist cars, two coaches, and the Pullman observation make up the elegant train.

The train briskly winds up the canyon until the gorge opens up into a broad valley. The stately Ramona Hotel sits on the hill above the conservatively poised Cascade House. The town is the first of the Ute Pass resorts. The train stops for water as well as passengers. The accommodations here are quite ample. A wagon road, visible to the rear of the old eating house, extends to the top of Pikes Peak.

The train pulls away after a few minutes, right on schedule. The grade has changed considerably since we left Manitou. The next siding is Culver. The area was known as Ute Park for several years. It was the site of an attractive stone depot, which was closed after the Ute Hotel burned down. The structure was as unique as the little depot. The railroad station, with its cupola and porches, was one of the most marvelous stations ever built by the Colorado Midland. The hotel, with its conelike towers, was to be the center of a communal village.

The railroad has entered a narrow canyon that is quite green. The train slows and stops at a depot identical to the one at Cascade. We have stopped at the largest resort community in Ute Pass—

Green Mountain Falls. The pause is all too short, and the locomotive pulls us away after leaving a dozen people on the platform.

The tracks curve around the side of the hill north of the depot, over the creek, and onto a hillside on the south side of the valley. A long sweeping curve leads through Crystola. The area is much less like a pass each mile we travel. Pikes Peak, which has been out of sight since we passed Manitou Iron Springs, is visible from here and becomes much fuller and finer for the next hour.

The little town of Woodland Park has a perfect view of Pikes Peak. The town was originally called Manitou Park Station. The park is located several miles to the north. Dr. Bell, the same man who developed Manitou, built a hotel at the park. One of the unusual features of the doctor's attention was a narrow-gauge lumber railroad. The line was abandoned a few years ago, and the lumber mill has fallen into disrepair. The property has been given to the Colorado College School of Forestry.

The present depot at Woodland, or Woodland Park, is the third building to be the depot. The Midland Hotel, across the street, was also a Colorado Midland depot at one time, but it was closed about ten years ago and moved to its present site.

The railroad swings sharply to the south, making a big "S" curve toward the upper mouth of Ute Pass. In the last few minutes we have climbed nearly one thousand feet. We are twenty-three miles from Colorado Springs, almost halfway to Cripple Creek.

Edlowe is a flag stop. The train roars right through, gaining speed as we move across the meadows filled with flowers. This is one of the favorite spots for wild flower excursions. Trains have been stopping here since late June, but there are plenty of flowers—pretty far from the track, however.

The railroad is climbing but much less severely than before. The town of Divide is ahead as we wind through the hills. In a few minutes the town of Divide, and the railroad station will be on our right. It is a small town, but it has been here longer than either of the railroads. Most of the inhabitants work for one of the two lines. The Midland Teminral has a small shop in Divide. Another building here has been used as an engine shed, but it is empty now.

The town developed on the wagon road traffic bound for Leadville, and the name Divide was used on and off by the wagoneers. The town once had a lively reputation, but that has settled down quite a bit. The old Cripple Creek toll road started here, but the toll station was at Midland. A lumber mill has kept busy shipping boards to Colorado Springs, Cripple Creek, and points along the Colorado Midland. The opening of the Midland Terminal killed the toll road.

The train pulls slowly into the station. The Colorado Midland main line swings slightly to the west, and we head a bit south. The brown building is on the eastern end of town. The platform has several people waiting for us to stop and let them on. A few of the crowd look like Easterners, probably going to the district for the first time.

The conductor carefully steps down off the platform before we stop near the door of the depot. The train stops a few yards later. On the track running through the center of town, a few boxcars are waiting to be coupled to Midland Terminal engine #5, which will be behind us on the way to Bull Hill. The crew is adjusting the switches to allow the locomotive to pick up the cars, and later the short MT way car. The car greatly resembles a CM way car but has no side door. A number of people on the platform collect their things. Several passengers on the train stand and gather up their belongings to leave the train. In a few minutes we will pull out, again heading for Cripple Creek, this time on the rails of the Midland Terminal.

Divide owed quite a bit of its affluence to the Midland Terminal. The tiny town was nearly 80% railroad employees. The view of the school blocks the railroad yards, partly visible just over its roof.
— CC

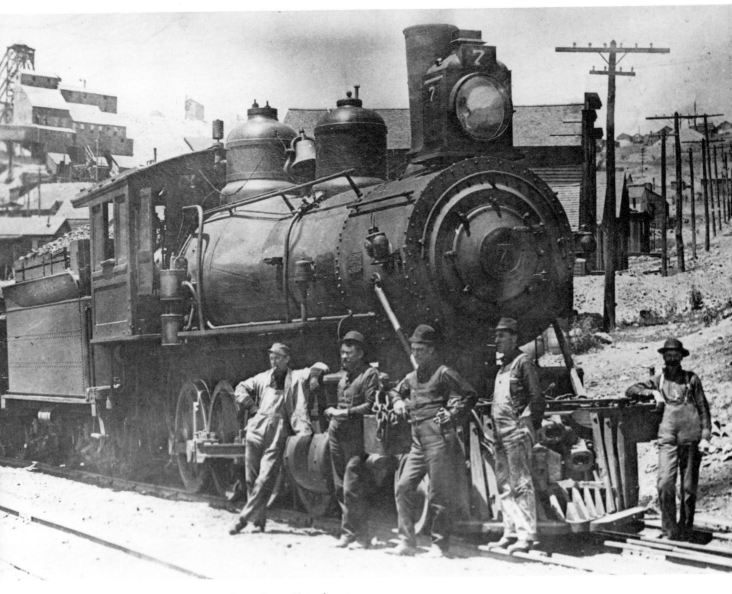

In 1904 #7 poses at Independence. Note the
dual gauge couplers, and the lack of a name
painted on the cab side. — AC

6. On the Midland Terminal

Midland Terminal #6 takes on water at Victor with one of the road's small cabooses a few years before its number was changed to 206. — Author's Collection

THE SUN IS ABOUT TO DROP BELOW the hills as we pull away from the Divide depot. The cut south of the depot casts a dark shadow on the side of the car. The wide cut is through red gravel, typical of the region. The road to Cripple Creek runs right along the railroad, but road traffic does not have the benefit of a cut. The high meadow is broad and rolling, bordered on the south by Pikes Peak and Raspberry Mountain and on the west by Twin Creek Canyon and assorted low rocky hills. The hills on both sides of the railroad, which are now part of the Crescent Cattle Company property, are covered with tall grass.

Prospect holes abound from Raspberry Mountain south to below Cripple Creek, and occasionally we might even see the lights from a cabin or two. Up on the slope of Pikes Peak is an area called Horse Thief Park, which is regularly visited by the sheriff.

The locomotive has started to work hard as we climb a hill. The sign for Murphy marks the first summit on the railroad. The station was originally called Tracy, since this is Tracy Hill, but it was renamed recently for an official of the railroad. Tracy Hill separates the Twin Creek drainage area from the Oil Creek drainage. A deep cut marks the top of the ridge. The drop toward Midland is quite sudden, and the cars lurch noticeably as we start down. The lights of a few buildings can be seen far down in the valley.

Midland is where the railroad "changed its mind." The grade between Divide and Midland was actually constructed by a company under contract to the Atchison, Topeka and Santa Fe. The railroad into Cripple Creek was originally to be a branch of the Colorado Midland. The lights and buildings ahead of us are the northern edge of Midland. The railroad was named for the proposed **terminal** with the Colorado Midland.

The town, called Midland City and Midland Junction, at one time had a population close to three thousand. The town, about three years older than the railroad, grew up around the stage and toll station. The valley becomes quite narrow, and the toll station was located here. Several streams run through the area, each joining Oil Creek. A section of town, where three or four buildings still stand, is north of the toll gate site. One of the buildings still bears a Terminal Hotel sign, but it is obviously empty. The railroad facilities and siding are between the north section and the main part of town. The buildings are now scattered out for nearly a mile along the valley. The lumber businesses and saloons seem to be the main money-makers now.

The train pauses long enough to take on water before we resume our climbing. One of the other passengers is quite familiar with the narrow-gauge grading. In the dark we cannot see the work on the hillside above us, nor can we see to our right. The wagon road continues down the valley to the right of the car toward the lower section, and actual center, of the village. The earliest railroad surveys were designed to follow the wagon road, but as the plans were refined, this route was selected. The old man relates that the surveyors crisscrossed the entire country between Divide and the Cripple Creek District until they had almost mapped the area better than the Hayden team. More than four routes were developed before this one was decided upon.

A spur track was built several years ago to serve the ice ponds and the lumber mills close the Midland. Two large ice ponds were dug, fed by the stream down Putney Gulch. A few of the local residents call this Canterbury.

One of the passengers asks, "Where did everybody go?" At one time there were ten times as many people living in this valley. But the people packed up and moved on into the next "end of track" town. The villages that grew up along the Union Pacific when it was being built across the grasslands are classic examples of these little boom towns, but we rarely think of this happening with a tiny little railroad. It did, though, and the majority of the people here moved on to Gillett in 1896.

The train sits long enough to take on water and a few passengers. The grade seems quite steep as we roll downhill around a corner and climb rapidly. The locomotive noise is obvious as we continue around the curve above the main portion of Midland. The moonlight is reflecting off the surface of the two lakes below us.

The main industry is logging, but in the winter, ice is cut from the ponds for the railroad. Early travelers tried mining, but there is little gold here (although some free gold was found in Oil Creek).

A passenger, obviously familiar with the region, explains a few of the local animals. He is an employee of the forest service and is on his way to the station at Clyde on the Short Line. In the daylight you can see woodpeckers, blue jays, eagles, or hawks, and even the Arctic ravens. The chickadee is one of the most common birds, but there are even hummingbirds. Gray squirrels and larger chipmunks are nearly everywhere. Porcupines are abundant as once were cottontail and snowshoe rabbits. The coyote is seen on occasion, and a few of the old-timers report a timber wolf. The bobcat is common, but the bear and mountain lion are becoming scarce. More than one train crew has reported chasing a bear out of the tunnel ahead. One crew reported that a bear actually climbed into a car once while the train was stopped at Gillett.

A few mountain sheep have been seen, but white-tailed deer are almost a staple in the diet of local residents. In the larger streams there are a few brook trout. The waters near Cripple Creek are spoiled, and few fish survive.

For more than a mile we have been climbing and curving through the hills, but now we have straightened out a bit. The people on the right side of the car can see the locomotive headlight on the red rocks along the tracks. The tunnel is upon us after several minutes of additional climbing. The roar of the engine and the smell of the coal smoke linger in the air for a few minutes. The aroma of the smoke lasts much longer than the sound. The car is rolling from right to left much like a boat at sea, and the motion, as well as the hour, have put most of the passengers to sleep.

The conductor enters the car a short distance past the tunnel to announce the arrival at Gillett. The car makes an obvious roll and lurches as we start down a fairly straight section of track toward the town.

Gillett was originally a railroad town. The Colorado Midland facilities in Colorado City were used for major work, but Gillett was the center of operations. The Denver and Southwestern changed things, and the new owner decided to build the large yards at Bull Hill and Divide. The heavy maintenance was done at Colorado City

An open inspection car is one mile out of Gillett, bound for Waters Tunnel in the late 1920's. The car was a regular sight along the line until it was replaced by a newer sedan. — Jeff Gillapsy Collection

until that also was moved, to Canon City. It was rumored that a big roundhouse would be built up here, but that never happened.

The train has pulled through a line of small stores and homes. A few of the buildings have lights visible. The small station is well lighted. A freight train is waiting in the yards and pulls away as soon as we come up to the depot. It is made up of a large number of Colorado Midland and Santa Fe cars and a few Midland Terminal cars. The little caboose bounces gingerly over the switches as our train starts to move again.

Gillett was named for W.K. Gillett. Twelve years ago it had about five thousand people. The town was able to support three daily newspapers, eighteen saloons, three dance halls, two livery stables, two churches, and the Monte Carlo. The famous gambling club sat high on the hill to the

east. It was built by the Woods brothers of Cripple Creek. A dam was also built by the brothers, and the lake behind it was named Woods Lake. For a while it was owned by the man who was the perpetrator of the great "Bull Fight." Two of the other proprietors were Johnny Nolen and Jeff White, who have establishments in Cripple Creek.

On the hill to our right is a moderately sized mill, but the El Paso Reduction Works has not been very successful because it is not close enough to the mines. Nevertheless, the railroad hauls several carloads of fairly good ore in some of the smaller mines every week. A majority of the large mines use the Cripple Creek District and Colorado City mills; however, the smaller mines try many of the smaller mills. The Gillett area has no large mines and only a few small mines. A large mine this far from the center of the district is a real rarity. There

93

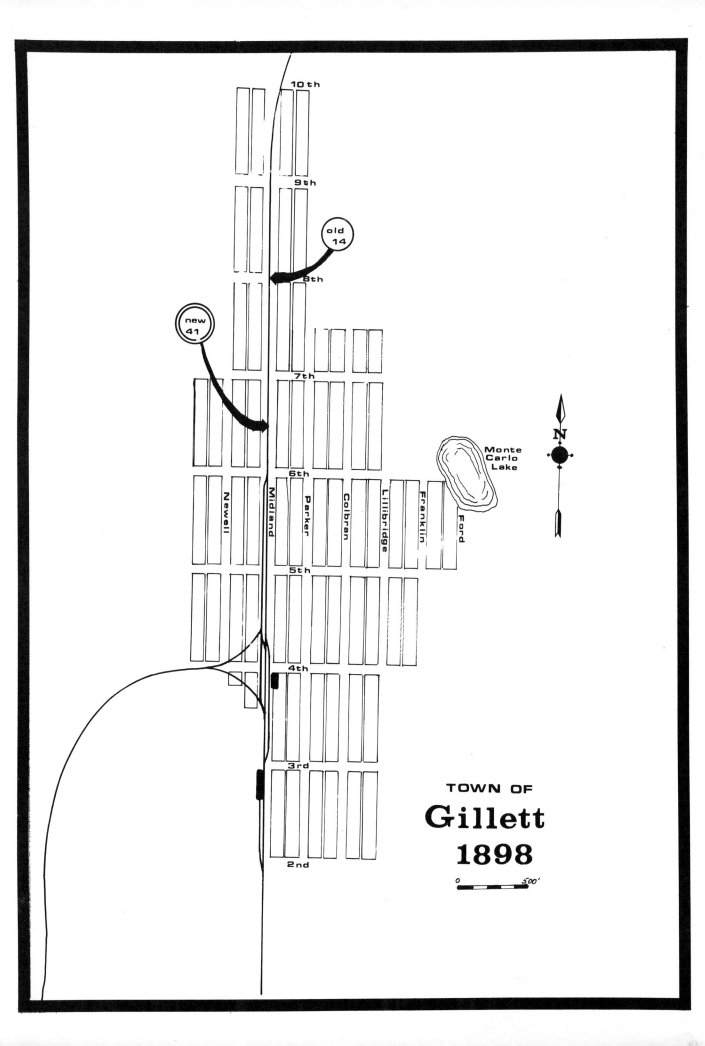

TOWN OF
Gillett
1898

N

Monte
Carlo
Lake

old
14

new
41

10th
9th
8th
7th
6th
5th
4th
3rd
2nd

Newell
Midland
Parker
Colbran
Lillibridge
Franklin
Ford

0   500'

The Gillett depot on the Midland Terminal was one of the coldest spots on the railroad, but the multipane windows on the end of the station are unique. — DPL

Gillett was still a fairly prosperous community in 1908. The old coal trestle had not been used for a couple of years, and the yards are completely empty. At one time shop facilities were planned for here. — CC

was one such mine near here, but it only lost money for the investors. Several claims have lasted longer than a few months, but not more than a year.

The population of Gillett is down to two hundred. A number of the people who stayed after the railroad moved on moved in 1898 or 1899 when huge windstorms blew down the poorly built homes. The area, unlike Cripple Creek and Victor, is not sheltered from the extremes of the weather. High winds are common, but the storms in those years were truly remarkable. The people who live here now often joke about what it takes to stay on the ground. One of the saloons has a stack of bricks in the window to loan to their slim clientele. The railroad has even had cars blow over and down the tracks.

A big hill to our left is reported to have a large ice cave in it. In the moonlight, descriptions of the local attractions are lost to reality. The return trip tomorrow morning will explain the features much more clearly. The dark blue sky is dotted with thousands of stars, more than one sees at the lower altitudes. The moonlight barely lights up the hills, but the outlines of the more prominent ones are detectable. The back of Pikes Peak is visible,

but the outline can be seen against a sky that is quite dark. One of the other passengers nearby explains to those of us who have never ridden the train to Cripple Creek just what is going on in the area.

The train has slowed again, and a sigh from one of the passengers arouses several others. The train is climbing, and on the left side, passengers can see another train. The railroad below is the Short Line, carrying passengers. Sparks can be seen around the locomotive's smokestack. Lights can be seen in some of the coaches. The train is the evening run from Colorado Springs that left from the Santa Fe station well after we left the Rio Grande depot.

The next stop is Cameron. The Short Line train will be behind us all the way into the station; its depot is only a short distance from that of the Midland Terminal. The two railroads run right along each other for a couple of miles. On the hills around the town a small number of large mines are in operation. On the hill to the south, the Cameron School Section is the closest to the tracks. The knowledgeable passenger explains that Cameron was the site of an amusement park, but it has now been closed. Residents of the entire

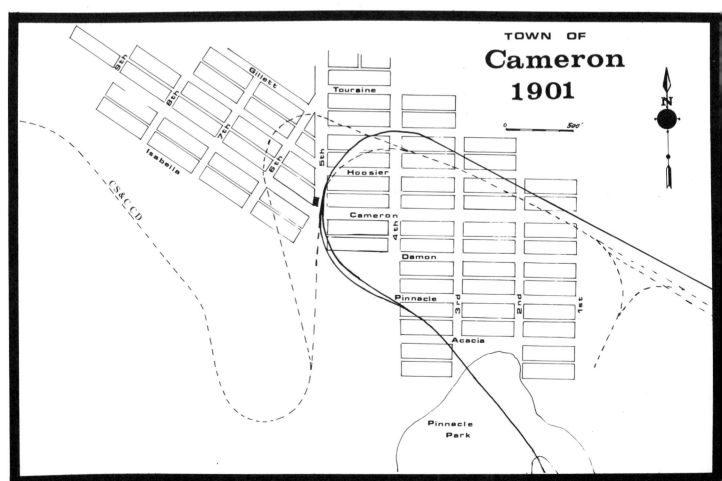

Cameron on the CS&CCD was the site of a wye, the Midland Terminal ran to the right, crossing the Short Line just beyond the wye. The two railroads had stations on the far side of town, near the trees. — CC

district would ride the electric line here for a Sunday outing. The district has noticed a decline in the output of the mines the last six or seven years, and the population has fallen with it. A short train is parked at an angle to our train as we pull into the yards. The train is on the tracks of the Short Line. It will probably leave after the passenger train arrives. The Short Line and the Midland Terminal lines meet here, and the tracks are connected.

Lights from the various mines can be seen on the side of the hill to our left. The train pulls up to the station, and passengers on the left side of the car can see the Short Line train pull up. The freight train is already moving away. Our train pulls out after a short pause. It takes five minutes to work our way up to the Bull Hill railroad yards. A locomotive can be seen working a string of cars near the mill below the yards. The building is actually a sampler—there are two in the area. A sampler only checks the value of the ore samples, and the material is then shipped to a mill. The larger mills have their own samplers. The sky is sparking, even at this hour, with the yellow lights from homes and the brighter white lights from the mines on the hillsides. The headlights of several

locomotives can be seen as the train stops at the station of Independence. The conductor calls out a list of town names for departing passengers: Independence, Goldfield, and Altman.

The town of Goldfield is quite large. A number of lights can be seen from as far right as the bright lights of a big mine, north to the railroad yards at Bull Hill. The business district is on the lower edge of town, well lighted. The glow from the Golden Cycle Mine, the La Bella power plant, and several other mine complexes can be seen. The sound of the mines surrounding the train is much louder than that of the train. One of the passengers points out that many of the buildings that we might think of as mines are really samplers. At one time there were over twenty samplers in the district, but now that number is less than ten, all privately owned.

A number of men boarded the train at Independence, and most of them look as if they might be miners. The trains up here are usually full. The Midland Terminal and the other railroads run short passenger trains through the day and night to provide transportation for the men who work in the mines and mills. The train has pulled away past the depot and stopped. A number of the

Looking at Bull Hill with its two large samplers, the Cripple Creek on the left and the Taylor and Brunton on the right (soon to be the Eagle) with a MT locomotive on the wye between them. — CHS

A washout sent engine 1, the WK Gillett onto the ground soon after its arrival in the district. The poor trackwork often sent engines and cars off the rails, but in this case it was weather. — PM

Victor in the winter of 1897 or 1898 would see a number of Santa Fe cars, however, the Hanrahan refrigerator car is unusual, seen behind the pine tree. — DPL

Anaconda was about half way between Cripple Creek and Victor, and was the scene of one of the first wrecks on the F&CC. The narrow gauge line is just below the road while the standard gauge is higher on the hill. — CHS

miners have gathered near the tracks and quickly climb aboard. After a few moments, the lights of Victor can be seen below us. The train passes the town and stops, and a few of the miners get off while we wait. The train is backing into Victor.

Victor is actually on a branch line. The Florence and Cripple Creek, and Mother Nature, prevented easy access to Victor. The two roads reached an agreement about several right-of-way problems several years ago. The agreements were brought about when the MT started a very interesting series of events. The MT actually laid tracks **over** the tracks of the F & CC at the Strong Mine.

The Victor depot was one of the first brick buildings in town, a feature that has saved it from a huge fire that in 1889 nearly destroyed Victor. The roof of the building burned, but the walls were saved and the building was easily rebuilt. The town has been completely rehabilitated, and most of the reconstructions have been of brick. The Gold Coin Mine, a short distance away, was burned to the ground. One of the interesting features of the rebuilding of the mine buildings is the style of architecture used. The mine's main building towers over the rest of the Victor buildings, but if one was not familiar with it, one might think it was an office building or even a church. It does not look like a mine. The splendid Gold Coin Club is across the street.

The train has emptied, only to be filled again. At 9:30 P.M. we pull away from the depot. For such an hour, the streets of town look fairly busy. The aroma of stale liquor drifts through the car, and it is clear that a few of these miners did not come from the mines above Victor, but had paused at some of the saloons. The saloons down the street in Goldfield, as well as in the many small communities, manage to do quite well, but Cripple Creek is the best known center of that type of entertainment. One of the male passengers, who has been with us since Colorado City, points out that the district towns are literally "wide open," as a story in the newspaper that he is reading points out.

A convention of national press reporters recently convened in Denver. The press clubs from Pueblo and Colorado Springs hosted visits to their towns, as well as a tour of the district. The Colorado Springs newspaper has reprinted a few of the reporters' stories about what they saw. Some of the local residents will not be very happy with this story.

The train has paused in Elkton during our discussion of the night life in the district. A few more miners find their way on and off as the movement of the train sends those standing to the nearest seat. The looks on the faces of many of these men show that they have come from a hard

The west (left) side of a 1910 panorama of Victor shows the location of Victor Junction on the MT, where the two lines on the hill at the left meet. The smokestack of the Gold Coin mine is quite visible in the town, with the Ajax above it. Looking up toward Goldfield the eastern (right) section of Victor extends well past the Strong, Portland and the dark sampler building at Bull Hill station is only slightly above the edge of town. — CC

The Cripple Creek Express is heading around the wye, and will back up to the depot. The Midland Terminal used Colorado Midland cars until the latter railroad closed. The cars here are coach 253 and 11. — Jackson Thode Collection

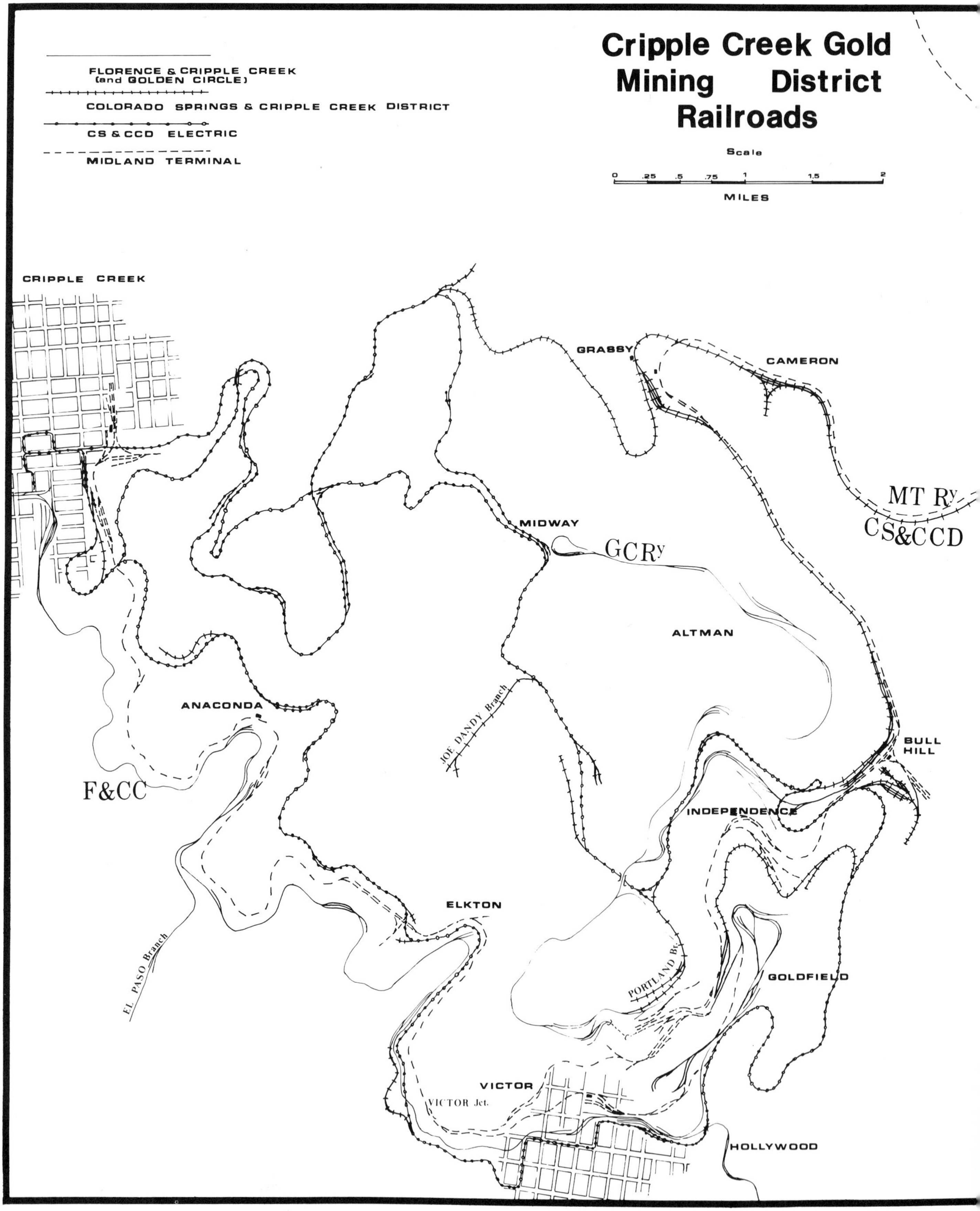

Cripple Creek Gold Mining District Railroads

Scale

0 — .25 — .5 — .75 — 1 — 1.5 — 2

MILES

FLORENCE & CRIPPLE CREEK
(and GOLDEN CIRCLE)

COLORADO SPRINGS & CRIPPLE CREEK DISTRICT

CS & CCD ELECTRIC

MIDLAND TERMINAL

CRIPPLE CREEK

GRASSY

CAMERON

MT Ry

CS&CCD

MIDWAY

GCRy

ALTMAN

ANACONDA

JOE DANDY Branch

F&CC

BULL HILL

INDEPENDENCE

ELKTON

PORTLAND Br.

GOLDFIELD

EL PASO Branch

VICTOR

VICTOR Jct.

HOLLYWOOD

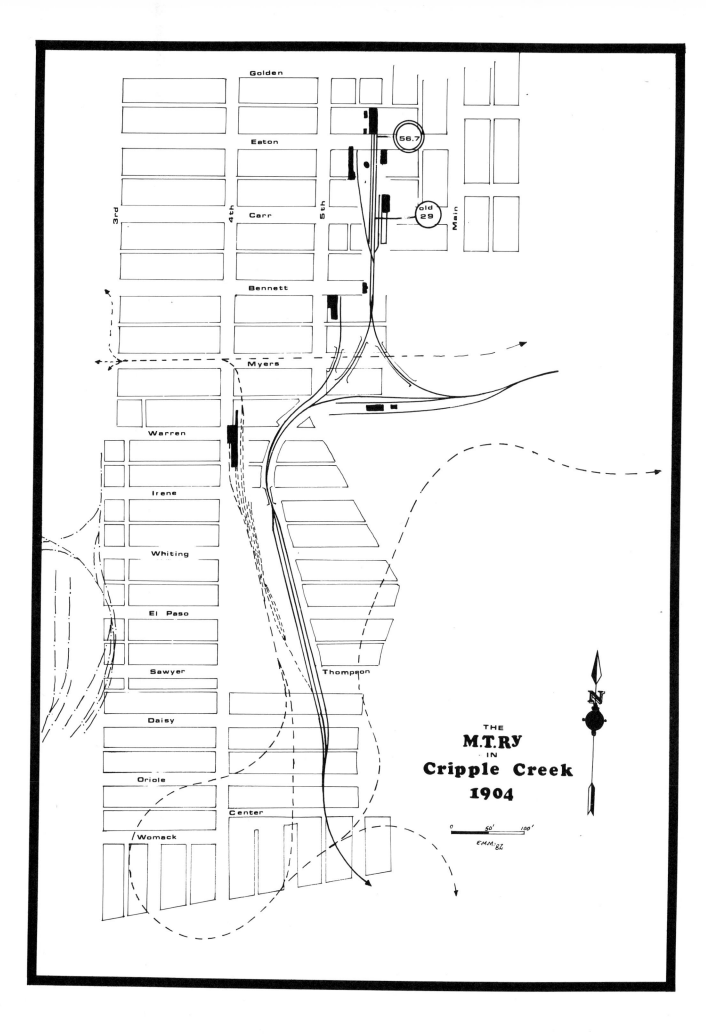

Golden

Eaton

Carr

Bennett

Myers

Warren

Irene

Whiting

El Paso

Sawyer

Daisy

Oriole

Center

Womack

3rd

4th

5th

Main

Thompson

56.7

old 29

N

THE
M.T.RY
IN
Cripple Creek
1904

0   50'   100'

E.M.M. '84

day's work. A number of the mines run two twelve-hour shifts, but most run three eight-hour shifts. In many of the mines, stopes or passages are leased to miners on a percentage basis, and they set their own hours.

There is not much left of Anaconda—it is about half the size it was ten years ago. The railroads and the electric lines have helped reduce the size of some of these towns Cripple Creek, Victor, and Goldfield have become the important places to live due to the conveniences available. The rapid forms of transportation have made living near the mines unnecessary. At one time almost everyone up here owned a horse, and many had wagons, but now many do not. It is much the same for sidearms. In the early days many wore them, but now only the guards, policemen, and a few of the rough crowd have them.

It is ten o'clock as the train turns on the wye and backs into the depot at Cripple Creek. The first floor of the building is well lighted, and the two main streets are clearly visible behind it. One of the streets is Myers, the other is Bennett, named for the two developers of Cripple Creek. Myers is the colorful section of town, even though it has quieted considerably from the rip-roaring days of the turn of the century. We will stroll down Bennett to our hotel. One can find hotels along the avenue that have rooms for a minimum of fifty cents to ten dollars a night, depending upon the degree of comfort required. While we walk from the depot, the railroad crew will uncouple the locomotive, reload the depleted coal pile, add water, and relubricate the engine. The locomotive may even receive a washing before tomorrow's return trip. The engine house is north of the depot, as is the small switching yard and the water tank. The Short Line also uses this depot now. For its first several years, the CS & CCD had a depot of its own not far away, but now it has consolidated services here. The large sign on the front of the depot clearly boasts of the railroads available here.

The most amazing thing on broad Bennett Avenue is the noise. The sounds of music blend with the blare of drills, pumps, generators, locomotives, and muffled explosions. The sound of an occasional horse cart is barely audible above the sound of an automobile. The even rarer truck with its hard rubber tires can be heard from somewhere on the hillside. The sounds pour out of every corner of town. The emanations from the saloons invade the ears of those walking up the street.

The best hotel is in easy view even at night in Cripple Creek. The New Midland Hotel is almost within yelling distance from the depot; however, it is fairly plain, even though it has seen remodeling recently. The National is Cripple Creek's **grand** hotel. It has all of the modern conveniences, including electric lights in all of the rooms and an elevator. The hotel, which was backed by one of the Midland Terminal's founders, W.K. Gillett, takes up almost one-fourth of the block and is four stories tall, not including the tower.

A number of other passengers seem to be heading for the National. The one-block walk takes only a few minutes. The lobby of the New Midland fills with customers from the train. The ceiling of the lobby of the National is open to the second floor, and an archway behind the cigar stand leads into the large dining room. The number of people who have arrived on the train does not even begin to fill the waiting area in the lobby. A huge man with a fine handlebar mustache is standing behind the counter as we come toward the desk. A small crowd has gathered, waiting their turn at checking in.

A nearby stairway leads to the upper ballroom. The room has seen the likes of Stratton, Penrose, Carlton, Tutt, and even Womack. A brass-trimmed elevator is located near the stairway. It is relaxing to rest on one of the fine, red-velvet–lined chairs in the lobby. The National is the finest hotel in the district. The present proprietors, John O'Riley and L.R. Barr, purchased the hotel a few years ago. Once we check in, at the rate of four dollars, we have a room overlooking Bennett Avenue on the third floor.

The ride in the open, brass-trimmed elevator lasted for only a few minutes. Our room is in the corner, near the bath. It is small but neatly arranged with two sets of windows, one on Fourth and the other on Bennett. A single bed, a dresser with a mirror, an easy chair, and a table with a small reading lamp furnish the room. The bath is across the hall. Each room is no further than twelve feet from a bath; each bath serves roughly four rooms.

The lights and sounds of Cripple Creek are interesting. The low rumble is accentuated by an occasional loud roar, steam whistle, clanging bell, and even a rare gunshot, but it is never absolutely silent. The miners are constantly coming and going, either to work, home, or for entertainment.

In the summer of 1911, CS&CCD train #3 approaches the Cripple Creek Union Depot. The MT had not built an engine house at this time, they might have been using the Short Line facility. — AC, H.E. High Photo

Cripple Creek was very busy in the late 1890's. The damage from the fire was almost completely erased. The Midland's wye is visible, but the depot is hidden. — CCDM

The town is tame now. However, a few years ago the scene was much different. Bennett Avenue is still off-limits to the citizens of Myers, but even Myers is quieter than it was only two years ago. The doors on the bars and **houses** on Myers are never locked, but a few are boarded up now. People roam the street at all hours of the night, many using the dark to conceal their identities. The police constantly patrol the area, but still trouble is likely to start at any time. A recent shooting in a saloon on Bennett was said to have been the result of a problem that started in on Myers.

The shades help block the lights, but the sound is still only muffled by the heavy brick walls. The large bed is very comfortable, and the night slides right past. In the morning the sound of a steam whistle from one of the mines awakes us, just as it is intended to wake employees. The street below is much as it was when we pulled the shade, except that the time of day has changed. A few women and children are visible. Delivery wagons are making the rounds of some of the businesses. The interurban cars are loaded with men on their way to the mines.

The hour is barely detectable. Our locomotive and cars are already parked at the depot. The preparation of the train started over an hour ago. Our preparations will not take quite so long. One more check out the window allows us to see a Short Line train approach the depot with four cars. The green cars are clearly different from the Midland's maroon cars. A glance at our watch as we finish dressing speeds us up a bit. A look at the lobby clock as we rush past the desk on the way to the street indicates just how early it is—6:45 A.M.

One thinks of the glamour of mining towns, but while walking up to the depot another thought strikes us. Nowhere in Colorado can another area of twelve square miles be found that shows on the surface so many shafts, tunnels, quarries, trenches, gopher holes, and all other sorts of mine workings. In places, ore has been shipped from the surface—shipping the scenery as it is called. The great terraced warts on the slopes of the hills are the dumps of waste rock hauled out of the mines. The larger buildings are the shaft houses, protecting the hoisting and pumping machinery. Tall and short gallows frames stick up amongst buildings and trees. Here and there, samplers, or their remains, can be detected. The air is filled with smoke and noise, and as we near the station the

sound of our locomotive is almost audible over the other sounds.

The red brick depot is dramatically situated. It almost commands your attention from any spot in western Cripple Creek. Rising above the street three stories, located up against a rocky hill, the station towers above surrounding buildings. On the south side of the depot is our next point of interest. The pedestrian bridge allows us, as well as area residents, to pass over the busy tracks to the hill above the station. A large number of people live and work in Poverty Gulch, the name of the area above the railroad yards.

The walk over the train allows us a smoky perch over the tracks and the two trains. The Short Line train will be leaving in a few minutes. The conductor of our train is already allowing passengers on. The crowd is large, but due to the confined location, the number is misleading. A number of the passengers seem to be business-men traveling to Colorado Springs with their wives. The schedule allows plenty of time for business and shopping in town before the return trip. The one major feature lacking in the schedule is a connection with westbound trains at Divide. The wait is over four hours, and many of the passengers choose to ride into Colorado Springs rather than wait at Divide. The cars load quickly, and the conductor seems concerned that there might not be enough room on the train.

The train is completely full when the final call for boarding is heard promptly at 7:15 A.M. The whistle sounds, and we pull away from the depot. As the station passes, we get a fine view of the entire town. A few years ago the valley was lined with buildings, but with the mining slump, many buildings have been torn down. A few of the city blocks are empty. The yards of the Short Line and Florence and Cripple Creek are below us. to the west.

As the train passes the coal bins, the smoke of another MT locomotive on a lower track blocks our view of town. On the crooked grade south of Cripple Creek, each person must be thinking especially of that which interests him most. The attraction of the geologist will be to the exposed railway cuts and the hundreds of prospect holes and trenches. He might note the great variety of colors due to weathering, with reds and browns predominating but with many a passing gleam of the peacock iron stain, and he can compare these colors with the greenish-gray tint of many of the

F.L. Ransome recorded the city of Anaconda and the many mines on the ridge east of it. The lower railroad on the hill, which runs through town is the narrow gauge F&CC. — USGS

F.L. Ransome saw a long line of Midland Terminal box cars near the mine at Elkton. The lower track is the narrow gauge F&CC. — USGS

Anaconda before 1903 shows signs of prosperity, all three of the district railroads are represented, highest to lowest they are: Short Line (CS&CCD), MT, and F&CC. A fire in 1903 destroyed many buildings. — AJ

Colorado Midland #12 with the Cripple Creek Express meets another, unidentified C.M. locomotive at the Victor depot. — AC

Not the best picture, but, one of the first five locomotives is seen in Victor at the turn of the century, pulling one of the new box cars. — PM

(Far right) The Independence depot was the scene of a lot of freight and passenger traffic, particularly in the late 1890's when the railroad had not reached Cripple Creek. — PM

dumps. The miner and prospector will especially note the number of mines about and the assorted prospect holes. The farmer will notice the grass still growing on these hills in spite of the tramping and will not wonder at the fact that before the discovery of gold, this broad range was considered one of the best cattle ranges. No matter what their taste may be, all travelers enjoy the wide panorama. The enjoyment will come from the effects of the colors—the reds, blacks, browns, blues, grays, and greens contrasting with the white of the snows on the distant peaks, and the billowing clouds that grow in the warm afternoons. A few light clouds can be seen to the west, but by midday they will drift in this direction.

The mines in the area appear to be busy. A look in the local morning newspaper would indicate a lively summer. The Joe Dandy is working three hundred feet, and General Manager Jim Wright is quoted as saying that new drifts are expected to be developed soon. The Portland, largest shipper in the district, is shipping 9,000 tons of ore each month. The Isabella, once owned by J.J. Hagerman, shipped thirty-five carloads last month. The Anchoria-Leland is projecting fifty carloads this month, at eight to fifteen dollars a ton. The Gold Sovereign on Bull Hill shipped sixty cars in July, averaging fifteen dollars a ton. The entire district shipped a record of 35,000 tons last month, or an average of seventy cars per day. The majority was shipped out over the Florence and Cripple Creek and the Short Line. The gold rate per ton is lower than it was in the past, but with the completion of the drainage tunnel, the mines hope to find more high-grade ore. The Roosevelt Tunnel is now 3,000 feet long and is progressing at nine feet per day. The tunnel is already draining some of the water from the mines on the north side of the district, and it will eventually drain most of the larger mines.

The towns between Cripple Creek and Victor look much smaller in the daylight, and the mines look nearly twice as large. At 7:30 the train pulls into Victor and a number of passengers get off. One who remains points out the important local buildings, but the amazing feature is the noise. Cripple Creek was very noisy, but Victor is also noisy in a different way. The noise in Cripple Creek is the sound of a city, plus the sound of mining. In Victor the sounds of mining are much louder, mixed with sounds of people. The sounds of the city are not so loud here.

The return to the main line and the ride around the end of Battle Mountain are marked by the numerous stops and pauses for other trains. The Short Line, Midland Terminal, Colorado Midland, F & CC, and the diminutive Golden Circle engines work around the mines, samplers, and mills at a feverish pace. The green electric cars dart around the streets of Goldfield, below us. One must only wonder, as we pass through Independence, what it must have been like eight years ago, at the peak of activity.

The brown depot at Independence is towered over by the piles of rock that have been rejected. The waste rock was worthless, but someday it may be possible to extract some of the low-grade ore that is mixed with ordinary granite. The miners talk of the huge caverns that have been excavated. Even now, inside the mountain, right under this car, men are working. The railroads all over the mountain are actually undermined by literally dozens of tunnels. It is only justice that there is at least one tunnel through a waste rock pile.

The train makes its way past Bull Hill and the tiny depot there. The two huge samplers tower over the railroad's facilities. A marvelous view of the lower railroads can be seen from here until the town of Cameron. An MT freight is just rounding the curve toward Gillett as we stop at Cameron, which is also known as Grassy. On Hoosier Pass, to our left, one of the green cars of the electric line is just coming into view. Once it has passed over our tracks, we can move on.

The sky is bright blue; not a cloud is to be seen yet. The train makes its way out of the district toward Pikes Peak, Gillett, Divide, and on into Colorado Springs. The retracing of our earlier path is highlighted by the memory of our visit to Colorado's greatest gold camp.

MIDLAND TERMINAL DEP
INDEPENDENCE, COLO.

Engine 64 and 65 pull through Woodland,
just beyond the depot heading south toward
the old wye. The railroad didn't really like
having the pumps on the front, but on the
side they often scraped the close sides of
cuts and tunnels. — HB/ESP

Book Three:

On an Ore Train

Introduction

NOW WE WILL RIDE AN ORE TRAIN MAK-ing a typical run to Bull Hill and back. The trip will follow a train on an average late summer day in 1939 or 1940. The Midland Terminal runs its passenger service during the day, while the ore train runs at night. The local switching at Colorado Springs and in the district is done during the day. The last chapter in this book concludes with a look at the switching operations typical for the same period inside the district.

This book could not have been written without the fond memories of several former Midland Terminal employees. It is through them that you are able to share the ride.

Local switcher #52 steams near the office
building near #58 and 57, while #60 waits to
go on the turntable, ready for a trip to Bull
Hill in 1948. — Herb O'Hanlon
Photo/Author's Collection

7. All Aboard!

Locomotives 64 and 66 in the Colorado City yards, steamed and ready to collect their crews, empties, and caboose for the trip west. — DPL

THE BUS RIDE FROM THE DENVER AND Rio Grande Western depot in Colorado Springs took about ten minutes. If we had wanted to spend the day, we could have ridden the motor car over at 8:30 this morning, when it came for the mail run. It would have made for a very long day and night. The bus stopped in front of the church on Colorado Avenue at Twenty-first Street. The neighborhood is where many old Colorado Midland employees lived, and where many Midland Terminal men still do.

The grocery store across the street is a likely place for the next stop. It seems very strange for the butcher to make up sandwiches for a lunch that we will not eat for another half a day. It might be a good idea to have an extra one or two, since it will also be our supper. The butcher entertains us with his knowledge of the **Midland** while he works. Most of the westsiders call it just that. The

butcher's father worked in the old Colorado Midland shops. The names Prosser, Pressler, Sullivan, Tait, and Groome are just a few that have been mentioned while the lunch was being made. The butcher than pops in a pair of boiled eggs as his gift to the occasion.

It is a short walk down the street to the railroad yards. One block from the grocery store, we cross over the D & RGW's Manitou Branch. The Colorado Springs switcher, steam engine #54, is one block away with an empty tank car that it is taking back to the Rio Grande yards. The gas station up the street gets its gasoline deliveries by tank car. The switch for the storage track is an old three-way stub switch.

On the hill across the way we can see the Midland Terminal's switcher with five empties crossing behind the Golden Cycle Mill. In a few minutes it will be picking up the last few cars and

113

An air view showing the Colorado City yards as well as the Golden Cycle Mill in the summer of 1947. Long strings of empty ore cars can be seen in the yards, one stretching past the coal trestle to nearly 25th Street ready to head up to Bull Hill. — USGS

The railroad end of the Golden Cycle Mill. To the right of the smokestack is the ore sorting building and unloading facility. — PPL

bringing them down the hill into the yards. Yesterday one of the cars derailed and went rolling into a man's backyard. It took most of the day to get it back. The track runs west across the hillside and swings down Arch Street to the yards. It should be pulling these empties into the yards while we are there.

The afternoon sun is warm, but the clouds are building up over Pikes Peak. It just might rain on us this afternoon. Our destination is in the far end of the roundhouse. We could walk around the back, around the coal trestle, and around the turntable pit, but there is a better route. If we go around the end of the coal trestle and between it and the roundhouse, we can see what is going on inside the roundhouse.

The stone structure is a very dirty building. The soot from the locomotives and dust from the tailings pile at the mill cover every inch of the buildings. Lunch bag in hand, dressed in dungarees, we can pass for any railroader or mill hand. The windows at the end of the roundhouse are filthy, but we can make out the shape of a man inside working on a big machine.

We step very carefully over the rails and round the corner. The big doors are open. This end of the building is filled with machinery: lathes, grinders, presses, and the like. The rails have been taken up inside this part of the building. The boilermaker has part of the space, as does the blacksmith. In the next set of stalls, a team of men are pulling the drivers from under an engine. It looks rather odd, like a smile with a front tooth missing. It is one of the older locomotives. A long pit runs across several tracks and is deep enough for a man and a big air-driven machine that raises and lowers the drivers. A long pit runs the length of another track

The cab on the engine has a coat of red primer, and we cannot detect a number.

In the next section the three engines for tonight's trip are being made ready. A fourth engine is in the adjoining stall. One of the engines for tonight already has steam up, and they are working on the second. The three will be pulled out, fueled, watered, oiled, and waiting on the ready track on the other side of the turntable by four o'clock.

One of the stalls on the end, usually occupied by a little yellow monster, is empty. The other converted streetcar is resting silently outside, while the #101 is running somewhere between Cripple Creek and Victor right now. In the #102's usual stall is one of the new locomotives from Alaska. The hostler's office is in the corner of the roundhouse. With a wave he gives us directions around the engine, while pointing to a locker where we can stick our lunch until the ore train leaves.

Trying to remember the list of names he rattles off, we start to walk in the direction of the office building. The next big building is only two hundred feet away, and the big doors are open. The two little buildings at the end of the roundhouse are for storage of the motor cars and the Pierce Arrow sedan. The automoile is now fitted with railroad wheels.

The big building ahead of us is the old machine shop, now more or less a carpentry shop. It was converted when the machines were moved into the roundhouse. The big building is virtually empty, except for a few machines, piles of new and used wood, and a few steel car parts. A few old wheels and axles line one of the walls, and the blacksmith uses the old parts to make replace-

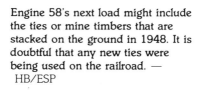

Engine 58's next load might include the ties or mine timbers that are stacked on the ground in 1948. It is doubtful that any new ties were being used on the railroad. — HB/ESP

ment parts for the engines.

A black, coal residue coats the floor and part of the walls. A few years ago the company was expecting a coal strike, and this building was empty. The railroad unloaded several dozen carloads of the commodity in the long building. As things turned out, there was no strike, and a scoop was used to move the coal to the coaling trestle, where it could be loaded into tenders. The pile took several months to move.

The windows are very dirty, and a few have been broken out. The sound of an engine signals the arrival of the Golden Cycle Mill switcher in the yards. The large building is silent except for the noises that we make. The sound of an engine moving the cars to the assigned track echoes around the room. Rubbing a bit of coal dust off the window we cannot see the switcher, but its smoke can be seen behind a large building west of the old machine shop.

A door opens on the north end of the building, closest to the office building. A large man, who has been told of our visit, heads quickly toward us and introduces himself as the shop foreman.

"We do not do much in here now, mainly repairing engine cabs and beams and such. At one time this place could turn out a completely new car. They had a coach shop, boiler shop, and the works. Not much left now, no real need. The last big project was converting the street cars." He takes us on a quick tour of the building. "That big building on the other side used to be a shop, now it is filled with junk," he says.

Our tour of the shop is over as he heads us out the door and points us toward the office building. "We get a few people in here in the summer taking pictures. It does not bother us too much, but the guys in the office get nervous. There are two or three guys that are seen here and there regularly. If you haven't done it yet, you better check in at the office."

The big office is on the end of this building.

Climbing up the steps, you get the idea that you are taking a stairway back in time. The big heavy door, the smell of the office, the old pictures on the wall and the desks—it looks like the twenties. The man at the desk turns and accepts our introductions.

"We have the permission forms ready. Here, sign this right here, and over here. Keep a copy of this in your pocket. Mr. McKay is rather busy, but if he has time he wants to talk to you. All of the train crew knows you are coming. Please stay off the cars and do not go into any building without someone with you."

Looking at the old clock, it is clear that we will not be roaming much more. In the background we can hear the engines being moved out to the ready track. Our little adventure is now about to get going.

The engine crew caller, Art Wilcox, who is also the Midland Terminal's Colorado City hostler, started calling for tonight's run to Bull Hill at 2:30 P.M. for the 4:30 run. The train crews, the brakemen, switchmen, and conductor, were called by Vern Clark. The three engines have been moved to a spot near the water spout, ready to go. We all stand around near the roundhouse, grabbing quick instructions. The train tonight is about average, but for the last several nights there were small trains with only a few engines and less than thirty cars each. Last week there were a couple of four-engine nights.

The tenders are all loaded, but the firemen doublecheck as they inspect their engines before climbing into the cab. There is little question of which crew has an engine, since most of the crews have been working together for many months, even years. Occasionally there is a new fireman or a brakeman, but all of the engineers are old hands at this.

Train orders in hand, the engineer of the lead engine climbs up to his cab and within minutes is ready to head west. The head brakeman is also in

Locomotives 64 and 65 are made ready for one of the last ore runs to Bull Hill. — Ed Heltemes Photo

Engine 59 was used for freight and ore trains between 1932 and 1949, and waits near the water tank in October 1939. — HB/ESP

Locomotive 60 is ready to join the empty ore cars for a trip to Bull Hill. The old roundhouse, snow plow, and office building have seen the passing of many steam locomotives, but by 1946, only a few more years were in the cards. — HKV

Ready to go, 60 is now ready to head away from the roundhouse probably on an ore train. — WS/EC

The depot at Colorado City needed a coat of paint on August 26, 1931. The building lasted only a short time after the passenger train was discontinued. — WM/BSM

the cab. The train is scheduled to roll at 4:30, but often if the general manager is not in his office, the train does not move until nearly five. Mr. McKay's car is here, so we start out right on time, choofing lightly up Twenty-sixth Street. The fireman has set a light fire that will keep us going for a few minutes. The pressure is up to its normal 150 pounds.

The fireman pauses, "Well, while it is fresh on my mind, did you hear about what happened to the old depot at Twenty-fifth Street? It was in the winter of '31, and Dave McDonald was the janitor. I guess he banked the fire in the waiting room with just a bit too much coal for that old cast iron stove. It just overheated itself and ignited the wall, with the dispatcher's office on the other side, it made Winslow's office just too hot for him. E.W. Winslow, who was the dispatcher, was at home, fortunately, but by morning there was nothing but ashes of his office, anyway they just moved his office up to the stone building."

The rear brakeman and conductor are riding on the footboard of the last engine; as they pass the caboose track they hop off. The last engine stops, and a switchman throws the switch to the caboose track, signaling the engineer to back up. There are two cabooses on the track, the regularly used #1, and the backup #2. There usually is only one train on the line at one time, so the only thing we will meet is the #101. The engineer has coupled to the first black caboose, #1.

While all of this has gone on, the other two engines are now ready to back toward the two lines of empty cars. The middle engine is backing toward the cars on yard 2. As soon as the engine is clear, we will back onto yard 1. We pull out as soon as we are coupled to the empties and head west, almost all the way to Thirty-first Street. You could easily think that we are on our way to Bull Hill, the way we pull away. The second engine is ready to pull out now. It pulls up to the rear of our cars, couples on, blocking Twenty-sixth Street. This shuffling is well known in this part of town, and the local people try to avoid it. The switchman is very busy resetting the switches so that the last engine can pull up to the train. Once the caboose is clear and he has thrown the last switch, he climbs onto the rear platform of the caboose.

The firemen are now getting their fires banked again. The last engine is ready, and he "whistles off." Two toots lets us know that he is ready and starting to apply steam. The engineer of the next engine has been listening very carefully, and when he hears the whistle, he whistles off and also starts to roll. The lead engineer whistles off, and the train is now moving up the hill. The last engine has pushed up any slack. The jolt in the second engine is light. The men up in our engine know very well that it is on its way, and they are ready as it hits us.

The last engine is now moving, and soon the train will be under full steam. When the train reaches Red Rock Canyon we are up to almost thirty miles per hour. Adam's Crossing is a short distance ahead and is a clue for the fireman to get back to his fire. This grade marks a marked change at the crossing, and more steam is needed. Our engine has already started up the climb above Manitou, and the second will be starting on it soon. The last engine will be there in a few minutes. The fireman is working hard, getting the fire ready to go through the first two tunnels.

Up until a few years ago, the Midland's siding and the Denver and Rio Grande's siding in Manitou usually had private cars parked on them most of the summer. A few of the cars were there every summer, as regular as a clock. Some of the cars would be here for a week or two, others would be here all summer.

A small, dark, stone building sits next to the tracks as we pass behind the high school. The obscure little building used to be the Manitou depot, but the building has not been used for several years. The little passenger car will stop here when flagged, but we do not even blink.

The first tunnel is just around the curve. We can look to the north and see the track coming back, as well as the lime kiln. The engine crews do not like rolling through the tunnels under full steam. The smoke from a working engine can choke you. The fireman banks his fires before we hit the first tunnel. He will check it again before we approach the second one.

The Colorado Midland used to double-head its engines that worked up Ute Pass, but the tunnels created a real heat problem. The smoke and heat from the second engine were enough to give the crew in the lead engine considerable problems. The heat would come right over the coal pile into the cab. The solution was to put the engines like they are run today, spread out through the train.

The fireman again works up his fire as we pass over Ruxton bridge. The grade is steep, and with the curve, the train's speed is down to ten or fifteen miles an hour.

The train crosses over two long fills above the

Engine 58 backs a string of empties in preparation for the run to Bull Hill. — EH Photo

The old Manitou depot had been used to store coal in the 1930's, and stayed boarded up until it was rebuilt into a fine, solid home, a few years after the abandonment. — HB/ESP

The train is now working above Manitou and engine 57 is in the middle of the train. — HB/ESP

It is unusual that the helper is behind the caboose, but perhaps it was added after the train left the yards in this November, 1948 photo. — HB/ESP

Engine 60 drags behind caboose 1, which had additional bracing added to lessen its swaybacked condition, unusually visible is its full lettering in this April 7, 1935 photograph in Ute Pass. — DPL

Veritable old 52 in August, 1935, with its long smokebox, still has two sets of square weighted drivers, but two newer sets. — William O. Gibson Photo

town. The fills cover old wooden trestles. In 1934 and 1935, a whole series of improvements was done along the line. The two old bridges had caused quite a few problems. Trucks from Pikes Peak Fuel, also owned by Golden Cycle Corporation, dumped waste rock from its coal mine on the tracks. The blackened rock looks like it might have coal in it. The trestles are now completely buried.

On the subject of coal, the fireman talks a bit about a coal experiment. "A while back the company tried using some of their lignite on these engines, 'bug dust' we called it. It caused some real headaches. It did not burn fast enough, we were losing a lot of it right out the stack. We had lots of fires caused by the hot cinders. The depot at Woodland was even set on fire. The Golden Cycle switcher runs on lignite still. It is okay in it."

The three engines are really barking as we pass the company lime kiln. A few loads are waiting on the siding, where we are to pick them up. The train will stop to switch them and pick them up on the way back.

The Lime Rock pickup is sometimes left for the ore train, but usually the Colorado City switch crew comes up this far. The cars on the track tonight are quite a conglomeration—a Midland lime car, Denver and Rio Grande Western box, and a Pennsy box. Non-Midland cars are rather unusual on the line, except for the Rio Grande, Santa Fe, and dozens of Rock Island cars. The lime, part of the Golden Cycle Mill's processing, is occasionally shipped all over the country.

The fireman on our engine has his fires set for our entrance to tunnel three. Three and four are long tunnels. The engineer eases back on the throttle a bit and pulls off his gauntlet glove. He casually bends over and breathes through his glove, and the other two men in the cab do similarly. The air in the tunnel quickly gets smoky. The train is now moving at five miles per hour. We hardly notice the flash of light that signals the gap between the two tunnels as we enter five. The fireman again hits his fire as we blast into the fresh air. The train doesn't jar noticeably as each of the engine crews go through the same sequence of events.

The engineer eases up a bit each time we enter a tunnel, powering up as we exit. The fireman is working steadily as we work our way up through the towering mass at Hanging Rock Cut.

The highway, off to our right, is fairly busy this afternoon. A few tourists stop occasionally to watch trains, and some even take pictures. The canyon is already starting to get dark, but we will be back in the sun as we get close to Cascade. The highway is right out the cab door after we pass a steel bridge. We are in the narrowest part of the pass. There have been many accidents along here, so the highway department keeps trying to widen the canyon by blasting out chunks of the hillside. The worst problem with the spot is from tourists who park too close to the tracks. These big, old engines can do wonders on a car fender. The remark goes around, "You remember that new 1937 Chevy we took the fender off of a couple of years ago? We whistled and whistled, and the little lady was out there with her Kodak, just kept waving back to us!"

One of the other favorite stories has to do with the amount of smoke the engines put out, if the engineer and the fireman want lots of smoke. "You can fill this pass with thick black smoke, some tourists just love it, but the railroad is **always**

getting calls about too much smoke."

The fireman points out the water glass and his pressure gauge. A red line marks where the pressure in the boiler reaches a danger point. The "pops" on the steam dome open, and the pressure drops to a safe level. He points out the proper level on the sig t glass and directs our attention to the injector handle. The injector pulls water from the tender to the front of the boiler, operated by the fireman. If the water level in the glass drops too far, more water is pumped from the tender. The main problem is that this water is often very cold, and it cools the boiler. The fireman must operate his injector very carefully, slowly adding water and keeping the water level in the center of the glass. The engineer watches ahead on the tracks while the fireman talks, and the head brakeman has about dozed off.

"You put in five scoopfuls every time. Put the first one to the right front corner, the second to the left front corner. You repeat that for the back corners, then dump the last one just inside the door." He instructs us not to worry about the center. The draft will pull the flame up toward the throat. We notice, through the intense flames of the firebox, that he has about two inches of flame along the bottom of the grate. The draft, from the rear of the boiler to the smokebox, makes the flames dance with each "choof" from the stack. He points out that a heavier layer of coal will cause some cool spots and may even cause clinkers. We need to keep heat at the side of the firebox, not so much in the center.

"The object in firing, now, on these steam engines is not to worry about the center. The center takes care of itself, but on the sides, that's where your water is. That boiler is hot, so you have got to keep the heat there, not in the center. Keep it against the sheets, so the water is boiling and steaming. Keep your fire uniform. If too much air comes in here at the back it will warp your gate."

The last shovelful goes in just as he instructs. The engineer calls out, "Cusack Corner."

The crews have named almost every landmark on the railroad, and each has a special meaning to the crew. It may be where a brake is set or released, or, like this corner, a warning to the fireman that Cascade is just ahead. It is time to shake the grates and get ready to dump the ashes.

The lead engine pulls into a shallow cut as the fireman works to dump the ashes before the train reaches the short bridge over the creek, on the east end of Cascade. The bridge and building department gets pretty mad if you set their bridge on fire. The majority of the engine crew have spent a little time on either the B&B crew or with a section gang before they were able to go on the road, so they have a healthy respect for the maintenance crews.

The yellow #101 waits for us at Cascade. Our train is slowing as we pull up right to the platform. The big depot was torn down in 1923, but the signboard tells us that we are at Cascade. We have to roll past the water tank, far enough to let the gasoline car out on the main. We hear a whistle blast, telling us that the last engine is under the water tank. While we wait, the fireman and the engineer are out looking over the engine and oiling the rods and other points. The engineer returns the signal, and we back up. With another blast, we

The train is clear of all of the tunnels in Ute Pass, but there is still a lot of work before the train reaches Cascade. The train is only doing about ten miles an hour. — HB/ESP

(Left) The last ore trip is half way between tunnel 8 and Crags bound for Bull Hill, working at about 15 miles an hour. — Ed Heltemes Photo

Engine 65 on the tail end of this January, 1949 train pushing a load of coal for Cascade and rock cars for the quarry. The fragile caboose is on the end. — HB/ESP

Ex-US Army, ex-0-6-0 with ex-Colorado Midland caboose wait at Cascade for their train to finish setting out a load, backs to the downhill end of the train. — HB/ESP

stop for the second engine.

The sequence is repeated, but it is our turn. The fireman has climbed back over the coal to take on our water. He pulls the rope for the chute, then, when it is in position, he pulls another rope on the control valve. It is not too bad this time of year, but in the winter there is ice in the water. It will freeze as soon as it hits you during the winter, and, in fact. the whole tank is coated in winter with icicles as big around as a tree. The water now is not exactly warm, observing the expression on the fireman's face as it wets his overalls.

The railroad has been a part of Cascade for over fifty years. The whistles from our train, which is ready to pull out, have echoed in this valley like a natural part of everyone's life. The three engines whistle off, again ready to leave. It is a little hard to believe the engineer's story of the old days on the Colorado Midland, when there were famous hotels and quaint little depots scattered along the railroad. Cascade has a little pavillion, water tank, and some scattered wood, but little to remind you of any grandeur. A few buildings further up the pass date back to those "grand old days."

The fireman is busy again, the engineer is watching the rest of the train as we pull away, and we are left to watch the trees go by. The area has overgrown to the point where there are weeds

right up to the rails. The engine rocks from side to side as we slowly pass over a bad section of track and go around a gradual curve. The brakeman stares out of the cab window as we pass through a grove of trees. The trees are lined up along the creek as if from a picture book.

The sun is starting to drop behind the ridge, and in a few more minutes we will be in the dark. We hardly notice the dropping temperature, but we do notice the darkness. The headlight can be seen as a glow on the rails. The smoke from a few of the yards along the grade is scented with the odor of food. The smoke from our engines will soon overpower the aroma, but within a few seconds of our passing, the smell of cooking will again fill the hills. Cars can be seen up on the highway. The engineer gets ready to blow the whistle, warning any cars approaching the grade crossing ahead. This was originally Ute Park, but now everyone calls it Chipita Park. Up on the hillside to our right, still in the sun, the head brakemen points out the shape of an old railroad car.

"See that? It used to be the Midland Terminal's business car." The sound of the whistle almost drowns his words: "It was named **Cascade** and the Carltons used it. The two traveled all over the country in it."

"You remember that long building where the

caboose was in the yards?" the fireman adds. "Well, that is the coach barn, now. When I came to work on the railroad that car was parked in there. I can remember seeing them roll it out for one of their special trips. About five years ago, about when L.G. died, they parked it in there for the last time. The new president did not like it all that well, plus it was getting old. You could see that it was a real fine car, but in a year it was just covered with pigeon droppings. The car was put up for sale and sold to a guy who had worked for the Santa Fe. The guys in the carpenter shop stripped off the rigging and the trucks. It was moved up here and put on a foundation. I can still remember those six-wheel trucks. It was the only car we had with those trucks, ran real smooth, too, even up in the district. I think those trucks are in the shed behind the carpenter shop now. I can still remember that gold lettering shining against the highly varnished green. Now, maybe you saw, it is as brown as a

barn."

A man on a horse, crossing the grade ahead, gets a blast from the whistle.

"Green Mountain Falls!" someone calls, and the engine crew is on the alert, looking out the front doors of the cab.

Why all the attention, we wonder. It seems that there has been a rash of problems along this section. A couple of weeks ago some fool was hidden in the trees along the lake. He threw a wine bottle full of gasoline into the cab. Had it not been for the engineer smelling it, the whole crew could have been burned. The gas did not splash around, and the fireman kept the firebox doors closed until it was swept away.

The fireman again hits his fire and returns to our lesson on firing, while the engineer whistles for the crossing west of town.

The next lesson is the operation of the firebox doors. The engines originally had a single door. In

Caboose #2 at Cascade tank on February 1, 1949 clearly showing its rebuilt underframe. — DPL/Joe Schick Collection

The Cascade pavillion and water tank. — HO/AC

125

the 1930s sometime, the engines were upgraded with these butterfly type doors. First the fireman presses an iron lever to open the doors. After he puts in his four or five scoops, he reaches back and releases the lever, and the doors close. In the old days, a lot of firemen burned their hands until they learned to kick the door open. The bigger roads have air-operated firebox doors.

"You have to do that and keep an eye on that sight glass, and the steam gauge. Try to keep it from five to fifteen pounds below the popping off point. The next thing is the water level. One time up here on number 60 we had just passed Crystola when the water glass broke. It had a little crack in it, and it finally gave up. There are three water gauge cocks over here on the side of the boiler, right here," and he points out the cocks.

"You can tell right where your water is, but they are hard to use, and fire at the same time. We felt around up here in this box," as he points above his head, over the side windows of the cab, "and found an extra glass." He reaches up and feels around for a few seconds. "Hey! Here is another one." He shows us a short section of heavy glass tubing.

"So the engineer throttled very carefully, back enough that we were still making smoke, so the others would not think that we were goofing off. I kicked on the blower and went right to work. The two shutoff valves, above and below the glass, were closed, and I dug out the alligator wrench. The Midland always uses these antique tools; anyway, I worked to get the hot, broken old glass out of there. It was quite a job working out the hot pieces of glass. I had to keep the fire up and check the gauge cocks. I was like a monkey on a flagpole. We were almost to Woodland Park before I finished, right on Paradise Ranch curve."

The train is rolling at about twenty-five miles an hour as we pass the guest ranch. The engineer whistles for the grade crossings, on the quiet side of the whistle. The head brakeman points out that they have had some complaints from the clientele. He also points out the creosote plant where the Midland Terminal ties are treated, as well as the dark shape of the little depot on the right side of the tracks, as we near the curve. It is lighted by a single light.

"That is all that if left of a real fine depot. There was a fire up here in the twenties, almost burned down the whole depot. The baggage end was saved. The B&B boys took what was left and built this building."

The engineer adds that there used to be a big hotel up to our right, along with a wye, the tail of which went almost up to the hotel. The wye was taken out in the early days of the Cripple Creek gold rush. Suburban passengers used to run up this far and go back to Colorado Springs, sometimes twice a day. The run was increased to Divide when the rush started. In a few years the Midland Terminal was built, and trains were started all the way into Cripple Creek. The old hotel became a tuberculosis hospital about thirty years ago and was only recently torn down. The old Colorado Midland depot is across the street and is now a rather seedy looking hotel.

A sixteen-degree curve, the sharpest corner on the railroad, is just above Woodland. A few trains have dumped cars on this curve on their way down from Edlowe. After we turn the corner, we climb on up to old Summit Park, now called Edlowe, where the grade will finally level out again, for the first time since Manitou.

The engineer looks around to the fireman and says, "Tell you what I think we ought to do tonight. I am going to ease up on it after we pass Edlowe and let those two other push us up to Divide, and on into Murphy." He pushes in the throttle enough so that the steam is still working, but it is not working very heavily. From the other engines it looks like we are working as hard as they are, but in the dark they cannot really tell. The guys in the cab will soon be munching on a sandwich and drinking their first cup of hot coffee.

One-half mile from Divide, we top a crest, and the engineer asks, "Well, how are you guys now?" He receives a few nods in reply as the fireman and brakeman continue to eat. "From here to Murphy we are not going to work up a sweat!" he chuckles as he gives the fireman a slap on the back. The engineer was a fireman on the old Colorado Midland, Short Line, and Midland Terminal, and he surely remembers how hard a job it is. It is rather interesting that many of the firemen are rather slight in stature. One might expect the contrary; in fact, only one of the fireman on the extra board is young and muscular. The cab is not big enough for many large men.

The fireman rebanks his fire and watches the pressure gauge. The train is rolling right along, but we barely detect the grade. The climb is nothing like the climb in Ute Pass.

The crew points out a few local landmarks as we

The train from Colorado Springs works hard past the little Woodland Park depot on February 1, 1949. — DPL

The main street of Woodland Park just about 1920 shows that the MT was very busy treating ties at their plant this side of the depot. — PM

One of the ex-USA ex-0-6-0's pulls one of the modified gondola cars westward into Woodland Park in 1948 at the head of an ore train. — LLW

Engine 58 and caboose 2 bring up the rear of one of the last ore trains in 1948. Woodland Park is two miles behind, and the crew will be working hard all the way to Edlowe, about two miles ahead. — HB/ESP

Cars for the quarry are a big part of the train between Woodland and Divide. The Rock Island cars will be left at Midland for loading. — HB/ESP

(Top) Water time at Midland, engine 64 moves out to allow the next engine to water up. The newer engines were able to drop their pans and clean the grates from inside the cabs, but on the older ones it had to be done from the ground. — HB/ESP

(Center) One of the last ore trains, after passing through Edlowe. This high meadow was once used by CM Wildflower excursions for harvesting Columbines. — Ed Heltemes Photo

Near Edlowe the ore train is still working very hard, but it will ease off a bit in a few minutes. — HB/ESP

near Divide. The Midland Termninal used to serve a big icehouse on this side of town, but it is closed now. The ice was used to help refrigerate lettuce, which was a big industry up here. The switch to the icehouse on Coulson Lake is still in place.

The Colorado Midland used to run west from Divide to Florisaant, and on to Leadville. The Midland Terminal's depot was originally a joint-use depot. The Colorado Midland had a smaller station, but when the Midland Terminal was being built, a fire destroyed the old building. The station sat between the two railroad tracks. A few of the old CM yard tracks are still used on the west end of the Midland Terminal's wye. The agent waves as we pass and turn south into the cut below the station.

The engineer points out that this is the main place where the railroad's old rotary snowplow gets used. The cut that the wye passes through regularly gets filled with winter snow. It is as deep as the height of an ore car, so it must be a job. The other spots where the plow is put to work are at Murphy and at Blizzard Point.

As we approach Murphy the head brakeman climbs up over the tender. We learn that he will work his way back to the last car in our string. The climb along here us quite gradual; in fact, we are heading almost downhill it seems. While the brakeman climbs over the cars we roll qucikly through the low hills. In a few minutes we pass over the highway to Cripple Creek, and the switch at Murphy is not far away. Our end of the train is now climbing sharply, and we round a curve and enter a cut. In a short distance we will start downhill. The train is barely moving, but once the brakeman "pulls the pin" on our section of cars, when we are about halfway over the crest. We now pick up speed and run ahead into Midland, leaving the second section still climbing, but with a lighter load. Our engineer blows for the grade crossing, as we cross the road to Cripple Creek again. The headlight bounces, barely illuminating the gravel pit. We can look back and see the headlight of the second engine coming out of the cut.

"I sure am glad that highway work is done," the engineer breaks the silence. "That old road was a real mess, the new one is much better. It was completely redesigned, and has been done for about a year."

We coast quickly right up to the Midland water tank. The fireman now climbs back up onto the tender to take on water. The man works quickly, and by the time he closes the manhole cover and jumps down, the next engine is a couple hundred feet behind the train. The engineer whistles off and pulls our section clear of the old wooden tank, and the second engine pulls under the tank. The engineer has oiled around while the fireman was taking on water. The engineer might also shake the grates and dump the ashpan while taking on water, too. If he did not, the fireman would do it while they wait for the other engines to take on water. It was preferred that the drop be made near the water tank, so any spilled water could quench the smoldering ashes.

"You ready for the big hill now?" the engineer asks the fireman. "I shook the pans, and dropped them, so let's get ready to go."

The fireman throws on three more scoops of coal, and we pull on down the tracks and wait for the rest of the train. The third engine is taking on water now.

The fireman points out the old passenger cars alongside the tracks. The section gang here lives in those cars. The crew is assigned to work from Murphy to Gillett. The cars were originally built for the Florence and Cripple Creek. In the early teens a big flood washed out the connection between

66 on the head end of the last ore train from Bull Hill as it leaves Midland, southbound in February, 1949. — Ed Heltemes Photo

The last ore train dropped into Midland after passing Murphy without dividing the train. — Ed Heltemes Collection

Engines 64, 61, 62 and 57 pound up the big hill out of Midland. Above them is the old narrow gauge grade, never used; below is the old Ice House grade in this 1947 scene. — HO/AC

Florence and Victor, and these cars were used in the district on standard-gauge trucks for a few years, and they were finally brought here and put on the ground. A few other old narrow-gauge cars can be found along the Midland Terminal, all the way from Colorado City to Cripple Creek.

The second section has whistled up and is ready to recouple. The third engine has finished, turned his headlight back on and is moving up to recouple with the rest of the train. Our engine is on the curve below the climb toward Waters' Tunnel. The last engine pulls up, and the train is complete again. All three engineers pull their whistle cords, in order, and the train starts to move.

The train is working hard; that is, the firemen are the ones who are really working! The long, climbing curve is quite spectacular. It is about the steepest section between here and Gillett. Up to when we enter the deep cut at the top of the big "C" curve, we can look back and see the lights of the last engine and caboose.

The grade lets up as we reach the other end of the cut, but we are still climbing. The headlight bounces through the trees, casting a strange pattern. The engineer has leaned back, and the fireman is working at a slow but steady pace. The head brakeman, who returned to the cab after we watered at Midland, is completely asleep. The fireman does not even look up as he works. A few minutes later the engineer taps him on the arm. The last tunnel is in sight. The engineer, who has barely moved for the last few minutes, now starts to adjust the power, and the fireman banks his fire. Somehow, since our experience in Ute Pass, it seems perfectly natural for the men to take off a glove and have it up to their mouths.

The curve through the tunnel is left-handed. In a few minutes we enter a right-hand, uphill curve, and the fireman again gets his fires ready. He shakes the grates and drops the pans about midway through the curve. A left-hand corner at the top marks the end of the climb. As soon as we round the corner we start rolling downhill toward Gillett. The fireman has rebanked his fires, but we are pulling the load. Up to here we have been pushed more than pulled. We have now taken the load off the second engine and will soon be pulling the train over the hump. The firemen on each of the following engines will take their turns shaking their grates and dropping pans, in about the same spot we did. A little stream there will cool the ashes.

We are starting to pick up speed after we are about fifteen cars onto Gillett Flat. In a few minutes we are really rolling—as fast or faster than we will ever get anywhere else on this trip, except on the way home. The rails and wheels really clatter as we whistle for Gillett. We actually hit forty to fifty miles an hour, and none of the engines is really working. The engineer has the throttle about halfway out, and is pulling back on it. The brakeman, now wide awake, has kept an eye on our speed, aware that we will be unable to stop before we reach the next upgrade.

The grade drops off as we roar through the remains of the town of Gillett and down into a wide valley. Finally the train starts to climb uphill again, and rather quickly. The fireman immediately feels the change. He knows that Blizzard Point is up ahead, and he banks his fire. The banking is not for any tunnel but because the grade levels off a bit there.

The engineer points into the darkness on our left. "That is the old Short Line grade below us, now the Corley Mountain Highway. I remember the old trestle on the curve down there. real washout-prone. We will run along the old grade up toward Hoosier Pass. I started out firing on the Short Line; there was work."

We make the corner past Blizzard Point. As we swing westward, the engineer points out the lights of Bull Hill. We have a long way to go to get there, because we have to skirt a deep valley between us and them. The engineer pulls out his watch. "We are early."

The train rolls quickly through Grassy, or as most call it, Cameron. The station on the Short Line here was called both, avoiding a decision. The track swings around from eastward to almost westward. The whole train can be seen again, lighted by the engine lights and the moon.

As we approach Bull Hill, the head brakeman gets ready to climb over the tender again. As we strain to reach the saddle north of the station, we have slowed to a walk. The brakeman pulls the pin between us and the rest of the train. The second engine is now lined to push the cars into the yards. As the second engine nears the switch for the storage track, his brakeman pulls the pin between him and the cars behind. The last engine will push those cars onto a second storage track.

The loads are ready on the tracks nearby, so we turn on the wye and back up to take on water while the other engines are doing their switching. The

The ore empties are about to peak
the hill near Gillett. In the old days
the lead locomotives would have just
dumped its ashes into the creek, but
the newer locomotives did not
require that. — HB/ESP

Gillett looking south from the water
tank in 1948. — Herb O'Hanlon
Photo/Author's Collection

On the south end of the wye at Bull
Hill, the empty cars are being traded
for loads to go back to the mill. —
Herb O'Hanlon Photo/Author's
Collection

next engine has pulled clear of the empties and is ready for water when we finish. We pull ahead and back onto the track with the first section of loads, while he takes on water. The last engine has finished switching and will be taking on water soon, the caboose still coupled on behind. The second engine backs and hooks onto the other string of loads while the third engine waters. We pull our loads up to the saddle. It is quite clear from the sound of our engine that we have hooked onto some heavy tonnage.

The second engine pulls up and hooks on, and we pull clear of the wye. Everybody is working. The third engine was finished and has backed way down on the tail of the wye. We then start to back onto the wye toward their engine. When the train is coupled and ready to head back to Colorado Springs, the brakeman sets his brakes, the fireman stokes and banks the fires, and everybody sits back for midnight lunch. A few tall yarns, not to mention a lot of ribbing about the running of the train so far and the like, will fill the air for a while.

The conductor is handed a train sheet, and once the crew has returned to their engines, or walked to the old depot, each will rest. The crews will be at Bull Hill for at least an hour. Looking around the area, it is littered with the remains of a large railroad and mining complex. Two large samplers stood within a hundred yards of the depot. The old depot itself was not originally here, but it was moved from Anaconda to Bull Hill in 1912. The old town, where the first railroad accident in the district happened, had just about died when the station was uprooted. The F & CC dumped its D & RG cars on the first passenger train out from Cripple Creek on the trestle west of Anaconda.

The crews are now gathered around the old stove in the depot. One or two of the men have their feet up on chairs, "resting their eyes," while others read. An old black coffee pot produces cup after cup of aromatic brew. One or two men are brave enough to refill their thermos bottles, while one refills his only with hot water and dips in a single tea bag.

With Hoosier Pass in the background the train rounds the corner at Cameron with everyone working. This was a town at one time, but nothing remains, even in 1949. One of the engineers on this train was born not far from this spot. — HB/ESP

65 and 66 are working a load of cars getting ready to return to Colorado City. The engines will not return coupled together, but a cut of cars will separate them. — HB/ESP

Engine 65 is half way between Cameron and Bull Hill with the ore train. — HB/ESP

Two of the moguls work the loaded cars, in the snowy yards at Bull Hill in 1948. — HB/ESP

Back to work, the engineer climbs
back up on 58 at Bull Hill. — Herb
O'Hanlon Photo/Author's Collection

8. On the Way Back

Water up, climb on, and let's get back to Colorado Springs with a load of ore. Ex-Army, 0-6-0, then MT 2-6-0 64 is watered at Bull Hill in 1948. — HO/AC

THE SKY AT MIDNIGHT ON BULL HILL is clear, and the air is actually cool. The only sounds to be heard are the muffled moans of the locomotives. The crews break up their conversations and gather their gear for the return trip. The men have caught up on the latest events in the district, and have passed on the most recent news from Colorado Springs.

The grabirons on the cab on the engine are cold to the touch as we climb up into the warm cab. The fireman gives the grates a shake before he turns on the blower and throws in his half-dozen scoops of coal. The clinker hook is already hanging back in its regular perch, the front number plate. The heaping pile of coal in the tender is more than half gone, which might cause some concern if it were not for the fact that we have a downhill trip ahead of us.

The last engine whistles up, followed by the second and then our engine. The lead engine pulls away first, stretching out the train, jerking lightly on the second engine. The jolt at the caboose is

enough to knock you down if you are not ready. The train rolls easily down the hill through Cameron toward Blizzard Point.

We are moving quite rapidly, and the weight of the loads behind us is evident. The speed is enough that the engineer and brakeman continually watch the air pressure and the handbrake settings for the first several miles. In the early days, there were several spectacular runaway trains that took a few lives and did a lot of damage, all caused by not keeping an eye on these two things. Gillett Flats is dead ahead. Occasionally a train will stop and take on water at the old Gillett water tank, but only in the summer. In the winter the small tank freezes almost solid. The train hardly slows as we pass through town, but we begin to slow down for the curve ahead.

None of the firemen are working very hard now, just enough to keep the pressure up. The work for them is ahead of us at Midland. The train sways gently as we take the curves heading to Waters' Tunnel. The head brakeman is asleep again, and

MT #65, 64, and 66, being made ready for their return to the roundhouse. — HO/AC

Bringing up the rear is engine 64 and caboose 2, as they pull away from Bull Hill storage tracks. — HB/ESP

The water tank at Midland has seen its last passenger train, as the last excursion looks back. — HB/ESP

somehow he manages to keep from rolling onto the gangway as we roll from side to side. The moonlight shines on the quarry, with highlights added by the locomotive headlight. The outline of the tunnel is easily detected as we round the curve and is almost eerie among the trees. The headlight bounces from timber to timber through the tunnel, and once out, it lights the trees on the far hill. We can look back and see the headlight of the second engine pop out of the portal. We round another curve before the third engine becomes visible.

The rear brakeman has started to crank in a little more brake as we start to drop into Midland. The two long fills alert us to the nearness of the next stop. The lights of Midland are much less evident at this hour.

Rattling down the hill and around the curve, the train almost seems as if it was running away, but the calmness of the crew gives us confidence. Our engine will pull under the water tank first, but before we reach the bottom of the hill, the fireman is shaking his grates. He is ready to drop the pan while we take on water. The train rolls up the hill toward the tank and the level spot. We take on our water, and while we do, the engineer drops the ash pans. We whistle up, and the train moves up for the second engine to take on water.

The quarry up ahead has often shipped out gravel to the Rock Island Railroad for ballast. The siding is empty tonight, but the tracks are often filled to capacity with Rock Island gondola cars. Midland Terminal cars are not used for the shipments because of the cars' bad condition. The Midland Terminal cars are not interchanged, and many of the gondola cars were almost ready for scrapping when they were bought from the Denver and Rio Grande. The Rock Island cars are not really that much better; often a car has to be repaired before it can be brought up Ute Pass.

The second engine has taken on water and whistles up. The fireman starts to fire up, just the normal five scoops into the firebox, and we start to pull out, slowly. Expecting to stop, we continue to roll.

"We have to break the train to get all this tonnage on over the hill to Murphy. The train was broken behind the second engine at Midland while he took on water. While we are running these cars up to Murphy, the third engine is taking on water. The divide here is steep, from both sides."

The reason is plain once we start up past the quarry. The two locomotives pound the rails unmercifully, really barking. "Chow, Chow, Chow," they sound as we slowly work our way across the highway. Once we enter the cut and start toward the siding, we are going downhill. As we reach the siding, we have the advantage over the rear engine, and it is cut off. The second engine will back up and pick up the cars at Midland.

While we sit and wait, the engineer explains how we would have done this little maneuver if we had brought only two engines.

"We would have put these cars in the siding, set three or four of the handbrakes, uncoupled, and run into the clear, then backed down to Midland. The other engine would have run around to behind the caboose and waited for us. To be safe we would have taken on water again, then grabbed this end of that string and brought it up over the hill. We would have cut off and run back to the head end and recoupled. We would have pulled the first string into the clear and waited for the second section. At Divide that second engine usually pulls the pin, and drifts on into Colorado City."

"You mean one engine takes the train on into Colorado City?" we ask.

"Usually, because there are no more hills to go up."

We hear the sound of the second section popping over the crest of the hill behind us.

"Watch this," the brakeman instructs.

When the engine is just over the top, he pulls his pin and lets the other engine push, and the weight of the cars on this side of the hill helps pull the other cars over. The engine that is now separated from any cars runs past us, heading for home. The engine that is now coming over the hill stops, and we pull our cars out onto the main line again. We have the train all hooked up again, except that we now only have two locomotives, one at each end of this long line of loaded ore cars.

The two engines whistle off, and we roll easily and slowly to Divide. On some occasions the rear engine will be cut off, too. Tonight our load is large enough that we need the extra air on that end. We carefully make the turn at Divide before we pick up speed to make the climb over the low hill east of town. The valley is dark. The shape of the dome rock ahead is barely lit by the headlight.

The head brakeman tells us about the body from caboose #3. It is on the ground at the quarry, and the diggings here go back to the

Steaming in upper Ute Pass near Paradise Ranch in 1948. — HO/AC

The track gang must be in the depot at Woodland, their tools are ready to go. — HO/AC

Old MT caboose 3 was retired at the gravel pit near Divide, it had been CM 409. — L. Williams Photo

Colorado Midland days. A few years ago the railroad decided that it really did not need the car. The rock from this area was being shipped to the Rock Island. The caboose body was set off here for the use of the foreman. At one time it had been a real deluxe caboose, and the trainmaster used it as his special car, but now it is in terrible shape. It still has the old style curved cupola with which the Colorado Midland and the Midland Terminal cabooses originally came equipped. All of the old MT cars cabooses are ex-CM way cars. The original MT cars were either sold or scrapped. The cupolas on #1 and #2 have been rebuilt a couple of times.

We start to climb a bit as we near Edlowe, but quickly we start to go downhill again. The outcropping of rocks that marks the official start of Ute Pass is just ahead. The headlight gives it a strange color. In a few minutes we are around the corner, and the sixteen-degree curve is upon us. We have slowed quite a bit. The engineer tells of the time that he came around this curve a bit fast and dumped his caboose and several cars at the end of the train, cracking the train like a whip.

The engineer pulls back on the throttle, and we enter the cut above Woodland Park. He pulls the train up well past the diminutive brown depot and we stop. The brakemen have already jumped down from the cabs and will walk the train, checking the wheels and the brakes as they walk. We are to wait here for at least fifteen minutes for things to cool. The fireman checks his fire, and the engineer pours himself a cup of coffee and picks up the last of the sandwiches in his lunchbox.

A car pulls up to the engine; we can see from here that it is a police car. The old Chevy is a sheriff's car. A tall, big man climbs out of the car and strolls over to below the cab.

"How is the run so far?" he yells up, and a conversation starts that is obviously the continuation of an earlier one. In the light of only the cab lights and distant street lights, the conversation lasts for nearly ten minutes, when the man returns to his patrol car. The taillights indicate that he is bound for somewhere toward the north.

"He's a frustrated railroader," the engineer offers. "He meets us here whenever he has this shift, and asks about this and that. I swear he knows more about this job than any of us."

"He gave a couple of section guys a bad time last summer," the fireman adds. "Once in a while the section men will go over and buy some beer at the store over there. The man was in there, and had started out the door when the deputy spotted him. He quoted Rule G to the poor guy before the section man knew what was happening. He had the guy half stuttering before he slapped him on the back and told him who he was. Most of us know him by name at least, but he still gave him what for, about Rule G. Not many on the section really watch it anyway."

"Oh, it is not like they are a bunch of drunks," the engineer barks. "Hey let's get this drag going; where is that brakeman?"

The fireman leans out his side of the cab. "Here he comes."

"Highball," the brakeman calls as he climbs into the cab. No sooner are the words out when we hear a blast from a distant whistle, followed by a return from our whistle. "That's it," and the last engine whistles off, and our next leg of the trip starts.

The engineer whistles off and we start to roll again. There is not a car moving on the highway as we parallel it down through the guest ranch. The train softly chuffs as we drift down along the road toward Crystola. A fog comes upon us as we reach milepost 17.

"This area is the worst on the road for fog. One time some guys on a handcar were leaving Woodland. The men were part of a gang working extra on a section below here and had gone into Woodland for something. In the fog they lost track of their speed and where they were. When they saw the other section car on the track, they could not stop, so they took to the weeds. The car hit the standing car, and the water in the water barrel on the first car shot up like Old Faithful. It wrecked both cars; old McKay was furious. You would have thought those old wrecks were gold plated."

We round the curve below Crystola, break out of the fog, and head for Green Mountain Falls., A few lights can be seen ahead from cars coming up the road. The brakeman points out a diner to our right as we round the corner into town.

"Can you make out that place?" he asks, as we try to look in the darkness. "Looks like a streetcar; well, it sure was. It was hauled up here and turned into a diner some time ago. The food is really good, but the coffee is deluxe."

We quietly breeze right through town. Our speed has increased again, but the engineer pulls back because we have another stop coming up. By regulation we must stop at Cascade to cool the

A track crew is working in the cut near Murphy as the inspection car waits in the late 1940's. The men in the car were from the Golden Cycle Mill. — WS Collection

brakes. The brakemen will walk around the train again, checking the wheels and the brakes. If we need water we can take it on, before we take the final step down into Manitou. The Midland relies on the friction of the wheel flanges on the curving track to slow the trains, as much as on brake shoes. The grade in the pass has taken a toll on the railroad, causing many a dumped load due to speed.

"Better water up," the fireman warns the engineer. "If we do not we might run out during that switching at Lime Rock."

The engineer pulls up under the water tank and stops. There is plenty of time, so the fireman leisurely tops off the tender. The engineer whistles up, and we pull out far enough for the rear engine to water. The train is blocking the road at Cascade. At this hour nobody cares anyway, but it is not advisable on Sunday afternoon.

The required time has passed, but the brakeman has not made it back to the cab yet. In a few minutes he can be seen running toward the engine.

"There is a bad truck on one of the old cars; we have to set it out. It is liable to come apart before we get to Crags."

"Where is the bad order car?" the engineer asks, with a touch of disgust.

"It is ten cars from the caboose. The conductor says to break the train, and the rear engine will spot it on the siding for now."

"Well, do it, don't just stand there. We haven't got all night!"

The brakeman turns and trots off. We can see the rear engine make the movement and put the car on the siding with a thud.

"Must have come apart. I think it went off on the north side, away from us; anyone see?"

"Nobody seems to be excited back there, so it cannot be too bad."

In a few minutes the train is reconnected, and the rear engine whistles off.

"It failed alright. One end of the car is down on the wheels; not much we can do now but let them know in the shop. The siding is blocked until they can get somebody up here with a new truck."

The riddle is solved, and the engineer is concerned with the trip down the steepest part of Ute Pass. The fireman shakes his grates again and dumps the ash pan right on his spot. The train is rolling very slowly but is gathering speed as we roll onto the top end of the 4 percent grade. The brakeman is carefully watching the train. There is no air problem as we drift over the bridge near Crags.

The engineer is watching ahead, concentrating intently; a serious mood has filled the cab.

"You never know this pass. This summer we have had more rocks on the track than we have seen in years," the fireman whispers in our ear. "He has been on at least one engine that went over the side because of a rock on the tracks, and so have I. It is no damn fun!"

Tunnel eight marks some relief, but tension is still evident. We pull up the long fill below the third tunnel and stop the train just above the lime spur. The second engine is just outside tunnel four. The brakeman has set the brakes on three cars behind us, and we uncouple. The lights of Manitou glimmer below us as we move quietly downhill past the Lime Rock switch. The switching takes a bit more than ten minutes, including the time it

Engine 65 and 66 at the water tank at Cascade. A load of coal is being set out in an old wooden gondola car, which was originally a box car. — HB/ESP

54 drifts downhill in upper Ute Pass with a long string of ore cars. The old locomotive developed a series of problems including crown sheet weakness, and it was decided to retire it rather than rebuild it. — Denver Public Library/Otto Perry

took to release the brakes on the cars that we left on the main line.

A track gang has to come up here every so often and keep the rails stretched out. The heavy braking coming down and the pounding going up move the rail downhill. This finally breaks rail joints, tie plates, and occasionally a rail. You can really tell when the rails are moved because there will be huge gaps between them. The wheels really "clunk" in the gaps, and on the lower end there will be no gaps at all.

The hard work is over as we roll easily through Manitou toward home. We stop at the Twenty-sixth Street switch. The train will be broken about midway. We pull the first section into yard 1, and the other crew will push the other cars onto yard 2. The full tracks will be unloaded by the switcher tomorrow. It will take four or five loads up the hill at a time and will bring back that many empties until the job is done.

The final movement for the other engine will be to put the caboose back on the storage track. We pull our engine up to the end of the turntable. The engine that we saw last at Murphy is just now being backed into the roundhouse. The crew has already gone home and is probably in bed sound asleep.

The other engine pulls up with the caboose crew on the footboards as we walk over to the roundhouse. The conductor and the engine crew trade a few comments over the problems of the night. The derailment and bad order car at Cascade are the prime objects of discussion around the crew caller's desk.

Yellow #101 and #102 are ready for their morning run, as is the Pierce Arrow, for McKay will be going up to Divide this morning. The ore train crew tries not to look at the "little gift from heaven," as one of the men calls the converted streetcars. The men, dirty and tired from the night's run, quietly find their way out of the roundhouse toward their respective homes. Most of the men are now gone, but the fireman has a few more bits of information for us.

"You see the new locomotives?" he asks, pointing toward the shop end of the roundhouse. "That one is about half finished, the both of them will be used to replace the engines we used tonight." He leads us over toward the locomotive over the pit. "I started here as a helper. This engine is being converted from oil to coal, and they are putting a new trailing truck under it."

The conversation continues as the eastern sky starts to turn blue. The fireman finally leaves us to look around the quiet building. The night ore run is finished and the roundhouse is left to the ghosts of the Colorado Midland and the night hostler.

Our trip was short, not at all like what might have been in the late 1890s or the early 1900s. It was a trip like many from 1935 until 1949. Next, let's have a look at how that ore moved from the mines to Bull Hill.

The old Ramona Hotel was long gone by the time 55 was captured near Elephant Rock at Cascade in the late 1940's. Soon the engine would be retired and slowly cannabalized to keep her sisters running. — HO/AC

An eastbound ore train winds down lower Ute Pass between Tunnel 7 and 8 in the 1930's. — AC
Standley Photo

An ore train also included two tank cars and a load of timber as it passed Hanging Rock Cut bound for Colorado Springs. — AC

Sam Bayless, and an unidentified man pose near newly shopped engine 62 freshly polished, probably for the last time in its life. — UPHS

Locomotive 59, still painted for her last passenger trips in 1949 pulls a variety of cars over Englemann Trestle, including a lime car, and three ex-CM ex-Hanrahan cars, as well as the homebuilt depressed center flat car. — DPL/Otto Perry Collection

Engine 60 in the Colorado City yards with the last freight in.
— PPL

Caboose 2 at the powerhouse at Colorado City after the last
freight run to Bull Hill. On board was a local radio announcer
and his recording equipment. — PPL

The Rocky Mountain Railroad Club has just
pulled away from the Cripple Creek depot. In
a short time the final cars will be taken home,
along with the district switcher, waiting in the
engine house. — HB/ESP

9. District Switching

Engine 56 was occasionally used as the Cripple Creek switcher, seen here outside the enginehouse at Cripple Creek in 1940. — DPL

THE MORNING AIR IS COOL, BUT THE temperature in the low forties is not surprising at this altitude. A light can be seen in the old engine house north of the Cripple Creek depot.

The crewmen were called at 4:30 A.M., and they are on their way. The engine is parked right where the crew left it last night. It is directly in front of the brick depot, headed toward the south. The slow "chuff" of the engine can barely be heard as we walk up the hill toward the still dark depot.

The Cripple Creek hostler has quite a job. He has fired up the engine and given it a complete check, and after he finished that, he called the four crewmen for today's run. His job will continue tonight when we return. He will turn the engine on the wye and refuel and water it. It will be backed into the old engine house, ready for the next run. The engine for today's run is old #53, one of the Colorado Midland engines that the Midland Terminal kept in 1920. Next week it will be going back to Colorado City to be retired. Number 54 was up here for #53 last time it went to Colorado Springs for work, but it is hard to tell just which locomotive might come up to replace it. Number 52, the other old CM engine, is the Colorado Springs switcher. The locomotives up here generally rotate with engines at Colorado City. The engines used on the ore trains are usually the same engines, but with the addition of the three new locomotives, that will probably change soon. Four or five locomotives are available for the assignment.

The conductor is the first to arrive. The switching list is ready on the hostler's desk. The fireman and brakeman arrive at the same time, followed by the engineer. Each man has a job to do before we can leave. The men go about their tasks with very few words, as if they are still asleep. In a few minutes each man has arrived at the engine, ready to go.

A few quick introductions, and a few grumbles about the lack of space in the cab of the engine, and we are ready to leave. The crewmen stash their thermoses of coffee in the various hiding places, and we are warned where to, and where not to stand as the fireman builds up the steam. The fireman has his own way of firing the engine, but it is similar to the lesson that we have already been given. A few quick and very muffled toots on the whistle, and we are moving.

The district is broken up into routes, and each one is serviced at about the same time each day. The mines can adjust the loading of the cars by a set schedule. The run up to Midway, for example, is a one-day-a-week run. The run up to the coal bin at the Cresson is usually a one-day-a-week run, also.

149

In April 1947 #52 steams out across the turntable. — Herb O'Hanlon Photo/AC

A cut of ore cars is being taken to Bull Hill yards on the main line above Victor in about 1942 as seen from the depot. — Morris Abbott Photo

(Right) Locomotive 58 switching empties at Bull Hill. — HO/AC

The crewmen are still very quiet as the train pulls out over the bridge south of the depot and climbs well above the road. The engineer points out that the Short Line and Florence and Cripple Creek yards were in the lower part of Cripple Creek. The present road is built on the old F & CC grade. The conductor mentions some of the mines along the way like the Abe Lincoln, the Index, and the Gold Bond.

The El Paso is ahead of us, on a spur. The old town of Anaconda is below us in the next gulch. The conductor points out the old location of the Midland Terminal's depot as we pass. On the hillside above us is the Mary McKinney. The brakeman steps down onto the front beam. The conductor checks his switch list, and the engineer slows the engine. Two cars are waiting on the siding and both will be taken to Bull Hill. The switchman jumps down and runs ahead to throw the switch.

The crew have an elaborate set of hand signals. It is obvious that they have worked with each other long enough to know each other's jobs, but still the signals are required. We pause for a moment as the conductor steps down from the cab. The engine rolls forward and is directed up to the waiting cars by the man on the ground. The switchman brings us right up to the cars as we couple. (In the days of link and pin couplers, a lot of switchmen lost fingers, hands, and even their lives.) He releases the brakes on the cars, and we slowly back out to the main line again. The

conductor is hanging onto the end of the first car, while the switchman runs to reset the switch onto the main line. Once we have crossed the switch, he signals us to stop, then move forward. The El Paso is next on the switching order.

The engineer pauses, and we proceed down the main line at a respectable pace. The locomotive will be loaded to near its maximum tonnage after we pick up the El Paso cars, and we will have to get them to Bull Hill.

The switchman grabs the side of the first car and climbs up with the conductor, jumping down again as we approach the spur to the El Paso. The fireman is working at a fairly respectable pace, keeping the steam up but below what we have seen used on the ore trains. The fire is smooth and even, and the exhaust is white and clear. The fireman and the engineer express some concern about the old boiler and that engine that might be sent up to replace it. The engine's tonnage rating is well under what it was originally able to handle, even with modern equipment.

The switchman has thrown the switch for the El Paso. The track is uphill but not steep. The conductor calls for a stop, and the brakeman jumps down to remove the derailer. The derail is kept there to prevent the cars that are spotted at the El Paso for loading from rolling down onto the main line. A few weeks ago the conductor and the brakeman were so busy discussing the day's switching that they forgot and put a car on the ground. It took about half a hour to get the mess

fixed up. The crew carries a rerailer at all times, just for such an incident. We start to roll ahead again, stopping short of the loaded cars. The engineer carefully pulls up to the cars, and we couple and back down to the hill toward the main line. Two cars are still on the El Paso's siding, and one is almost half loaded. It will be ready by the time we get ready with empty cars, but otherwise it might wait here for a couple of days. It was a week ago that the cars we have picked up were left at the mine. The derail is replaced, and we move out onto the main line.

The next stop is Bull Hill. The little locomotive works carefully past Elkton and Victor Junction. The track is in fairly good condition, but combined with the old ore cars, accidents can happen suddenly. The engineer is extremely cautious of the track condition. A weakened tie or cracked or spread rail can put them on the ground for more than a day. Last summer several sections of old track were completely rebuilt after being torn up in wrecks.

The brakeman has a running commentary about some of the mines we have seen. The Cresson, one of the biggest producers in the district, uses trucks to haul its ore to a loading bin. A couple of years ago it had a major subsidence. One of the methods of mining that is used a great deal in the district is called "stope mining." A large room is literally carved inside the mountain, with timber bracing used to hold things in place. The old stopes have started to collapse recently, and that is what happened at the Cresson. An old stope, some say a hundred feet or more tall, collapsed. The hole opened up slowly, but before it was finished, it had gobbled up a pair of buildings. A bulldozer was used to push rock into the hole—rock that was hauled from several waste piles. The Cresson used to get coal for its steam boiler by way of a tramway up to a short spur track, but now the lower end of the tram is buried in the remains of the Cresson subsidence.

The engineer reminds us of a more recent subsidence at the Queen. It did not involve a train, but it could have. One of the local Romeos had the habit of making the area near the Queen his parking spot. He had been there for nearly an hour when he heard a rumble, and before he could move the car, he was surrounded by a dust cloud. The two in the car were in certain fear for what might have happened. It certainly interrupted what they had in mind for the evening, because

when it cleared they found a very, very deep and dark hole less than three feet from the front of his car. A long section of the grade was gone, too! The rails and many attached ties hung in the air. He slowly backed away from the pit after regaining his composure and went home, calling the hostler at Cripple Creek to warn him of the problem. One of several old stopes in the area had collapsed, but that one could have taken at least two lives.

Pikes Peak is red as we get our first view of it. The loaded cars at Bull Hill will be spotted on the tracks near where the empty cars are located. The empty cars are right where we had seen empty cars placed the night we rode up on the ore train. It looks like there are a few more cars on the siding than we brought up. It has taken nearly two hours to work our way around the hill, and the engineer tells us that the average trip from Bull Hill to Cripple Creek is forty-five minutes, without stops. The engine is turned on the wye and spotted under the water tank. The conductor has jumped down from the engine and walked into the depot for a list of the empty cars. The fireman is cleaning up his firebox while the engineer checks around the locomotive.

The sky has turned bright blue, and there is not a single cloud visible, even to the far west. The conductor returns with a handful of papers. The engineer backs the locomotive toward the long lines of waiting cars, while the conductor and switchman walk along the row of cars until they reach a certain one. The switchman motions to the engineer to pull ahead, and he lifts the coupler arm, breaking connection. The conductor and the man grab onto the car, a tank car, and we move westward. The load is a tank car, two loads of coal, and three empties. The train stops after we clear the wye, and the conductor jumps down and walks forward to the engine. We will be moving the cars down into Victor. The "gas can," as it is called, and the coal will be switched onto the tracks near the coal bins. The empty ore cars will be moved to the El Paso later in the day. The mines order cars in advance, for there is a long waiting list for available cars. The company likes to keep it that way. It is their opinion that having a lot of extra cars sitting idle is a waste of money; they would rather be short of cars.

The gasoline tank car is a real problem on the rough track, for it has a tendency to sway as the liquid inside sloshes on the curves and undulations. The conductor compares it to an old car with

Switching into Victor, 58 has ore cars, a box, and a tank car. — HO/AC

Waiting at Victor on August 21, 1941, #56 was switching in the district. Motor Car 101 was parked at the depot also. — Gordon C. Bassett Collection

Motor Car 101 at the Victor depot, attracts a little attention. — L.W. Moody Photo/John McCall Collection

old shock absorbers on a rough road, and there are more than a few of those up here, too!

The train carefully works past the remains of old uninhabited claims and tumbledown shacks. The dying town of Independence is nearly deserted. A few older people can be seen working in their yards. The entire district is littered with ruins, many of which are now the homes of stray animals. Dogs roam the hills in packs. Many of the canines were dumped here, unwanted by people from as far away as Colorado Springs who hoped that the dogs might perish in the darkness of an old mine.

A half hour later we arrive at Victor Junction. The switchman jumps down to throw the switch as we pass over it, and the engineer carefully backs the train around the curve. The cars rock on the extremely rough track. The switchman throws another switch, and we find ourselves backing down an even rougher track. The coal and gasoline are soon safely uncoupled, and we are on our way up the hill. Once we clear the street, the engineer stops the train, and we back toward the depot. The locomotive is stopped across the street from the depot at a water column. The engineer, fireman, and the rest of the crew leave the train and head down the street for breakfast. The old Victor depot is locked and empty, but the conductor still has a key if we would need to get inside.

The stop for breakfast can take from half an hour to nearly an hour. The conversation centers around the day's pickups and deliveries but is spiced with comments on the Colorado City and Bull Hill operations, as well as with a few colorful stories. The coffee is consumed by the quart while the men devour their breakfasts. One or two of the men have brought along their empty thermos bottles for refilling. The conductor prods the crew into motion as the meals are finished, and the conversation starts to slip into a series of tall tales.

The sun is now high, the sky is still virtually cloudless, and the temperature has started to warm the streets. The side of the engine is now warm. The fireman soon has his fire back up to normal and is rebuilding air pressure. The grate will need to be shaken before we move, and the conductor is anxious about getting underway. The locomotive finally starts to roll away with the empty cars, leaving Victor. Once we have cleared Victor and are nearing the switch at Victor Junction, the empties are cut off and left at the switch. We will come back and deliver these cars on the way back to Cripple Creek tonight.

The crew takes a few minutes during the switching to get reorganized. The conductor and the brakeman are riding on the tender as we back toward Bull Hill. The conductor checks his watch to be sure that we back to the wye on time. The "puddle jumper," as it is called up here, is due to arrive at about the time that we make it into Bull Hill.

The engineer heads into a line of cars, while the conductor and brakeman count off the required number of cars. The sound of the little bus is different from what we have heard this morning. It is much like the sound of an ordinary truck, but noisier. The contraption has a strange bounce as it moves along the track.

The car has five people on board this morning—an older man, and four women. The people remain seated as the vehicle parks in front of the depot. The driver climbs down from his perch, walks around to the rear door, and pulls out several boxes and stacks them on the platform. The agent has stepped out with a large R.R.B. (railroad business) envelope. The two men chat for a few minutes, joined by our conductor. The conductor and the driver the of "bus" trade barbs and head back to their respective vehicles after a quick slap on the back. The conductor turns, remembering that he has one more remark.

"Hey Truman, we left the El Paso empties on the Victor spur, at Victor Junction. You going into Victor?"

The driver turns, half in jest, half in seriousness: "No, but I wish you guys would find another place to stash your junk."

The engineer has pointed out the old cars that are on the ground near the tracks. "Those are old F & CC, Short Line, and Midland boxcars. The coaches are old Colorado Midland cars. The sectionmen use most of them for one thing or another."

"Water up, Midway is next," the fireman warns.

The run up to Midway is a weekly trip, that is, one trip per week. The crew does not like the trip, but it will be over before lunchtime. The locomotive pulls the assigned cars backwards toward Independence. The trip to the Portland sign takes nearly fifteen minutes, and the old mill site is littered with scrap iron. The brakeman jumps down from the end car and sets the switch, and the train starts to push the cars up along the hillside high above Goldfield. The track was originally narrow gauge, part of the old Golden

154

Circle Railway. The cuts are narrow, and the grade is very steep. Two mines on the branch are still shipping ore by railroad, another is shipping ore by truck. The empty cars are traded for the loads, and we continue toward the Midway saloon. The Golden Circle had to use a loop for turning around up here. The brakeman has set in braking on all of the cars as we head down the hill back to Portland.

The trip to Midway and back will take nearly two hours. The crew will break for lunch once we drop off the loaded cars at Bull Hill. The tender is again filled with water—a never-endinhg process, for each visit to Bull Hill requires water. The load of coal will last until we return to Cripple Creek. The grates are shaken again, and the engine is checked before the crew stops for lunch.

Looking across the valley toward Victor, we can see only a few of the mines that are operating in the district. The hillsides at one time were busy with operating railroads, mines, mills, and all of the assorted towns. Thirty years ago you could stand on the same spot and see more than thirty operating claims, served by the four railroads. The smoke from the mines, mill, railroads, and homes filled the air. Today there is little smoke in the sky, mainly from a trash fire in Goldfield.

The trip this afternoon is the biggest one, up in the Battle Mountain mines. The Portlands and the Ajax are the major mines on that route. The Ajax is the Golden Cycle's main producer now, with an output of about 100 tons a day, but the output has been higher than that lately, by about double. The run today has eight cars to set out and five to pick up at the Ajax. The crew's movements are much slower than during the morning run. The run around Battle Mountain will take over two hours.

The line of loaded cars pushes the engine down the hill from the Portland Mill site toward Bull Hill. In the distance we can see the yellow "puddle jumper" pulling into the depot for the return trip to Colorado Springs. The conductor barely looks up from his switch list as we pass the Vindicator Mine.

The engine crew will take an afternoon break after leaving the loaded cars at Bull Hill. A second string of seven empty cars is consigned for the Portland mines on Battle Mountain. The weight of the cars was too much for old "53" to handle with the Ajax turn. The crew is not very ambitious about

In 1942 Morris Abbott stopped at the Bull Hill depot and Motor 101 was there. — Morris Abbot Photo

155

the trip back up the hill, but once they have rested, the trip is repeated. The Portland mines are producing nearly as much ore as the Ajax, but the value is considerably lower.

The crewmen bring four loaded cars back to Bull Hill. One more short run will take care of the mines right here near the yeards, and then the last run will take us back to Cripple Creek. The string of loaded cars is nearly four times as long as the line of empty cars. The agent sticks his head out of the door of the depot as we return to the main line after watering up again.

"Hold up! The sedan is on its way up. McKay is bringing up some people from Golden Cycle. He should be between here and Gillett by now, so he'll be here in a few minutes."

The crew scans to the north, watching the track near Cameron for the vehicle. The car is just a speck when it first appears. The sound of the automobile is about half as noisy as the old streetcar. The grimy black car, with railroad wheels, stops at the front of the depot, and the agent meets the driver.

"That's not McKay," the conductor mutters, "that's a bunch of guys from Golden Cycle. How did they manage that? Old McKay rarely ever lets anyone but Truman drive it."

The car pulls away after stopping for a few minutes. The agent scratches his head as he turns toward us. A quick motion signals us to pull ahead. The agent calls out to the engineer as we near the platform.

"You going to near Elkton in the next two hours?"

"No, we still have these to take care of around here," he replies with a motion toward the string of empties.

"Check in before you go back to Cripple Creek; those Golden Cycle guys are working near Elkton."

The switching of the cars near the Goldfield and Bull Hill mines takes almost until sunset. The sun has already hidden behind a row of clouds as we pick up the last few empties on the last switching run for the day. The trip is delayed for a few minutes as the company car rounds the curve and bounces along toward Colorado Springs.

The train from Colorado Springs has already left, and this crew has just finished spotting the last of the loads. A few more empties will be dropped off at a couple of locations on the way back to Cripple Creek, as well as two loads of coal. The trip back to

the "barn" starts at seven o'clock. It has been a long day, but for this crew that is all normal.

"I sure am glad we got some new cars," the brakeman adds. "These old wooden wrecks we still have are about worn out."

"These old engines are about worn out, too!" the engineer adds.

"Now don't you call old #53 worn out," the fireman chirps up.

"I know that at one time this old kettle was really strong, but like anything old, its time has come. The maintenance crew just can't keep these things in top shape anymore."

"I am really glad we do not get that new engine, #61."

"I hear that the firemen down in the Springs really hate that one. The engineers claim she doesn't stay on the rails. The new Alaskan engines should really be something, too, whenever they get rebuilt from burning oil to coal. I guess the first one is in the shops now. The other is still out somewhere in transit. Did you see it when you were in the shops?" the fireman rattles off.

We relate our observations about the locomotive that we saw up in the roundhouse and assume that it is the locomotive in question.

The crew now works quietly in the dark. The cars that were left at Victor Junction have been recovered and delivered. The brakeman and conductor work with lanterns checking switches and car numbers. The headlight has been visible for nearly two hours when we finally see the lights of Cripple Creek. The brakeman and conductor do not even get back onto the train after we clear the switch to the coal track. We move back onto the main line and pull up past the depot. The fireman is now busy getting the firebox ready to clean, and the hostler is waiting to climb into the cab once the train is stopped. The crewmen know that their job includes getting as much done as possible before they turn the engine back over to him. The engineer sets the air brake and climbs down, followed by the fireman, then us. On the way out of the cab, we reach up above the cab window and feel around in the darkness until we find what we are looking for. Sure enough, we find a short section of glass tube.

"What are you looking for?" the fireman asks.

"Just checking," we reply, "just curious."

"Hey, look up in the one on the engineer's side," he adds.

The light of the cab does not illuminate the box,

The inspection car, and an old dog, wait at the Bull Hill
depot in the late 1940's. — HO/AC

The last two eras of operation are depicted here, steam
engine 59 before being dolled up for the last runs, and the
converted auto that was used as an inspection car, under the
coal trestle at Colorado City. — WS/EC

This group posed with the Motor 101 at Cripple Creek, before it turned to make the trip back to Colorado Springs in 1942. — Morris Abbott Photo

but with our hands we find a smooth, but dirty, glass ball. Once we have it in the light, we can see that it is a lantern globe, still emblazoned with a C.M.Ry. We take one last look around the cab. The single light bulb in the cab and the yard lights give the inside of the cab a strange appearance like we may never see again: the dark leather seat that the engineer used; the well-worn wooden cab, which has a layer of metal covering the outside; the silvery floor, which is now covered with a fine layer of fine coal dust and cinders; and the globe, which is returned to its rightful place.

"Hey, throw me down my water bag, I forgot it."

The canvas bag, hanging on the coal door of the tender, is now dry. The fireman grabs it as we start down from the cab.

"Thanks for the ride," we call out to the crew that are now heading away from the engine.

The sky is filled with twinkling stars, and a few lights are visible off of Bennett Avenue. A single car, a grey Chevy with a star on the door, is in the parking lot at the front of the depot. The hostler has already moved the engine to the wye to clean out the firebox. Tomorrow the same four men probably will be here at 4:30 A.M. to do pretty much what they did today. In the winter, the schedule changes with the weather, but it goes on nearly every day between late April and October in exactly the same way.

Down, and out. The tracks are gone, and soon the water tank will be gone, too. One of two at Midland, only the foundations remain in 1984, however, the well is still furnishing water. — HO/AC

Conclusion

THE MIDLAND TERMINAL ENDED OPER-
ations in 1949, and by 1950 it had started to
to disappear. Today there are still quite a few signs
left of it, and many people still remember the
Midland Railroad. Each day more of it is lost. In the
district, as the operations resume in the mines and
at the Carlton Mill, the ghost of the Midland
Terminal still rumbles.

Bibliography

Bryant, Keith K., Jr. **History of the Atchison, Topeka and Santa Fe,** New York: MacMillan Publishing Company, Inc., 1974.

Cafky, Morris, **Colorado Midland** Denver: Rocky Mountain Railroad Club, 1965.

_____, **Rails Around Gold Hill** Denver: Rocky Mountain Railroad Club, 1955.

Carter, Harvey L., ed. **The Pikes Peak Region, A Sesquicentennial History,** Colorado Springs: Historical Society of the Pikes Peak Region, 1956.

Howbert, Irving, **Memories of a Lifetime in the Pikes Peak Region,** Glorietta, N.M.: The Rio Grande Press, Inc., 1970.

Jackson, William S., "Railroad Conflicts in the Eighties." **Colorado Magazine** 23 (January 1946).

Lipsey, John J. **The Lives of James John Hagerman** Denver: Golden Bell Press, 1968.

Marshal, James, **Santa Fe: "The Railroad That Built an Empire"** New York: Random House, 1945.

McConnell, Virginia, **Ute Pass Route of the Blue Sky People** Denver: Sage Books, 1966.

Midland Terminal Railway, **Annual Reports,** 1900-1949.

Midland Terminal Railway, Records, Interstate Commerce Commission, Washington, D.c., National Archives and Record Center.

Midland Terminal Railway, Records, United States Railroad Administration, Washington, D.C., National Archives and Record Center.

Midland Terminal Railway, Right-of-Way Maps, General Land Office, Washington, D.C. National Archives and Record Center.

Midland Terminal Railway–Golden Cycle Corporation, Annual Reports, 1934-1949.

Ormes, Manley, **The Book of Colorado Springs,** Colorado Springs: The Dentan Printing Company, 1933.

Overton, Richard Cleghorn, **The Burlington Route, A History of The Burlington Line,** New York: Alfred A. Knopf, 1965.

Poor's Manual of Railroads, 1900-1940.

Sanborn Map Company, Insurance Maps for Cripple Creek and Victor, updated from 1905.

Stone, George W. **Midland Terminal Guide Book,** Unfinished manuscript, Colorado College.

Wilkins, Tivis E. "Florence & Cripple Creek RR," **Colorado Rail Annual Number Thirteen.** Golden: Colorado Railroad Museum, 1976.

Newspapers

Colorado City **Iris,** 1891-1918.

Colorado Springs **Gazette, Telegraph** and **Gazette Telegraph,** 1890-1963.

Colorado Springs **Free Press,** 1950-1963.

Appendix

Stations on the Midland Terminal

Milepost	Station		
000.0	North Point, Colorado Springs wye	041.3	Gillett
000.2	C & S Junction	043.9	Sylvanite
000.4	Tejon Street	046.6	Cameron
000.8	Wandell	048.3	Bull Hill
001.5	Hulbert	049.1	Independence
003	Colorado City	049.9	Franklin
004	Red Rock Quarry Spur	050.0	Portland
004.7	Becker's Spur		
006.1	Manitou	Branch Line 050.2	Taylor
006.9	Manitou Iron Springs	050.5	Switchback
007.5	Lime Rock	051.0	La Bella Junction
009.5	Crags	051.6	Portland Mill
011.5	Cascade		
014.9	Green Mountain Falls		
017.6	Bison	051.0	Victor Junction
020	Woodland		
023.3	Edlowe		
024.7	Quarry	Branch Line 051.6	Victor
026.8	Ice House Spur	052.2	Strong Junction
026.9	Divide (originally MT Mile Post 0)		
030.4	Murphy (Tracy)	051.9	Eclipse
032	Mile Post 32 (Quarry)	052.2	Elkton
033.1	Midland	052.8	Beacon Hill
033.3	Ice House Spur	053.8	Anaconda
037.2	Waters Tunnel	055.7	Cripple Creek
037.8	Mile Post 38 (Quarry)		
	(originally Log Spur at MT Milepost 11)		

Locomotive 58 sits just outside its stall at the Colorado City roundhouse on August 28, 1941. In the foreground is a set of old cylinders which may have come from a damaged engine. The post at the top of the building on the second stall to the right of the locomotive was used as a mount for block and tackle when working on engines. — DPL

A Look at the Condition of the
Midland Terminal in 1921

The Colorado Midland had just folded, and the Midland Terminal had just absorbed the 27 miles of trackage to Divide, and in an astounding few years the trackwork would receive many changes. This list indicates the condition at that instant of change. The Midland Terminal had one concrete bridge and seven trestles that totaled 1240 feet, not including trestles at mines and mills, which were actually property of the industrys.

Rails: MTRY		Rails: CMRY	
45 lb.	.679 miles	45 lb.	.014 miles
50 lb.	.083 miles	56 lb.	16.407 miles
52 lb.	.373 miles	60 lb.	1.162 miles
55 lb.	.638 miles	75 lb.	16.790 miles
56 lb.	4.014 miles	80 lb.	7.888 miles
60 lb.	27.183 miles	85 lb.	.554 miles
65 lb.	.290 miles	Switches 101	
75 lb.	3.686 miles	(13 stub switches)	
80 lb.	.018 miles		
Switches 115			
(27 stub switches)			

(Above) Pikes Peak as seen from above Woodland Park on the Midland Terminal, was used on many advertising brochures, including those of the railroad. — JGC

The Colorado Midland's rotary is about to depart from the Cripple Creek depot after one of its many visits to the district. In 1913 the plow was instrumental in clearing the massive drifts from the district's railroads. A number of people must be removed from the track before the return trip. — Cripple Creek Museum Collection

162

Buildings on the Midland Terminal

A number of lists have been compiled on the Midland Terminal, each reflecting the period selected. I have chosen to list only the buildings on the Midland Terminal prior to the addition of the 27 miles of Colorado Midland trackage. The list is based upon early tax inventories and the Interstate Commerce Commission's valuation inventory. All of the buildings are assumed to be of frame construction, the exceptions being: (I) Iron, (B) Brick, (BC) Boxcar body; also included is the year built if it was available.

Divide: Office and Store Room 14x44, Engine House(I) 22x70 (1895), Boiler House (I) 11x26, Sand House 14x18, Car Inspector's Shed 12x15 (1893), Telegraph Office 10x12 (1893).

Midland: Water Tank 16x24, Tool House, Bunk House (1914), Section House (1914), Pump House, Station 14x28 (1895).

Gillett: Station 20x56 (1894), Freight Warehouse 28x62 (1894), Pump House 14x16, Material Shed 9x23, Track Scales, Coal Chute 42x20 (1896), Water Tank 15x24, Coal Shed 10x24.

Cameron: (Grassy), Station 16x42 (1895), Section House 12x16, Bunk House 16x20 (1895).

Bull Hill: Station 12x20 (First-1904), Station 15x40 (Second-1912), Tool House, Car Repair Shop 17x23 with two additions 9x23, 10x12, Water Column, Water Tank 16x24, Section House (4 BC).

Independence: Station 18x52 (First-1894), Station 20x60 (Second).

Portland: Station 10x14 (1897).

Victor: Station 27x70(B) (1895), Water Column, Ore Loading Ramp.

Elkton: Station 24x16 (1899).

Anaconda: Station 15x40 (1895), moved to Bull Hill in 1912.

Cripple Creek: Station 23x61(B) (1895), Freight Station 24x105, Car Repair Shop 8x15, Track Scales, Water Tank 16x24, Two Water Columns, Overhead Foot Bridge, Tool House, Pump Houses(2) 7x7, 5x5, Engine House (1913) (With 1 indoor pit), Outdoor Engine Pit (1906), Oil House and Office(BC) (1913), Sand House (1895), Four Pocket Coaling Station, Track Scales.

Colorado City coal trestle on February 1, 1949. — DPL/Joe Schick Collection

Photographer Stan Payne climbed upon a Midland Terminal
box car in January 1949 to capture this view of the freight
cars in the Colorado City yards. On the left is an ex-Colorado
Midland Hanrahan refrigerator car. On the right are the
newer ore cars. In the distance are the office building and
machine shops.— Penrose Public Library

All was quiet in the yards as everyone waited for the last
train from Bull Hill to arrive. — PPL

A few months after the Midland Terminal had been scrapped a photographer recorded the derelict roundhouse. Of interest is the collection of outbuildings that were used for storage, including the box car and a half tall shed. — PPL

The tracks are cleared, the turntable pit is filled and soon the old roundhouse would be sold. This view in 1951 shows the building as it would look for several more years. — PPL

The old Machine Shop in 1953 stood empty, but a few years later it became a local attraction called Ghost Town. The small building on the left, the tin shop, was connected to the Ghost Town building through a walkway. — PPL

Seen in January 1949 the Divide depot will only see a few more ore trains, mostly day runs. — HB/ESP

This old coach was used on Bull Hill by the track gang, having served the Colorado Midland as a coach, and combine. — MM

The enginehouse at Cripple Creek would only last a few weeks after the last run in February, 1949. — HO/AC

Midland Terminal Passenger Equipment

The Midland Terminal owned only one piece of passenger equipment before absorbing the Colorado Midland and Cripple Creek and Colorado Springs equipment, Business Car 99 *Colorado*. The ex-Union Pacific car was purchased in about 1908 and was sold or scrapped in about 1920.

19	Open Observation	Ex-MT 1, EX-CM ?
20	Coach	Ex-CM 251
21	Coach	Ex-CM 252
22	Coach	Ex-CM 253
23	Coach	Ex-CM 254 (note A)
23	Baggage	Ex-CM 304 (note B)
24	Baggage Mail	Ex-CM 316
25	Coach Baggage	Ex-CM 8
26	Coach	Ex-CM 107
27	Chair	Ex-CM 109
28	Chair	Ex-CM 110
29	Chair Observation	Ex-CM 111
99	Business *Colorado*	Ex-UPD&G 99
100	Business *Cascade*	Ex-CM 100
411-415	Coach	Ex-F&CC (411-61, 412-62, 413-63, 414-65, 415-66)
451	Coach	Ex-F&CC 60

451	Retired 1930
411, 415	Retired 1932
413	Retired 1932
25	Converted to 036 in 1932
20-22	Rebuilt as Combination Cars 1932
28	Converted to 037 in about 1930

A. First 23 retired in 1924, replaced by 304.
B. 304 and 316 were alternately numbered 23 and 24, and 304 carried it's CM number First 23 went out of service.

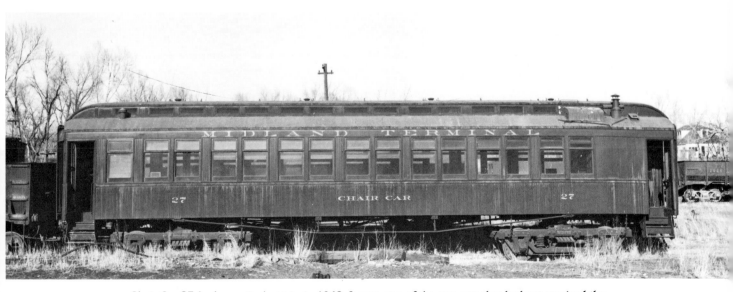

Chair Car 27 had seen its last trip in 1948. It was one of the two cars that had not received the baggage doors of a combination car. — HB/ESP

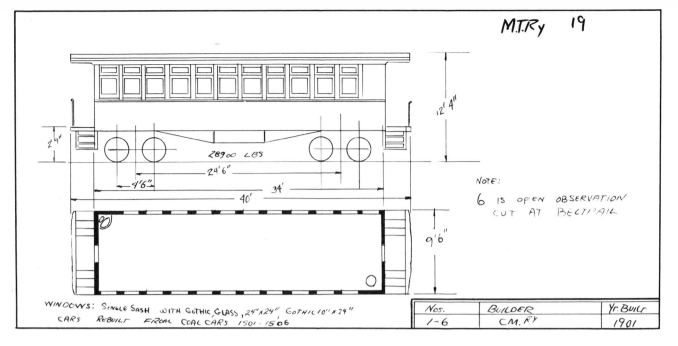

M.T.Ry 19

12' 4"

2' 4"

28900 LBS

24' 6"

4' 6"

34'

40'

NOTE:

6 IS OPEN OBSERVATION CUT AT BELTRAIL

9' 6"

WINDOWS: SINGLE SASH WITH GOTHIC GLASS, 24"×24" GOTHIC 10"×24"
CARS REBUILT FROM COAL CARS 1501-1506

Nos.	BUILDER	Yr. BUILT
1-6	C.M. RY	1901

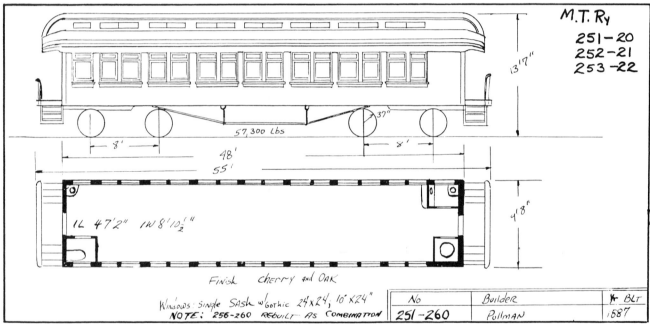

M.T.Ry
251-20
252-21
253-22

13' 7"

32"

57,300 Lbs

8'

8'

48'

55'

1L 47' 2" 1W 8' 10½"

4' 8"

Finish CHERRY and OAK

WINDOWS: SINGLE SASH w/GOTHIC 24×24; 10'×24"
NOTE: 256-260 REBUILT AS COMBINATION

No	Builder	Yr BLT
251-260	Pullman	1887

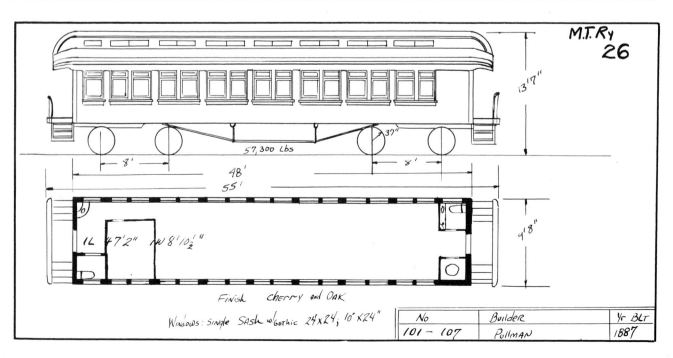

M.T.Ry
26

13' 7"

32"

57,300 Lbs

8'

8'

48'

55'

1L 47' 2" 1W 8' 10½"

4' 8"

Finish CHERRY and OAK

WINDOWS: SINGLE SASH w/GOTHIC 24×24; 10'×24"

No	Builder	Yr BLT
101-107	Pullman	1887

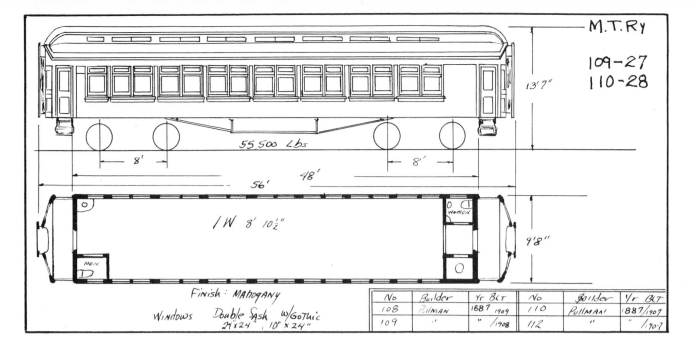

Finish: MAHOGANY

Windows Double Sash w/Gothic
24 x 24, 10" x 24"

No	Builder	Yr Blt		No	Builder	Yr Blt
108	Pullman	1887	1909	110	Pullman	1887/1907
109	"	"	/1908	112	"	" /1907

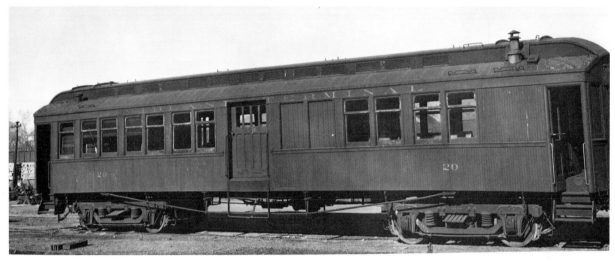

Coach/Combine 20 was one of the last usable cars, and rode on the l ast two passenger runs. —
HB/ESP

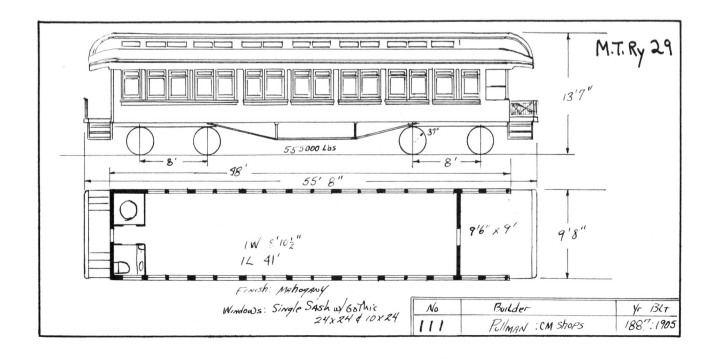

Finish: MAHOGANY

Windows: Single Sash w/Gothic
24 x 24 & 10 x 24

No	Builder	Yr Blt
111	Pullman :CM Shops	1887:1905

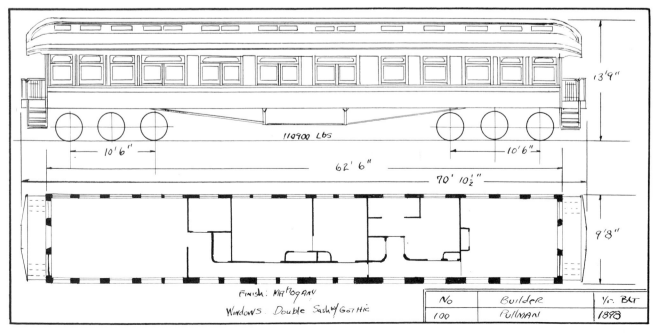

Finish: Mahogany

Windows: Double Sash w/ Gothic

No	Builder	Yr. Blt
100	Pullman	1898

13'9"

10'6"   10'6"

62' 6"

70' 10½"

9'8"

110900 Lbs

The plush interior of the business car Colorado, when it was used by the Union Pacific, Denver and Gulf. — CHS

Union Pacific, Denver and Gulf Business Car 99, became Denver and Southwestern 99, and was used by officials of the Midland Terminal about 1916. — Colorado Historical Society

Ex-Florence and Cripple Creek coach once CS&CC 414 sat behind the Colorado City roundhouse until it was moved to south 26th Street. — Ray Hilner Photo/Art Gibson Collection

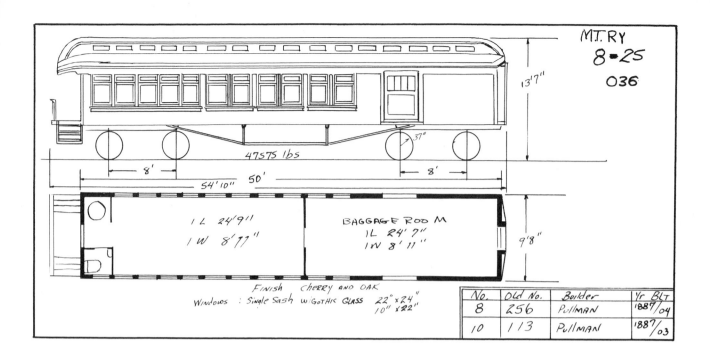

MJ.RY
8-25
036

47575 lbs

13'7"

37"

8'   50'   8'
54'10"

9'8"

I L 24'9"
I W 8'77"

BAGGAGE ROOM
I L 24'7"
I W 8'11"

FINISH CHERRY AND OAK
WINDOWS : SINGLE SASH W/GOTHIC GLASS 22" X 24"
10" X 22"

No.	Old No.	Builder	Yr Blt
8	256	Pullman	1887/04
10	113	Pullman	1887/03

Old CM Combine 8 was used by the
MT finally as a work car, and as a
shed at Victor. Today it is rapidly
deterioriating, a far cry from its glory
days as a wildflower excursion car.
— MM

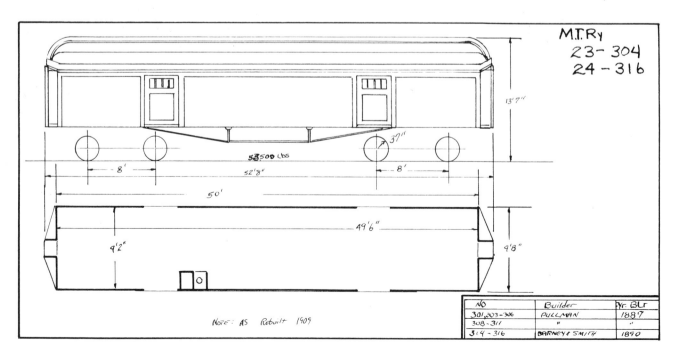

MJ.RY
23-304
24-316

13'7"

53500 lbs

37"

8'   52'8'   8'
50'
49'6"

9'2"   9'8"

NOTE: AS REBUILT 1909

NO	Builder	Yr. Blt
301, 303 - 306	PULLMAN	1887
308 - 311	"	"
314 - 316	BARNEY & SMITH	1890

List of Freight Equipment

1900 — Original Equipment

Number	Built	Builder	Length	Width	Capacity
Cabooses:					
20-25	1897-8	Wells & French	28'2"	8'6"	
Tool:					
01	1894	CM Shops	34'	9'	Unknown
Flat:					
30-32	1896	St. Charles	34'	9'	50,000 lbs
Boxcars:					
200-399	1896	St. Charles	34'	9'	60,000 lbs

The cabooses replaced Colorado Midland furnished equipment. Tool car 01 was purchased from the Colorado Midland. Flat car 33 was added in 1901, constructed from a wrecked boxcar. The equipment list remained stable until 1917.

1917 — Before addition of CMRR and CC & CS Equipment

Number	Built	Builder	Length	Width	Capacity
Cabooses:					
22, 23, 25, 26	(26 Rebuilt from 24; 20, 21 Destroyed)				
Tool:					
01					
Flat:					
30-33					
Box:					
200-299					
Coal:					
100-170	1915-7	MT Shops	34'8"	9'8"	60,000 lbs
Refrigerator:					
701-703	1917	MT Shops	34'7"	9'	60,000 lbs

Coal cars built from heavily damaged boxcars starting in 1915, program continued until 1922 concluded with 282. Flatcars 32 and 33 as well as Tool 01 were rebuilt into Bunk Cars 032-034. Only thirty boxcars from the 200-399 class survived at the start of 1917.

1922 — After initial Culling of Added Equipment

Midland Terminal equipment list swelled to nearly 100 times yearly average size. All remaining Colorado Midland equipment was absorbed by the Midland Terminal, however, most of those cars were in the process of being scrapped and sold. Three ex-Colorado Midland cabooses replaced old Midland Terminal cabooses, which were scrapped or sold. Ingoldsby dump cars were purchased from the Portland Gold Mining Company in 1915 by Cripple Creek and Colorado Springs, which in turn was absorbed into the Midland Terminal in 1921.

1924 — Return to a Normal State

Cabooses:

1-3	Ex-CM (one, #3 was originally CM 409)			

Flat:

40-42	CM/MT Shops	36'4"	Various	60,000 lbs
43-50	CM/MT Shops	34'	Various	60,000 lbs

Coal:

100-282

Stock:

601-607	1900	Pullman	37'	9'4"	60,000 lbs
4211	1900	Pullman	37'	9'4"	60,000 lbs

Refrigerator:

701-703				
704-719	1897	Pullman	36'	9'	60,000 lbs

Box:

301-329	MT Rebuilds	Various	60,000 lbs

Tank:

500	MT Shops	41'	
501-504	Var.	CM Shops	Various	80,000 lbs

Steel Dump:

801-804	Unk.	Unk.	37'8"	41,600 lbs
805-810	Unk.	Unk.	41'	42,400 lbs

Wooden Dump (Ingoldsby):

1601-1610	1904	Mt. Vernon Car Co.	40'	9'5"	40,000 lbs

1925

All remaining Colorado Midland stock cars were finally refurbished and renumbered 608-618, including 4211. Ralston Steel Dump cars 811-815, 42' in length were purchased. Tank car 500 was sold, and 501-504 were converted to flat cars.

1931

The last five Ingoldsby cars were scrapped, as well as flat cars 501-504.

1935

Steel Hopper cars 901-937, 27'6" long, were added.

1937

An equipment rebuilding program was started, old wooden cars were gradually upgraded, put into M-O-W or company service. Old boxcars were converted to additional wooden coal cars, expanding the number to 96-299.

1941-1949 — The End

Steel Dump cars 2001-2004 were added in 1940, Ex-D&RGW. In 1945 and 1946 2100-2120 were added, ex-D&RGW. After 1941 the railroad no longer interchanged their equipment with other railroads. A dropcenter flatcar was built in the shops for hauling large milling equipment to the district. In 1946 a proposal for upgrading road and maintenance equipment included a variety of equipment, but the majority of it was cancelled when the shop men went on strike.

Dispositions

MT 220 sold January 1947, Iron & Steel Products Co. Chicago, Illinois. One hundred additional wooden gondola cars were sold to the same company in March and April 1947.

All remaining equipment was sold to Commercial Metals, who sold the majority of the remaining steel cars to various Mexican railroads. The two remaining caboose bodies could be seen in Colorado Springs until the 1960's serving as a sand pit office and a shed.

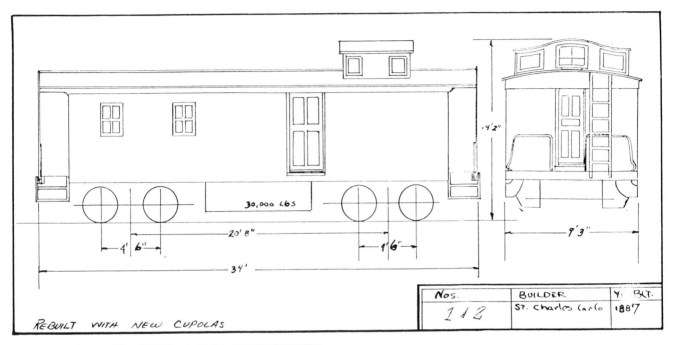

30,000 LBS

20' 8"

4' 6"

1' 6"

34'

4' 2"

9' 3"

REBUILT WITH NEW CUPOLAS

Nos.	BUILDER	Y: BLT.
1 & 2	St. Charles Carlo	1887

Midland Terminal caboose #2 a short time before it was destroyed at a gravel pit near Colorado Springs in 1975. — Richard Hatch Photo.

MTR Caboose #1 on the work train. — RH/AG

Caboose 2, freshly painted, at Midland on August 27, 1927. — JS

Caboose #2 in its better days was a Colorado Midland car, but the MT rebuilt it with a steel underframe, on the end the sign states "Glass Do Not Bump"; there must be a sort of interesting story there. — RH/AG

Not much was left of 409 when it was photographed in the late 1960's. Number 1 and 2 went on to similar fates, but much earlier. — Tom Daniels Photo

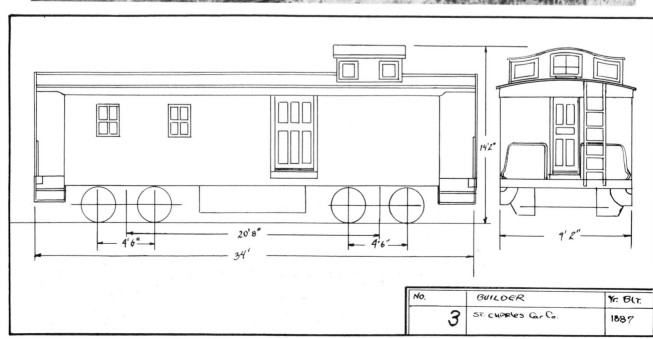

NO.	BUILDER	Yr. BLT.
3	St. Charles Car Co.	1887

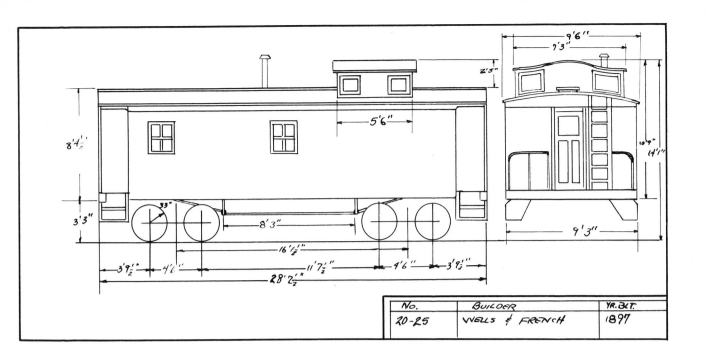

NO.	BUILDER	YR. BLT.
20-25	WELLS & FRENCH	1897

MTR Flat Car 51 had a heavy load of timbers and ties on August 28, 1946. Note the steel frame. — RH/AG

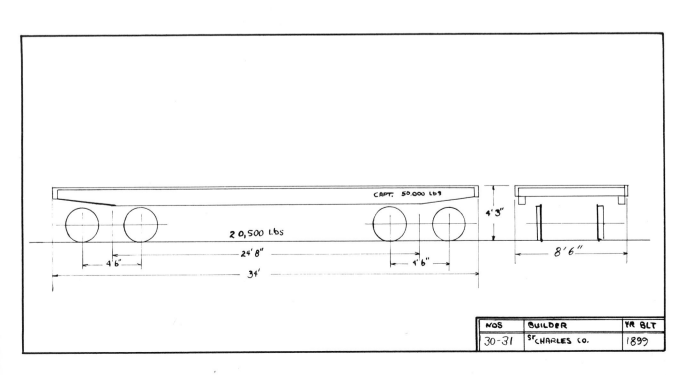

NOS	BUILDER	YR BLT
30-31	St CHARLES CO.	1899

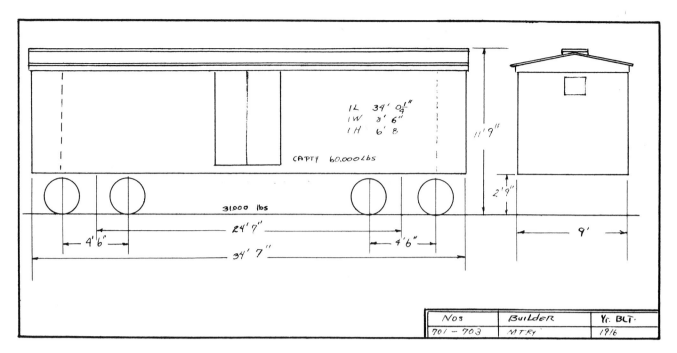

1L 34' 0¼"
1W 8' 6"
1H 6' 8

CAPTY 60.000 lbs

31000 lbs

11'9"

2'9"

24' 7"

34' 7"

4'6"

4'6"

9'

Nos	Builder	Yr. Blt.
701 — 703	M.T.Ry	1916

Midland Terminal 707 was originally a Colorado Midland Hanrahan refrigerator car, the off-set door distinguishing it apart from an ordinary car. — HB/ESP

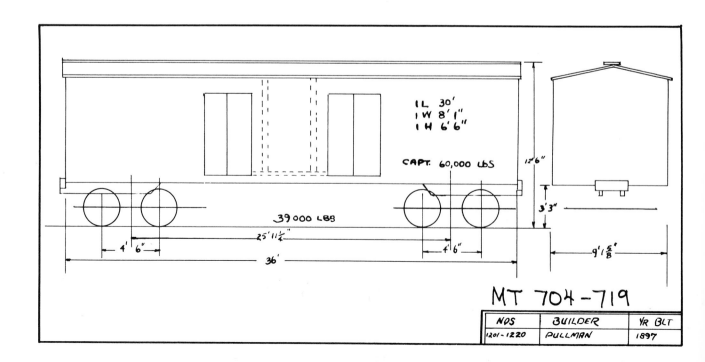

1L 30'
1W 8' 1"
1H 6' 6"

CAPT. 60,000 lbs

39000 lbs

12'6"

3'3"

25' 11½"

36'

4'6"

4'6"

9'1⅝"

MT 704-719

Nos	Builder	Yr Blt
1201-1220	Pullman	1897

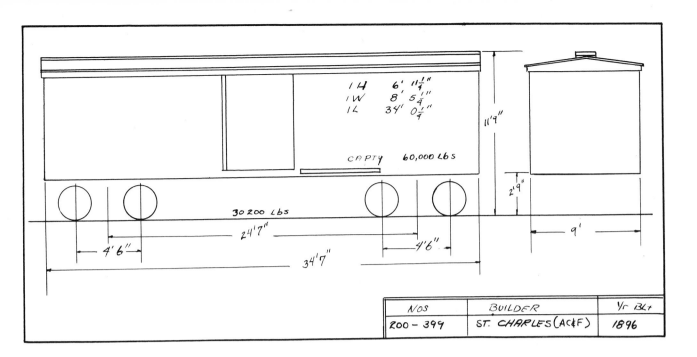

NOS	BUILDER	Yr Blt
200 - 399	ST. CHARLES (AC&F)	1896

Detail measurements on drawing:
1 H 6' 11¼"
1 W 8' 5¼"
1 L 34' 0¼"

CAPTY 60,000 LBS

30 200 LBS
24'7"
4'6"   4'6"
34'7"
11'9"
2'9"
9'

MTR 612, originally a Colorado Midland Palace Stock Car, hauled a variety of material in later years including coal. In 1946 it was parked in Colorado City. — HKV

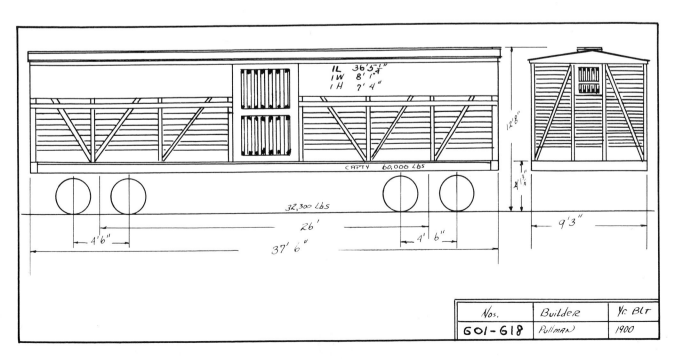

Nos.	Builder	Yr. Blt
601 - 618	Pullman	1900

Detail measurements on drawing:
1 L 36' 5¼"
1 W 8' 1¼"
1 H 7' 4"

CAPTY 60,000 LBS

32,300 LBS
26'
4'6"   4' 6"
37' 6"
12'8"
4'1¼"
9'3"

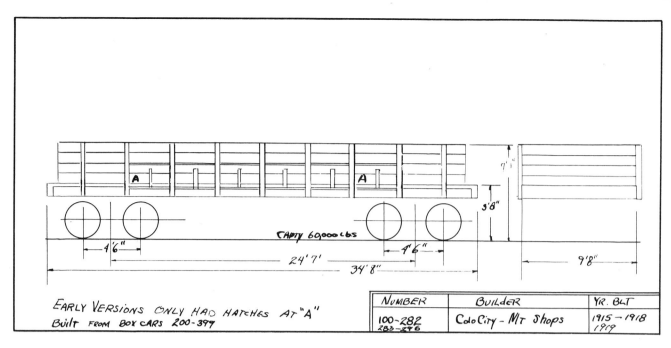

EARLY VERSIONS ONLY HAD HATCHES AT "A"
BUILT FROM BOX CARS 200-399

NUMBER	BUILDER	YR. BLT
100-282 283-296	Colo City - MT Shops	1915 - 1918 1909

MTR 108, Built in 6-1915 from an old box car, in Colorado
City, August, 1946. — RH/AG

Steel gondola 2037 was among the last batch of cars
purchased by the MT. It was sold to one of the Mexican
railways in 1949. — HKV

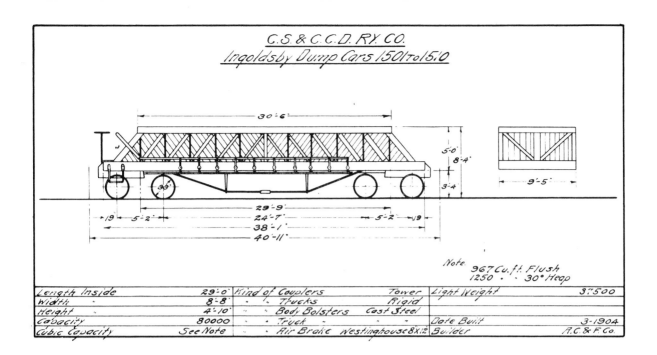

C.S. & C.C.D. RY. CO.
Ingoldsby Dump Cars 1501 to 1510

Note. 967 Cu. ft. Flush
1250 " - 30° Heap

Length Inside	29'-0"	Kind of Couplers	Tower	Light Weight	37500
Width "	8'-8"	" Trucks	Rigid		
Height "	4'-10"	" Body Bolsters	Cast Steel		
Capacity	80000	" Truck	"	Date Built	3-1904
Cubic Capacity	See Note	" Air Brake	Westinghouse 8x12	Builder	A.C.&F. Co.

Gondola car 813 was built in 1913, seen in August, 1946. —
RH/AG

Ore Car 924 would eventually go to Mexico. — W.A.G.

Maintenance-Of-Way

(The compilation given is based upon equipment post-1921)

04	Derrick	(Ex-CM 05)
05	Wrecking Tool Block Car	(Ex-CM 011)
06	Wrecking Diner	(Ex-CM 014)
07	Rail Loader	(Ex-CM 08)
08	Tool Car at Bull Hill	(Ex-CM 010)
09	Scrap Flat	
010	Cinder Car	(Ex-CM 0552)
011	Cinder Car	(Ex-CM 0553)
012	Cinder Car	(Ex-CM 0557)
013	Cinder Car	(Ex-CM 0558)
014	Coal Storage Hopper 60,000 lb.	(Ex-CM 3004)
015	Coal Storage Hopper 60,000 lb.	(Ex-CM 3007)
016	Coal Storage Hopper 60,000 lb.	(Ex-CM 3013)
017	Coal Storage Hopper 60,000 lb.	
018	Rail Loader	
031	Tool Car	
032	Bunk Car (Dismantled 12-7-26)	
033	Bunk Car	
034	Bunk Car - Lineman's Car	
035	Coal Storage for Store Room 60,000 lb.	
036	B & B Bunk	(Ex-MT-25)
037	B & B Bunk	(Ex-MT-28)
038	Tool Car	
039	Ditcher	
A	Rotary Snow Plow	(Ex-CM A)
B	Snow Cut Widener (Spreader)	

Derrick 04 was originally steam shovel 05 on the Colorado Midland. — LLW

Work Train equipment included, left to right, 05, 06, and 04, seen in Colorado City in 1949. — LLW

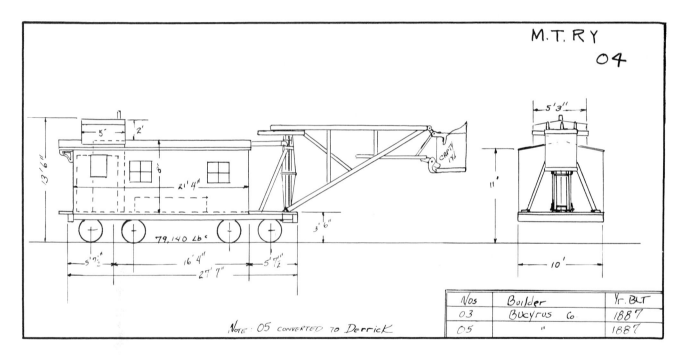

M.T. RY
04

CAP'TY 1¾

13'6"

5'   2'

21'4"

79,140 Lbs

5'7½"   16'4"   5'7½"

27'7"

3'6"

5'3"

11"

10'

NOTE: 05 CONVERTED TO DERRICK

Nos	Builder	Yr. Blt
03	Bucyrus Co.	1887
05	"	1887

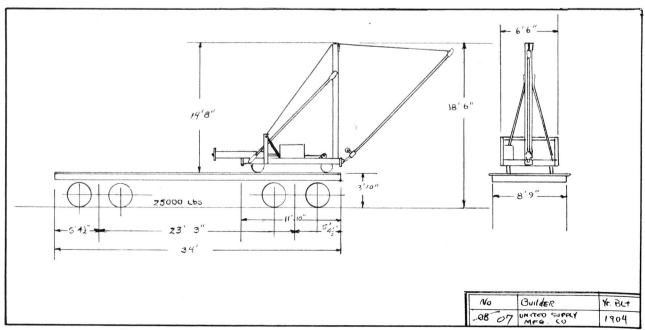

14'8"

18'6"

6'6"

25000 Lbs

3'10"

5'4½"   23'3"   5'4½"

11'10"

34'

8'9"

No	Builder	Yr. Blt
08 07	United Supply Mfg. Co.	1904

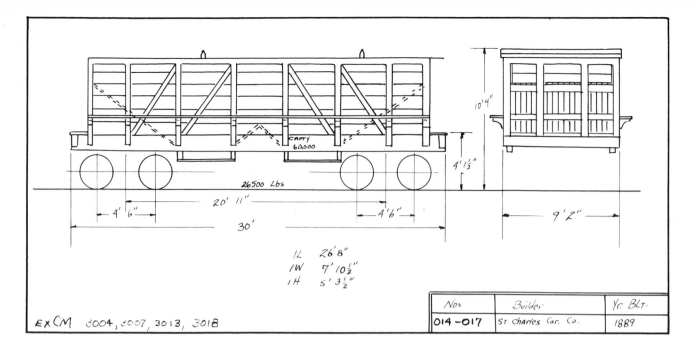

IL 26'8"
IW 7'10½"
IH 5'3½"

EX CM 3004, 3007, 3013, 3018

CAP'Y 60000
26500 Lbs
20' 11"
30'
4' 6"
4' 6"
10'4"
4' 1½"
9' 2"

Nos	Builder	Yr. BLt.
014 –017	St. Charles Car. Co.	1889

Cinder car 013 served the CM and the MT, but not without extensive rebuilding. — HB/ESP

Cinder car 012 was rebuilt from a Colorado Midland car, seen here in August, 1946. — William A. Gibson Photo

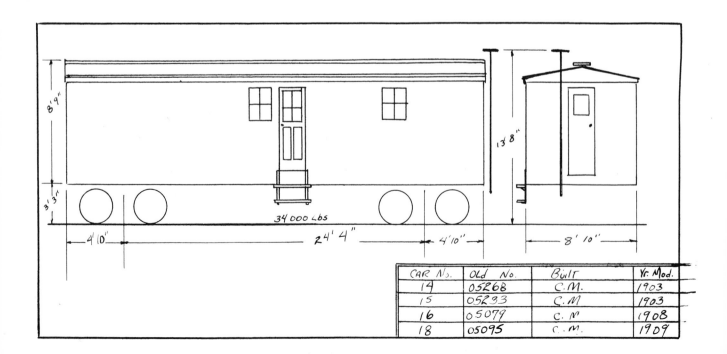

8'9"
3'3"
34000 Lbs
4'10"
24' 4"
4'10"
13'8"
8' 10"

CAR No.	Old No.	Built	Yr. Mod.
14	05268	C.M.	1903
15	05233	C.M.	1903
16	05079	C.M.	1908
18	05095	C.M.	1909

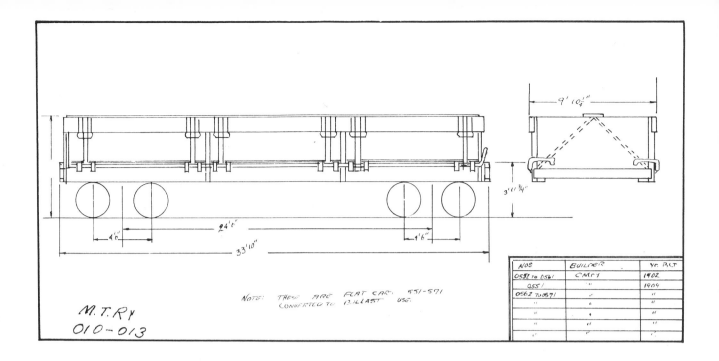

NOTE: THESE ARE FLAT CARS 551-571 CONVERTED TO BALLAST USE.

M.T.RY
010-013

NOS	BUILDER	Yr. BLT
0552 to 0561	CMrY	1902
0551	"	1904
0562 to 0571	"	"
"	"	"
"	"	"
"	"	"
"	"	"

MTRy 016 was originally one of the "Battleship" gondola cars that hauled coal on the Colorado Midland. The Midland Terminal hauled and stored coal in the few ramaining cars. The Broadmoor Hotel also bought four of the cars. — HKV

Midland Terminal coal storage car 016, was originally a "battleship" gondola car on the Colorado Midland. — HB/ESP

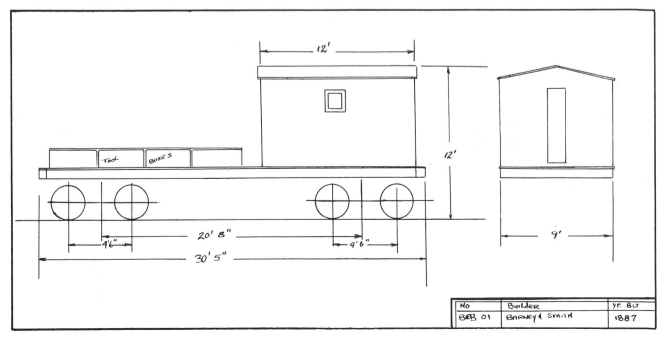

NO	BUILDER	Yr. BLT
B&B 01	BARNEY & SMITH	1887

Rail loader 018 was used during the scrapping, and two loaded cars of rail can be seen ahead of it. — DPL

The rustic steam shovel that was used at the quarry at Midland. — LLW

F&CC (and Leased Lines) Ditcher #1, served mainly the MT, and was recorded at the American Hoist and Derrick factory in St. Paul before delivery. The disposition is unknown. — Frank Ellington Coll.

Maintenance of way car 037 was originally a coach on the CM, and then was put to work on the MT. It was involved in a runaway and rather than rebuild the car it was diverted to use on the B&B gang. — HB/ESP

187

Midland Terminal tool car 031 at
Cripple Creek in 1942. — MWA

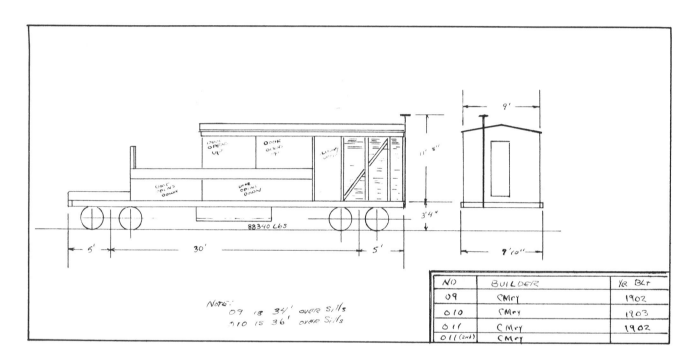

DOOR OPENS UP

DOOR OPENS UP

LIGHT

DOOR OPENS DOWN

DOOR OPENS DOWN

11' 8"

3' 4"

5'   30'   5'

88340 LBS

9'

9' 10"

Note:
    09 is 34' over Sills
    010 is 36' over Sills

NO	BUILDER	YR BLT
09	CMRy	1902
010	CMRy	1903
011	CMRy	1902
011 (2nd)	CMRy	

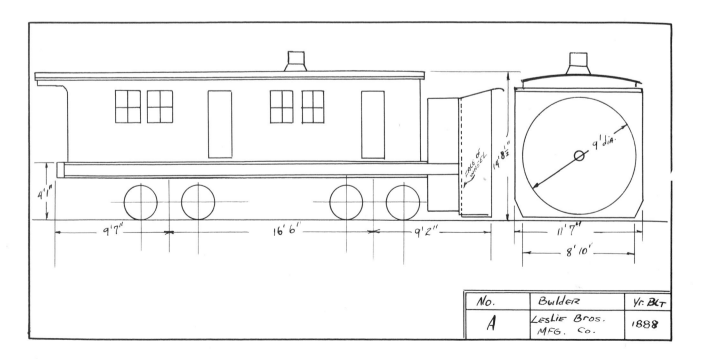

4' 1"

EDGE OF WHEEL

14' 8½"

9' dia.

9' 7"   16' 6"   9' 2"   11' 7"

8' 10"

No.	Builder	Yr. Blt
A	Leslie Bros. MFG. Co.	1888

Record of Locomotives

2-8-0 Type:

Number	Builder	Year	Builder's Number
52	Baldwin	1897	15131
53	Baldwin	1897	15134
Driver Size	Cylinder Size	Boiler Diameter	Weight of Engine
52 inches	21x26 inches	62¼ inches	154,000 pounds

Number	Builder	Year	Builder's Number
54	Schenectady	1896	4427
55	Schenectady	1896	4428
56	Schenectady	1896	4429
57	Schenectady	1896	4430
58	Schenectady	1896	4431
59	Schenectady	1898	4741
60	Schenectady	1899	5178
Driver Size	Cylinder Size	Boiler Diameter	Weight of Engine
52 inches	21x26 inches	62¼ inches	150,500 pounds

Number	Builder	Year	Builder's Number
61	Brooks	1910	47769
Driver Size	Cylinder Size	Boiler Diameter	Weight of Engine
51 inches	21x28 inches	80 inches	194,280 pounds

2-8-2 Type:

Number	Builder	Year	Builder's Number
62	Brooks	1915	55490
63	Brooks	1917	58164
Driver Size	Cylinder Size	Boiler Diameter	Weight of Engine
48 inches	20x28 inches	73 inches	195,000 pounds

2-6-0 Type:

Number	Builder	Year	Builder's Number
64	Lima	1944	8385
65	American Loco.	1942	70410
66	Lima	1944	8384

0-6-0 Type:

Number	Builder	Year	Builder's Number
4064	Lima	1944	8398
4070	Lima	1944	8404
4014	American Loco.	1942	70390
Driver Size	Cylinder Size	Boiler Diameter	Weight of Engine
50 inches	21x28 inches	64⅞ inches	163,500 pounds

Remarks:

Locomotive 52 was Colorado Midland 50 purchased 3-2-21.

Locomotive 53 was Colorado Midland 53 purchased 3-2-21.

Locomotive 54 was originally Midland Terminal 1, 201, and 41.

Locomotive 55 was originally Midland Terminal 2, 202, and 42.

Locomotive 56 was originally Midland Terminal 3, 203, and 43.

Locomotive 57 was originally Midland Terminal 4, 204, and 44.

Locomotive 58 was originally Midland Terminal 5, 205, and 45.

Locomotive 59 was originally Midland Terminal 6, 206, and 46.

Locomotive 60 was originally Midland Terminal 7, 207, and 47.

Locomotive 61 was originally Buffalo and Susquehana 174, purchased by Chicago and Illinois Midland as 510. Purchased by Midland Terminal in 1938, rebuilt into 2-8-2, and returned to 2-8-0.

Locomotive 62 was originally Copper River & Northwestern 70, purchased 1940, converted to coal burner.

Locomotive 63 was originally Copper River & Northwestern 74, purchased by Midland Terminal 1940, converted to coal burner.

Locomotive 64 was originally U.S. Army 4051, purchased 1946 as an 0-6-0.

Locomotive 65 was originally U.S. Army 4028, purchased 1946 as an 0-6-0.

Locomotive 66 was originally U.S. Army 4050, purchased 1946 as an 0-6-0.

Remaining locomotives were ex-U.S. Army, but were not rebuilt or renumbered and were probably never used.

Workhorse 52 on June 22, 1941, coaled and ready. — John McCall Collection

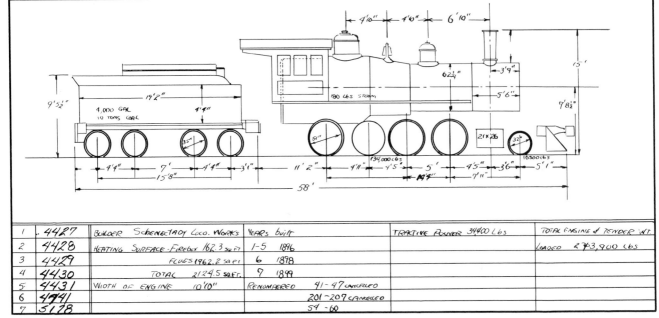

1	.4427	BUILDER SCHENECTADY LOCO. WORKS	YEARS built		TRACTIVE POWER 34,400 LBS	TOTAL ENGINE & TENDER WT.
2	4428	HEATING SURFACE - FIREBOX 162.3 SQ FT	1-5	1896		LOADED 293,900 LBS
3	4429	FLUES 1962.2 SQ.FT.	6	1898		
4	4430	TOTAL 2124.5 SQ.FT.	9	1899		
5	4431	WIDTH OF ENGINE 10'0"	RENUMBERED	41-47 CANCELLED		
6	4941			201-207 CANCELLED		
7	5178			54-60		

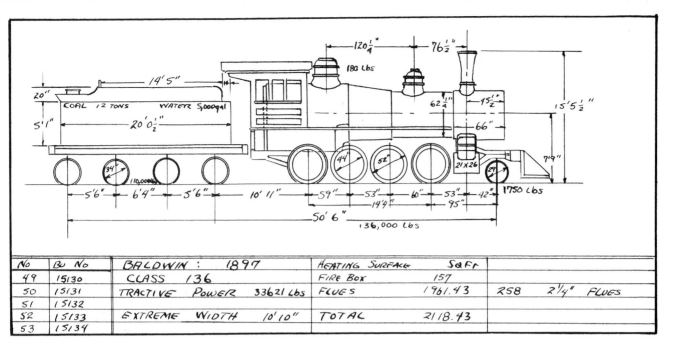

No	Bu No	BALDWIN : 1897		HEATING SURFACE	SQ FT			
49	15130	CLASS 136		FIRE BOX	157			
50	15131	TRACTIVE POWER 33621 Lbs		FLUES	1961.43	258	2¼"	FLUES
51	15132							
52	15133	EXTREME WIDTH 10'10"		TOTAL	2118.43			
53	15134							

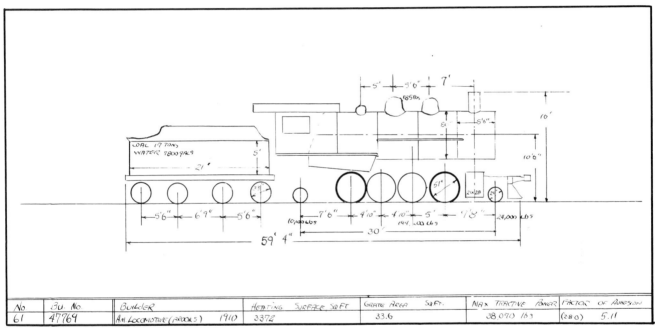

No	Bu. No.	BUILDER		HEATING SURFACE SQ FT	GRATE AREA SQ FT.	MAX TRACTIVE POWER	FACTOR OF ADHESION
61	47769	Am. Locomotive (Brooks)	1910	3372	33.6	38,070 lbs	(280) 5.11

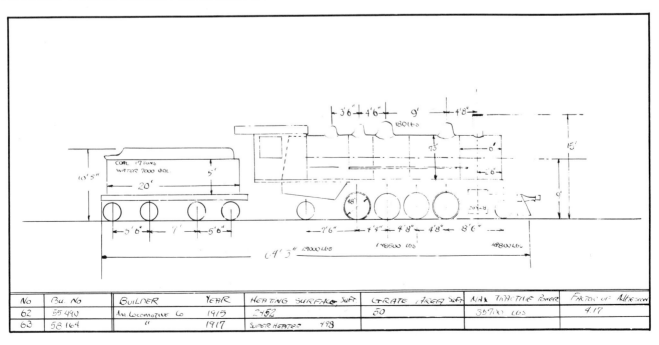

No	Bu. No	BUILDER	YEAR	HEATING SURFACE SQ FT	GRATE AREA SQ FT	MAX TRACTIVE POWER	FACTOR OF ADHESION
62	55490	Am. Locomotive Co	1915	3452	50	35700 LBS	4.17
63	58164	"	1917	SUPER HEATER 798			

Engine 53 had some good miles left on it when it was used on the work train near Murphy. The air dump cars were borrowed for the summer's work. — DPL

Locomotive 53, once Colorado Midland 53 was out of service by 1940, and occasionally steamed up for use as a stationary boiler. It would be scrapped in a few years. — DeGolyer Collection

Engine 54 was primarily used as a spare engine in the early 1940's, but after the newer engines arrived it was used as scrap. The parts were used to keep mainly the oldest engines running. The rotary plow is parked behind the engine. — HB/ESP

Originally #1, #54 working on August 27, 1938. — Gordon C. Bassett Collection

The lettering on 55 is bright and vivid, a rare scene, fresh from the roundhouse. — L.W. Moody/John McCall Collection

Engine 55 had been wrecked several times, and after WWII it was put on the rip track near the machine shop, where it was used for parts to keep other engines running. — HB/ESP

Ready to roll off the turntable, #56 on September 8, 1936. — W.A. Gibson Photo

The opposite side of #56, with the water tank in the background. It is unusual to see the both sides of an engine on the same date. — W.A. Gibson Photo

Ready for an ore run, #58 & #59 (behind) wait on September 8, 1936. — W.A.G.

Engine 59, with the old self trimming Colorado Midland tender, waits at the Colorado Springs, D&RGW depot with one of the last passenger runs under steam. The tender had an interesting reputation and reportedly the high center of gravity caused it to sway on the curves. — LDM

Locomotive 59, seen here with her freight coloration would be dolled up to pull the last two passenger trains. The old Colorado Midland tender that was regularly behind 59 had been scrapped a few years earlier. — HKV

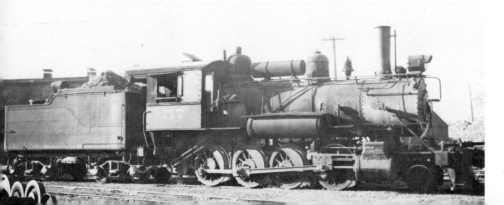

Locomotive 57 was used on the September 8, 1936 run to Bull Hill, sporting its rebuilt tender and resplendent with air tanks. — William A. Gibson Photo

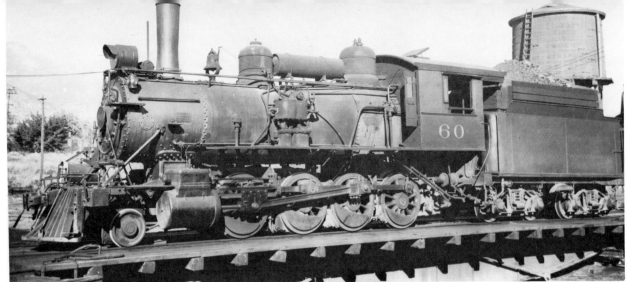

In September 1936, engine 60 was very clean as it was being made ready for that night's run to Bull Hill, seen on the Colorado City turntable. — William A. Gibson Photo.

In 1947 #60 was found in Cripple Creek, near the depot. — HO/AC

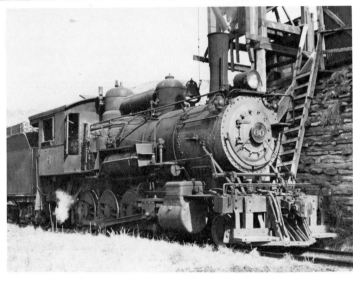

Snuggled up between 60 and 64, 61 sports her new look without her experimental trailing truck in 1947. — HB/ESP

On July 24, 1939, #61 still had its trailing wheels, however, in a short time they would be removed. — DPL

The changes in 62 included a new trailing track and conversion from oil to coal, and included a new tender. The engine had been Copper River and Northwestern #70. — HB/ESP

Engine 63 is being prepared for the nightly trip to Bull Hill in August 1948. — DPL

Engine 4064, ex-US Army, saw only mileage in the yards and was not rebuilt like her mates, 64-66. She still carried 4064 when shipped east to Norfolk, Virginia. — PM

Engine 4070, another ex-US Army locomotive, was like 4104 and 4064, never placed in service on the Midland Terminal. — R.H. Kindig, Colorado Railroad Museum Collection

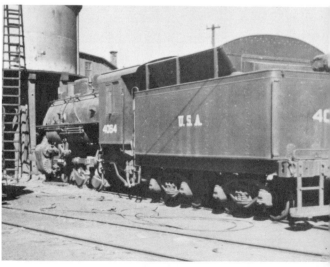

USA locomotive 4051 in Topeka before shipment to Colorado on the Santa Fe. — W.A.G.

Former USA locomotive 4051, Midland Terminal #64 at Midland tank, November, 1948. — EP/HJB

Engine 66 takes on water at Midland while the crew check over a load of coal bound for Victor. — HB/ESP

Engine 65 takes on water at Midland. — HB/ESP

Disposition of Locomotives

52	Scrapped 1949
53	Retired September 1940, scrapped by 1947
54	Scrapped November 1946
55	Scrapped October 1947 — Boiler in Carlton Mill
56	Scrapped September 1948
57	Scrapped June 1948
58	Scrapped 1949
59	Scrapped 1949
60	Scrapped 1949
61	Scrapped 1949
62	F.C. Nor Oeste de Mexico 200, December, 1948
	F.C. Chihuahua al Pacifico 200, Scrapped
63	F.C. Nor Oeste de Mexico 201, December, 1948
	F.C. Chihuahua al Pacifico 201, Scrapped
64-66, 4064, 4070, 4014	
	Norfolk & Portsmouth Belt Line Railroad

Engine 61 in the process of being cut up in the spring of 1949. — PPL

Lima's were numbered 53-56, American Locomotive Works were numbered 64 and 65, all as 0-6-0s. Scrapped in the late 1950's and early 1960's.

Gasoline cars 101 and 102 were scrapped by the Midland Terminal, but the bodies could be seen at various locations as late as 1965. It is rumored that one was burned (probably 102) and that one is now located on a farm in eastern Colorado.

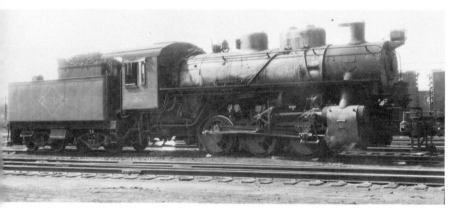

At Portsmouth, Virginia in March, 1955, #55 is reported to be Ex-MT, Ex-USA 4064 or 4077. — HKV

Upon looking this could be an ex-Short Line 0-6-0, however, it is **NOT**, matter of fact, the MTRy is not in Colorado. It is Minnesota Transfer Railway #10. — Gordon C. Bassett Collection

Chihuahua al Pacifico 200, in February, 1960, with yet another tender, was originally Copper River and Northwestern 70. — H.K.V.

The inspection car at Colorado City in 1946. — MA

(Above—left) Motor car 102 was quite different from 101, since it hauled mainly freight and the mail. It has just arrived from the station in Colorado Springs on July 24, 1939. From the back it still looked like a street car. — DPL

The remains of Motor Car 101 and 102 sat east of the Golden Cycle mill site for several years, exact disposition of the pair is unknown. — L.D. Mitchel Photo

Motorcar 101 with its original nose seen at Cripple Creek in 1936, not long after it was finished. It was altered after a slight accident, with a more streamlined nose, quite visible here is its streetcar heritage. — DPL

Only diesel to operate over the MT was the scrapper's engine a former US Army locomotive, number 53, seen here at Colorado Springs. — HB/ESP

A Partial List of Employees

This list, like the trips described here, was built using the memories of former employees. A complete list was shipped to the Railroad Retirement Board upon the closing of the Midland Terminal in 1949. The truckloads of records included the records of men who had worked for all of the Cripple Creek railroads as well as the Colorado Midland. The list *is not* 100% accurate, and only a lengthy search of those 1949 records (if they still exist) could make make it so.

Officers

H.P. Lillibridge	President	1892-1894
H. Collbran	President/General Manager	1895
D.R.C. Brown	President/General Manager	1895-1898
W.K. Gillett	President/General Manager	1898-1905
J.H. Waters	President/General Manager	1905-1912
H.M. Blackmer	President	1912-1916
J.H. Waters	General Manager	1912-1914
J.J. Cogan	General Manager	1914-1931
A.E. Carlton	President	1916-1920
Spencer Penrose	President	1920-1934
E.W. Winslow	General Manager	1932-1941
Merrill Shoup	President	1934-1949
Wm. McKay	General Manager	1941-1949
Richard Newell Jr.	Chief Engineer	1892-1894
W.H. Leffinwell	Chief Engineer	1894-1895
M.J. Burgdoff	Chief Engineer	1895-1899
Wm. Murphy	Roadmaster	1894-1897
J.C. McCullough	Roadmaster	-1922
W.B. Wreath	Roadmaster	1892-
Wilmot Brown	Roadmaster	1941-1949
E.E. Rittenhous	Trainmaster	1893-
J.B. Flaherty	Trainmaster	1905-1915
Leonard Butler	Trainmaster	1938-1949
W.A. Mattlock	Traffic Manager	1904-1908
F.C. Matthews	Traffic Manager	1908-1914
	General Freight/Passenger Agent	1914-1931
D.C. McWatters	General Passenger Agent	1900-1907
William Meyer	Traffic Manager	1941-1949
May O'Brien	Secretary	1920-1949
Sadye Rabbitt	Stenographer	-1949
M.E. O'Brien	Car Accountant	1917-1923
P.E. Brooks	Surveyor	
E.F. Schumm	Timekeeper and Paymaster	1928-1949
E.W. Winslow	Colorado City Agent	1921-1932
George Deikster	Colorado City Agent	
E.W. Meyers	Woodland/Divide Agent	1924-1949
Mr. Webb	Woodland/Divide Agent	
Vern Clark	Colorado City Dispatcher	1925-1943
Ray Murphy	Colorado City Clerk	

Sam Bayless, Master Mechanic, poses alongside the new locomotive 61 in 1939. — JG

The roundhouse crew at Colorado City poses with wheels and tires at the turn of the century. — Mrs. D. Butler Collection

Julius Meyer	Colorado City Clerk	-1949
Dave McDonald	Bull Hill Dispatcher	1901-1917
Charles Steele	Freight Clerk Cripple Creek	
A.P. McCarthy	Chief Dispatcher	1900-1906
Robert Reagal	Weighmaster	1935-1949
"Doc"	Weighmaster	
George Tait	Lineman	1925-1949
John Vidmar Sr.	Coal Chute/Sand House	1925-1934
Roy Kent	Coal Chute/Sand House	1934-1949
Andy Butler	Timekeeper	1926-1949
Wilmot Brown	Storehouse Manager	1930-1935
William C. Meyer	Storehouse Manager	1935-1941
Dave McDonald	Janitor/Reliefman	1918-1932
Paul Haulderman	Security Guard	1938-1940
Martin Novlan Sr.	Janitor	1931-1941

Mechanical Department

Frank Singer	Master Mechanic	1900-1910
H.W. Bleeze	Master Mechanic	1911
N.J. O'Connor	Master Mechanic	1912-1913
C.A. McCarthy	Master Mechanic	1913-1917
M.J. Powers	Master Mechanic	1917-1922
J.H. Dummer	Master Mechanic	1922
P.E. Brooks	Master Mechanic	1923-1925
William McKay	Master Mechanic	1925-1941
Sam Bayless	Master Mechanic	1941-1949
O.R. Owen	Foreman Mechanical Dept.	1917-
William McKay	Machinist	1911-1925
Sam Bayless	Machinist	1921-1941
George Nichols	Machinist/Drill Press	1920-1942
Frank Nichols	Machinist	
Ed Weller	Machinist	1928-1946
Charley O'Brien	Machinist	1918-1949
Bill Lewis	Machinist	1913
T.D. Burke	Machinist	1914-1917
Al Whitman	Machinist	1927-1936

Mr. Miller	Machinist	
Jack Buckman	Machinist	1946-1949
"Shorty" Mathews	Machinist	1937-1943
Carl Otto	Machinist	1935-1943
Frank McCaffrey	Machinist	1920-1943
Harry Horr	Tin Shop/Pipefitter	1927-1944
George McCaffrey	Machinist Helper	1914-1916
Woody Ralston	Machinist Helper	1942-1945
Roy Kent	Machinist Helper	1932-1934
John McGrady	Shop Helper	1936-1944
Tony Vidmar	Shop Helper	1938-1942
Elmer Skalla	Shop Helper	1939-1944
Fred Schumm	Shop Helper	1945
Andrew Schooley	Mechanic/Extra Train Crew	1941-1949
Jimmy McGrady	Head Blacksmith	1920-1942
Bert Bender	Blacksmith Helper	1925-1942
Joseph McGrady	Blacksmith Helper	1929-1936
John Manick	Welder	1925-1949
Walter Titus	Welder	-1949
Harvey Cline	Boilermaker	1915-1949
Orey Gephard	Boilermaker	1934-1946
Sammy Crain	Boilermaker	-1949
John McLaughlin	Boilermaker	1920-1936
George Giesing	Welder	1919-1920
Al Schilling	Boilermaker/Sheet Metal	1910-1941
Fred Ward Jr.	Engine Cab Carpenter	1922-1941
Henry Weber	Bolt Shop	
Frank Wreath	Section/Motor Car Repair	1921-1949
S. LeRoy Bowling	Handyman/Watchman	1914-1949
Jess Wreath	Rip Track/Wreck Train Cook	
Jack Ward	Car Repair Foreman	1918-1935
George Hill	Car Repair Foreman	1935-1949
Dan Grace	Rivetor	
Frank O'Lear	Car Repair	
Delbert Marsh	Roundhouse Helper	1920-1929
Jim Marsh	Roundhouse Helper	1920-1929
Charles Grainer	Car Repair	1931-1940
Joseph Scheider	Coach Cleaner-Cripple Creek	1908-1919
A. Shane	Car Repair-Bull Hill	1915-1917
Wm. C. Day	Car Repair	1916-1918
R.L. Eastham	Car Repair	1920
C.V. Johnson	Car Inspector-Bull Hill	1912-1913
T.C. Rhoades	Car Inspector-Divide	1905-1906
R.C. Stewart	Car Inspector-Bull Hill	1916-1917
James Varley	Car Repair	1931-1940
Marge Moyher	Car Repair	1920-1929
Jerry Jernigan	Car Repair	1935-
Andrew Trickak	Car Repair/Painter	1919-1939

Taken for a retirement memento; back row left to right is Sam Bayless, A.P. Schilling, John Manick, Andy Schooley, Edward Weller, Charles O'Brien, Jimmy McGrady, and Harvey Cline; front row, S. Crane, Billy Henderick, Carl Otto and Elmer Skalla.
— AC

Thornton Tait Jr.	Carman/Carpenter	1933-1941
Dale Wright	Car Repair/Welder	
Frank O'Lear	Carman/Air	1930-1941
Joe Marsh	Air Inspector	1918-1925
Clarence Milner	Air Inspector	1921-1941
Timothy Driscoll	Air Inspector	1920-1941
Al Decker	Air Inspector	1918-1942
Charles Murphy	Air Serviceman	1925-1943
Henry Weber	Scrap Dock	
C.C. Williams	Scrap Dock	
Henry Vogelsang	Scrap Dock	
Lewis Chambon	Scrap Dock	
J.H. Blanton	Scrap Dock	
C.E. Westcott	Scrap Dock	
H. Carroll	Scrap Dock	
Robert Painter	Scrap Dock	
Fred K. Whitaker	Scrap Dock	
Wilmot A. Brown	B&B Superintendent	1936-1942
Frank Craig	B&B Foreman	1914-1930
Ben Wreath Jr.	B&B Foreman	
Johnny Sherbak	B&B Foreman	1942-1949
Johnny Sherbak	B&B Carpenter	1926-1942
W.E. "Newt" Newton	B&B Carpenter	1927-1942
"Doc" Worf	B&B Carpenter	1927-1942
Ed Palko	B&B Helper	1931-1940
Frank O'Lear	B&B Helper	1935-1937

Jack Sullivan	B&B Helper	1936-1938
Homer Vandenberg	B&B Carpenter	
Otto Brandenberg	B&B Carpenter	
Dewey Fitzgerald	B&B Carpenter	
Ralph Bishop	B&B Truck Operator	1944-1949

Colorado City Track Gang

Dennis Corbitt	Track Foreman	1919-1936
John Keliher	Track Foreman	-1926
Jimmy Wood	Track Worker	1920-1939
Chris Miller	Track Worker	1921-1941
Carl Hansen Sr.	Track Worker	1921-1941
Carl Hansen Jr.	Track Worker	1928-1941
Pete Vidmar Jr.	Track Worker	1929-1940
Charles Chonka	Track Worker	1930-1940
Al Palko	Track Worker	
Henry Nance	Track Worker	
Ray Marsh	Track Worker	
Claude Schubarth	Track Worker	
Ed McCaughey	Track Worker	

Cascade Track Gang

Ed Sherbak	Track Foreman	1925-1947
Hoot Sullivan	Track Worker	1929-1935
Jack Sullivan	Track Worker	1929-1934
Fred Gallardo	Track Worker	1928-1941
Woody Ralston	Track Worker	1936-1941
George Mikita	Track Worker	1939-1941
Edgar Hansen	Track Worker	1940-1941
Bill Johnson	Track Worker	
Spencer Marsh	Track Worker	1922-1925
Joe Petrinko	Track Worker	1928-1934

Woodland Tie Plant

Bill Wright	Plant Foreman	1928-1942
Glen Baldwin	Worker	1929-1934
Henry Rogers	Worker	1929-1933
Don Workman	Worker	1918-1933
Stanley Baldwin	Worker	1929-1934

An unidentified man, Hoot Sullivan, and Ralph Bishop work under and around the B&B truck after it suffered a broken axle. — RB

Divide Track Gang

Frank Countryman	Track Foreman	1927-1940
Ted Weaver	Track Foreman	1940-1949
Connie Countryman Jr.	Track Worker	1929-1934
Frank McCumber	Track Workman	1928-1939
John "Blackie" Rife	Track Worker	1927-1949
Frank Kayhill	Track Worker	1928-1939
Sommer Osborne	Track Worker	1928-1932
Bob Weaver	Track Worker	
Ted Weaver	Track Worker	

Midland Track Gang

Clifford Hook	Track Foreman	-1949
Bud Kirkbride	Track Foreman	1925-1931
Ben Wreath Jr.	Track Foreman	1931-1939
Bud Wellinton	Track Worker	1925-1932
Joe Bishop	Track Worker	1928-1936
Clarence Wilkins	Track Worker	1930-1942
Irving Gray	Track Worker	1931-1937
Frank Kovosi	Track Worker	1925-1940
Ben Wreath Jr.	Track Worker	1929-1930

Bull Hill Track Gang

Pat Kinney	Track Foreman	1917-1931
Ben Wreath	Track Foreman	1931-1942
Sam Houston	Track Foreman	-1948

Midland Gravel Pit

Frank Lovejoy	Steam Shovel Operator	1925-1936
George Bilbrey	Steam Shovel Operator	1926-1945
Walter Crain	Helper	1932-1934
Bud Wellington	Helper	1927-1937
Joe Bishop	Helper	1928-1934
Pascal Morris	Helper/Powderman	1928-1934
Roy Fivecoats	Helper	
Cliff Hook	Helper	

Section Foremen—Assignment Unknown or Incomplete

Fiedler

Schreck

The old maintenance-of-way truck was built from an old sedan and scrap by the MT shops. The rugged vehicle rests quietly in the Colorado City yards in 1948. — WS/EC

The Cascade section crew on April 30, 1937 included, from left to right, Henry Nance, Fred Gallardo, Ed Sherbak, Bill Johnson and Woody Ralston. — JS

This proud track crew includes Woody Ralston, standing left, at Murphy Cut. — PM

Section Foreman—Divide

Tom Heath

Section Workers—Assignment Unknown or Various

Walt Burkhart
Joe Vidmar
Al Treiner
Roy McGee
Bill Weber
Andrew Sanders
Lance Howard
Fred Ramsell
Claude Heath
Dwight Stanton
Harry Stevens
Johnny Mosco
Joe Sherbak
Pat Hankins
Joe Sawyer
Carl Stevens
George Perry
Tim Finnucan
Joe Angland
Steve Snodgrass
Charley Stevens

The tracks came up in April 1949 near Manitou, here just east of Tunnel Two. — DPL

Bull Hill Yardmaster

Dave McDonald	Yardmaster/Agent	1901-1917
Bert Fleming	Yardmaster	1917-1925
Vern Clark	Yardmaster	1925-1928
Leland Evans	Yardmaster	1928-1942
Rex Edwards	Yardmaster	1942-1949

Roundhouse Foreman—Cripple Creek

F.W. Milburn	Foreman	1917-1923
Arthur Stone	Foreman	1923-1949
Art Wilcox	Extra	
Frank Vogler	Extra	

Hostlers—Colorado City

Ed Dagley	Hostler (Day)	1918-1949
Art Wilcox	Hostler	
Charles O'Brien	Hostler	
S. LeRoy Bowling	Hostler	
Keith Schooley	Hostler	1948-1949
Gail Winters	Hostler	1945
Lloyd Lundsten	Hostler	1940-1941
Harry Sanders	Hostler	1924-1930
Buck Wilkins	Hostler Helper	1938-1942
Woody Ralston	Hostler Helper	1942-1943
F.W. Oswald	Hostler Helper	1912-1913
Mr. McGillicudy	Hostler Helper	

Hostlers—Cripple Creek

Charles Pressler	Hostler	1916-1920
C.A. Nulph	Hostler	1920-1923
Nick Calmes	Hostler	1923-1928

Motor Car

Carl Truman	Motor Car Operator	1932-1942
Don Workman	Motor Car Operator	1936-1938

Switchmen

Walter Crain	Switchman	1939-1942
Bill Hendricks	Switchman	1937-1939
Andrew Schooley	Switchman	1936-1939
Frank Nulph	Switch Foreman	1921-1938

Trainmen

(all were Brakemen and Conductors, all held rights on all jobs)

James Prosser	Conductor	1917-1930
J. McCaffery	Conductor	1918-1940
Thomas J. O'Connell	Conductor	1917-1949
Lenord Reeder	Conductor	1920-1942

Mike Jeter	Conductor	1917-1929
Paul Hammond	Conductor	1916-1918
Al Hammond	Conductor	1916-1924
Pardon Jordan	Conductor	1921-1928
Frank Nulph	Conductor	1921-1938
William Richardson	Conductor	1923-1949
K.H. Edmiston	Conductor	1924-1942
D.E. Nulph	Conductor	1926-1947
F.W. Ferguson	Conductor	1923-1942
Vincent Lynn	Conductor	-1949
Frank Barnhardt	Conductor	
Dave Martin	Conductor	

Brakemen

Wally Harmonson	Brakeman	1930-1941
Dave Miller	Brakeman	1930-1942
Merrill Willson	Brakeman	1930-1942
Charles Gallager	Brakeman	1939-1942
Frank Callom	Brakeman	1920-1930

The engineer and fireman of 59 pose after the last trip from Bull Hill in 1949. The two men, Ralph Hubbard and Jack Hartman grimy from their work in the cab, look ready to make yet another run, but all that was left was the scrapping train. — PPL

'ORM 154 500-8-15—C

THE CRIPPLE CREEK & COLORADO SPRINGS RAILROAD C
AND LEASED LINES.

OFFICE OF **Superintendent Motive Power**   Letter No.
and Car Department   Impression copy to be taken is
kept for that purpose.

Colorado Springs, Jan. 20, 1920

In specifying reasons for leaving service insert the words "Resigned," or "Discharged," only

This is to Certify, That **William Webster Quinby**
has been employed in the capacity of **Locomotive Fireman on Midland Term**
At **Cripple Creek, Colorado**
Fireman
From. **February 10, 1899.**
Engineer
To **April 6, 1902. From April 6, 1902 to July 21, 1906.**
Left service account. **Decrease in business.**

Services satisfactory.

Signature of Proper Holder:

S. M. P. & C. D

George Wilkinson	Brakeman	1922-1928
Jack Ward	Brakeman	
Andy Hawkins	Brakeman	1917-1930
John Bishop	Brakeman	1919-1930
John L. Morgan	Brakeman	
C.W. Duncan	Brakeman	
Richard M. McComb	Brakeman	
Andrew Schooley	Brakeman	1937-1941
Jack Sukllivan	Brakeman	1938-1949
Walter Crain	Brakeman	1938-1942
Archie Ketchell	Brakeman	1938-1940
Fred Haitz	Brakeman	1939-1941
Don Patterson	Brakeman	

Engineers and Firemen

(Engineers time as Fireman [or other] included)

Joe Logan	Engineer	1900-1941
James Dooner	Engineer	1900-1925
James Doris	Engineer	1900-1922
James Garber	Engineer	1900-1921
James George	Engineer	1899-1930
"Buckshot" Bartlett	Engineer	1900-1924
"Smoke" Harris	Engineer	1900-1928
Dave Lynch	Engineer	1900-1930
Leonard Butler	Engineer	1918-1938
Mike Butler	Engineer	1920-1949
William Britzman	Engineer	1922-1928
Clyde Prosser	Engineer	1918-1949
Charles Pressler	Engineer	1920-1949
Guy White	Engineer	1920-1936
Jack Kelly	Engineer	1920-1936
Joe Stewart	Engineer	1922-1949
F.W. Cummings	Engineer	1922-1942
C.A. Nulph	Engineer	1923-1942
Jack Hartman	Engineer	1928-1949
Everett Decker	Engineer	1935-1949
Harry Sanders	Engineer	1930-1940
Gail Winters	Engineer	
Hansen	Engineer	
Ed Dagley	Engineer	1918-1930
Jim Johnson	Engineer	1920-1939
Hoot Sullivan	Engineer	1936-1949
William Keating	Engineer	
Ernest Steele	Engineer	
William Quinby	Engineer	1902-1906
Leonard W. Richards	Engineer	1913-1920
James Sennett	Fireman	1919-1924
Walter Kling	Fireman	1923-1941

Charles O'Brien	Fireman	1920-1923
Art Wilcox	Fireman	1920-1928
Wyborn Cline	Fireman	1934-1943
Don Workman	Fireman	1933-1943
Charles Workman	Fireman	
Danny Rodgers	Fireman	1938-1942
Frank McCaffrey	Fireman	1919-1924
Monnison	Fireman	-1949
Weaver	Fireman	-1949
Schwartz	Fireman	1934-1938
James Gilland	Fireman	
Ralph Hubbard	Fireman	1937-1949
Marshall Johnson	Fireman	1928-1930
Ceryl Colby	Fireman	1929-1930
Robert Lynn	Fireman	1948
Solomon	Fireman	1939
David Butler	Fireman	1934-1937
Jim Adams	Extra Fireman	
Wm. F. Oswald	Fireman	1913-1917
Charles N. Pressler	Fireman	1917-1918
Joseph Scheider	Fireman	1896-1908
William Quinby	Fireman	1899-1902
John Welsh	Fireman	1919-1920
Leonard W. Richards	Fireman	1906-1913
Sauer	Fireman	-1949

Additional

Charley Marsh	Switchman-Safety Switch
Joe Stephan	Switchman
Jack Hanes (Haynes)	
Ray Potts	

Seen from the air, the old MT yards have been virtually erased. The roundhouse and machine shop are visible, but Midland Expressway covers most of the old yards. A few old relics were uncovered when many of the buildings and roads were constructed. — AC

← Two locomotives, at the end, under the torch at Colorado Springs in 1949. — HO/AC

ROUND HOUSE REGISTER

Report of Arrival and Departure of Locomotives, Engineers and Firemen at _Pueblo City_ Station on the _12_ day of _June_ 19_39_

	No. of Engine	Time	ENGINEER	FIREMAN	No. of Train	No. of Engine	Time	ENGINEER	FIREMAN
			ARRIVAL					**DEPARTURE**	
1	55	5³⁰ₐ	Cummings	Decker	rd	52	6⁰⁰ₐ	Prossler	Kling
2	58	6³⁵ₐ	Logan	Cline	Mo1	102	7½	Truman	
2	61	6⁵⁵ₐ	M Butler	Johnson	31	60	6pm	Prosser	Sullivan
d	52	5²⁵		Kling	"	61	"	L. J. Butler	Decker
2	102	1³⁵	Truman		"	56	"	Logan	Cline
3			June 13-39		"	55	"	M.G. Butler	Johnson
	55	4⁴⁰ₐ	M. Butler	Johnson					
	53	5⁴⁵	Logan	Cline	rd	52	6⁰⁰ₐ	Prossler	Kling
3	60	6⁵⁰ₐ	Prosser	Sullivan	Mo1	102	7½	Truman	
1	61	6⁵⁰ₐ	L.J. Butler	Decker	31	55	6⁰⁰	M. Butler	Johnson
1	52	4⁵	Prossler	Kling	"	58	6⁰⁰	Logan	Workman
2	102	6¹⁵	Truman		"	61	6⁰⁰	Prossy	Hartman
					"	10	6⁰⁰ₚ	Butler L.	Decker

Index

A

Aircraft Mechanics 63
Ajax Mine 58, 75, **100**, 155, 156
American Locomotive Works 40, 57
Anaconda 38, 75, **99**, 104, **107**, **108**, 134, 163
Aspen 8, 18, 23
Atchison, Topeka & Santa Fe Railway 6-23, **29**, 36, 40, 44, 45, 56, 91, 98

B

Bayless, Samuel N. **146**, **200**, **203**
Bear Creek Canyon 6, 7, 25
Bear Creek Toll Road 8, 12, 47
Bear Creek Trestle 43
Beaver Park 6, 8, 11, 12
Beaver, Penrose & Northern Railway 50, 51, 60
Bell, Dr. William A. 86, 88
Bennett, Horace W. 4, 104
Blackmer, Henry 38, 200
Blizzard Point 75, 130, 132, 137
Broadmoor 49, 50, 56, 60
Broken Box Ranch 4, 5
Brown, D.R.C. 23, 200
Bull Hill 12, 14, 30, **38**, **71**, 75, 92, 97, **98**, **101**, 109, 116, 132, **133**, 134, **135-7**, **151**, 152-**157**, **166**
Butler, M.J. 68

C

Cameron 14, **24**, 30, 43, 50, 96, **97**, 109, 132, **134**, 137, 161, 163
Camp Carson 63
Canon City 3-6, 32, 36, 38
Carlton, A.E. 29, 31, 38-57, 104, 124, 200
Carlton, L.G. 38, 53, 57, 124-5, 200
Carlton Tunnel 31, 57-59
Carlton Mill 68, 70, 72, 75, **77**, 159
Cascade 60, **87**, 88, 121, 124, **125**, 142, **143-4**, 161
Chipita Park 124
Cheyenne Mountain 49, 60
Chicago, Rock Island & Pacific Railway 12, 35, 45-6, 54, 58, 62, 66, 82, **83**, 139
Clough and Davidson 6, 12
Cogan, J.J. 40, 46, 200

Collbran, Harry 5-11, 15, 23
Colorado City 3-12, 18-20, 31, 36, 43, **78**, 84, 86, 92, 99, **114**, 118
Colorado Springs 7, 8, 20, 36, 41-3, 49-56, **82**, 83, 99, 106, 109, 156, 161
Colorado Midland Railway 3-36, 40-47, 83-130, 141, 144
    Abandonment 43-6
    Business Cars 7, 60, **61**, 124
    Cabooses 89, 139, **140**, 141, 173, 176
    Cripple Creek Survey 6-8
    Engine 12 **108**
    Engine 14 83
    Engine 15 **19**
    Engine 42 **17**
    Engine 205 88
    Operations 26, 43, 83-6
    Passenger Cars 84, **101**
    Refrigerator Cars 50, 174, **178**
    Shops 84
Colorado Philadelphia Mill 20, **22**, 30, 31, 36, 38, 84, 86
Colorado & Southern Railroad 35-45
Colorado Springs & Cripple Creek District Railway 13, 20-35, 41-49, **54**, 84, 96, 97, 104, **105**, 106
Colorado Springs and Interurban Railway 53, 56
Colorado Trading and Transfer 26, 29, **30**
Commercial Metals Company 68, 72, **75**, **199**
Corley Mountain Highway 47, 132
Corley, W.D. 47, 51
Crags 86, 142, 161
Cresson Mine 38, 40, 58, 59, 149
Cresson Vug 38, 40, 152
Cripple Creek 4-18, 23, 26, **36**, 72, 83, 89, 96, **101-5**, 106, **148**, 149, 154-163, **166**

Cripple Creek Central 35-49, 53, 84
Cripple Creek & Colorado Springs Railroad 12
Cripple Creek Express 13, 18, 83, **101**
Cripple Creek Mining District 5, 18
Cripple Creek Fire 22
Cripple Creek Labor Troubles 12, **32**, 33, 35

Cripple Creek Terminal 8-10
Crystola 88, 126, 141, 161
Culver 88

D

Denver & Rio Grande 6-11, 17, 24, 29, 40, 50, 54, 56, 60, 64, **68**, 75, **82**, 83-4, 113, 119
    Manitou Branch 84, 86, 113, 119
Denver & Colorado Southern Railway 19
Denver & Southwestern Railway 26, 29-32, 92
Divide **4**, 6-12, **10**, 17, 30, 41, 50, 72, **73**, **89**, 91, 106, 126, 130, 161, 163, **166**

E

Eagle Sampler **31**, 36
Edlowe 89, 126, **129**, 161
Elkton 56, 70, 99, **107**, 152, 156, 161
El Pomar Foundation 60
El Paso Mine 4, 5, 38, 151, 152, 154, 161
Engleman Canyon **74**, 119, **146**

F

Floods 56, 65
Florence 6, 7, 36
Florence & Cripple Creek Railroad 8-52, **31**, **42**, 99, 106, 151, **171**
Florissant 5-7, 84, 130
Fountain Creek 24, 54, 65, 84, 86
Fremont 4-6

G

Garden of the Gods 86
Gillett 12, **13**, 17-19, 23, 43, 50, 72, 75, **79**, 92-96, **95**, 130, 132, **133**, 137, 161, 163
Gillett, W.K. 11, 15, 22, 93, 104
Gold Coin Mine 26, 99, **100**
Golden Circle Railroad 23-26, **35**, 43, 109, 154, 155
Golden Cycle Mine **34**, 37-40, 97, **101**
Golden Cycle Corporation 38-81, 121, 156

Golden Cycle Mill 36-38, 50-57, 63, **67**, 68, 72, 84, **85**, 113, **114**, 116
Goldfield 23-25, 33, 84, 97, **101**, 104, 109
Grassy **24**, 109, 132
Great Mexican Bull Fight 18, 93
Green Mountain Falls 88, 125, 161

H

Hagerman, J.J. 7, 109
Hanging Rock Cut 86, 121, **145**
Hayden Survey 3, 92
Hoosier Pass 30, 35, 109, 132, **134**
Horse Thief Park 91
Howbert, Irving 7, 20
Hundley's Stage Line **4, 5**, 6, 24

I

Independence **14, 15**, 29, **35**, 36, 90, 97, **109**, 154, 161, 163
Iron Springs 86, 161

J

Jackson, W.S. 20

L

La Bella Mill, Water and Power 26, **34**, 97, 161
Leadville 4-7, 18, 26, 45, 51, 86, 89, 130
Lillibridge, H.P. 8-15
Lime Rock 121, 142, 161

M

Manitou 56, 65, **67, 73**, 86, 88, **119**, 120, 144, 161
Manitou & Pikes Peak Railway 12, 51, **55**, 56, 60, 75, 86, 144
Manitou Park 88
Manvel, Allan 8-10, 17
McKay, William 53, 55, 56-7, 65, 68, 116, 118, 141, 156, 200
Maps ix, 9, 94, 96, 102, 103
Mary McKinney Mine **44**, 151
Myers, Julius A. 4, 104
Midland **5**, 6, **8**, 9-12, **32**, 52, 58, 72, 75, 89, 91, 92, 130-139, **131**, **138**, **159**, 161, 163
Midland Expressway 211
Midland Terminal Railway
    Abandonment 68, 72, **73, 74**
    B&B Department 56, 122, 126, 187, 203, **204**, 205-6
    Cabooses 118, **125**, 139, 140,

    141, **147, 175, 176**
    Car Diagrams 168-188
    Car Roster 167, 173, 182
    Colorado City Yards 54, 65, **75**, **114**, 115, 144, **164, 165, 211**
    Construction 11-15
    Freight Cars 19, **49**, 50, 54, 57, 64, 121, **128, 135**, 139, 150, **177-181**
    Inspection Cars 156, **157, 199**
    Last Runs 70, **71**, 72, **148**
    Locomotive Diagrams 190-1
    Locomotive Roster 189
    Locomotives
    #1 (201, 54) 19, **20**, 35, **42**, 64, **98**, 113, **143**, 149, 190, **192**
    #2 (202, 55) 19, **21**, 35, 64, **65**, 77, **144**, 190, **193**
    #3 (203, 56) 19, **21**, 35, **41**, 70, **149, 153**, 190, **193**
    #4 (204, 57) 19, **31**, 35, 70, **87**, **112, 120, 131**, 190, **194**
    #5 (205, 58) 19, **21**, **35**, 89, **112**, 115, **119, 128, 136, 151**, **153, 161**, 190, **194**
    #6 (206, 59) **26**, 35, **49, 52**, 70, **71**, 72, **73, 76, 91, 117, 146**, **157**, 190, **194, 208**
    #7 (207, 60) **vi**, 26, **27**, 35, 72, 75, **90, 112, 117, 120**, 126, **147**, 190, **195**
    #52 i, 70, **112, 121**, 149, **150, 190**, 191
    #53 60, 62, 149, 156, 190, 191, **192**
    #61 **57**, 72, **76**, 131, 156, 190, 191, **195, 198**
    #62 60, **61**, 72, **76**, 131, **146**, 190, 191, **196, 198**
    #63 60, **61**, 72, **76**, 190, 191, **196**
    #64 **110**, 113, 116, **119, 131**, **137, 138**, 190, **195, 197**
    #65 **110**, 113, 116, **123, 135**, **138, 143**, 190, **197**
    #66 **113, 130, 135, 138, 143**, 190, **197**
    Observations 29, 70
    Operations 18-23, 29-52, 60, 64, 81, 97, 109, 111, 126, 134, 137, 149
    Organization 8-10, 23, 26, 53
    Passenger Cars 47, 49, 52, 130, **166, 167**, 169, 171, 173
    Passenger Motor #101 **48, 53**, 56, 115, 118, 122, 144, **153**,

    155, 158, 199
    Passenger Motor #102 **56**, 115, 144, **199**
    Plow **162**
    Shops 115
    Station List 161
    Strike 65, 68
    Structures **78, 79, 118, 163, 165**, **166**
    Surveys 9
    Work Cars **182-188**
Minnesota Transfer Railway **198**
Moffat, David 11
Mollie Gibson Mine 8
Monument Creek 54, 56, 65
Mount Pisgah 3-5
Mount Pisgah Hoax 3-4
Murphy 8, 58, 91, 126, 130, **131**, 139, 142, 161

N

National Hotel 22, 104
Newell, Richard 9, 13-15, 32, 200
Nye, S.N. 5

O

Oil Creek 6, 91, 92
Ore Treatment 84

P

Pikes Peak 88, 91, 96, 109, 115, 153, **162**
Pike View Mine 47, 51, 54
Penrose, Spencer 6, 20, 29, 38, **40**, 45, 47-51, **55**, 60, 104
Portland Mill 22, 36, 51, 84, 154, 161
Portland Mine **33**, 36, 38, **100**, 109, 155, 156
Poverty Gulch 3, 4, 106
Price and McGavock 8

R

Ramona Hotel **87**, 88
Requa, B.F. 3
Rhyolite 8
Ristine, George W. 17
Rocky Mountain Railroad Club 70, **71, 148**
Roosevelt Tunnel 38, 53, 109

S

Schilling, A.P. 7, **201, 202, 203**
Snow 26, **39, 162**

Short Line, see CS&CCD
Shoup, Merrill E. 57, 64, 65, **68**, **77**, 200
Standard Mill 30-38, 84, 86
Stratton, W.S. 6, 20, 29, 104
Strong Mine 24, 25, 99, **100**, 161

T

Teller County 25, 72
Thomas, Lowell 68, 72, **77**
Toll Roads 6-8, 89, **92**
Tracy 91, 161
Tutt, Charles L. 6, 20, 29, 38, **40**, 50, 60, 104

U

Union Pacific Railway 92, **170**, **171**
United Gold Mines 38, 56
U.S. Army 63, 64, 70, 72
    #4051 **197**
    #4028 **63**
    #4064 63, **76**, **196**
    #4070 **196**
Ute Pass 3-10, 47, 53, 65, 72, 83-88, **87**, 121, **122**, **123**, **140**, 142, **143**, **145**

V

Victor 14, **17**, 23-**28**, 38, 72, **74**, 96, 99, **100**, 104, **108**, 109, **150**, 152, 154, 155, 161
Victor Fire 26, **27-9**
Victor Junction 100, 152-6, 161
Vindicator Mine **66**, 155

W

Waters, Jesse 24, 38, 44, 200
Waters Tunnel 75, 93, 132, 137
Wildflower Excursions 43, 50, 83, 89, 129, **172**
Womack, Bob 3-6, 104
Wood, H.T. 3, 93
Woodland Park 56, 75, 88, **110**, 121, 126, **127**, **140**, 141, 161, 162
Woods Lake 93

Z

Zoo Special **55**, 56